Cosmic

B2

Students' Book

Rod Fricker

Suzanne Gaynor

Unit	Reading	Vocabulary	Grammar	Listening	Speaking	Writing
1 **Your True ID** **page 5**	Four-legged friends Matching headings with paragraphs Multiple choice	Personality and feelings Word formation: from text Word formation: nouns from adjectives Negative prefixes Accidents and health Phrasal verbs	Present tenses Stative verbs	Picture multiple choice True or false	Personal questions Talking about family and friends	Letter of Opinion
Revision 1 page 16						
2 **That's Entertainment!** **page 17**	Celebrities we love Multiple matching	Entertainment Word formation: from text Art Adjectives with *-ed / -ing* Phrasal verbs Prepositions + nouns Collocations Word formation: nouns from verbs	Past tenses *used to / would* Future in the past *It's time, I'd rather*	Sentence completion Multiple matching	Comparing two photographs	Discursive Essay
Revision 2 page 28						
3 **Sweet Success!** **page 29**	Dream jobs Multiple matching Multiple choice	Jobs and work Word formation: from text Work Compound nouns Workplaces Education Collocations Phrasal verbs	Future forms Comparatives Superlatives Quantifiers	Multiple choice Table completion	Making a choice	Report
Revision 3 page 40						
4 **Extreme!** **page 41**	Thrills, danger and … cheese! Missing sentences	Activities, equipment and dangers Word formation: from text Sports and equipment Verbs for sports Phrasal verbs Word formation: adjective prefixes	*too / enough* *so / such* *few / little* *Not only … but also* *So do I / Neither do I*	Multiple choice True, False or No Information	Reaching a decision	Letter of Complaint
Revision 4 page 52						
5 **Cool Computing!** **page 53**	Teen Hacker Saves the Day! Help Desk Horror Stories Completing sentences Open questions	Computers Word formation: from text Computer equipment Verbs related to computers Minor disasters	Modal verbs	Picture multiple choice Multiple choice recorded questions	Role play	Informal Email
Revision 5 page 64						

I've just done one of those magazine quizzes that tell you what type of person you are. It says I'm 'sociable and love going out' but I 'could be more sensitive at times'. What about you? What sort of person are you?

Your True ID

Vocabulary Starter

Personality and feelings

1 Do the quiz and find out what type of person you are.

The TRUE YOU!

A = 3 points
B = 2 points
C = 1 point

1 Your friend wants you to go to a party. You don't feel like it. What do you do?

  A You go. You know you'll feel great when you get there.

  B Stay at home. There will be more parties.

  C You don't want to upset your friend, so you go but leave early.

2 A friend isn't keen on your new jacket. What do you say?

  A I don't care what you think. I love it.

  B I wish I hadn't bought it now.

  C But it's really fashionable. I thought you'd like it.

3 You've just won two tickets to see your favourite pop group in concert. The concert is the same night as your friend's birthday party. How do you feel?

  A Excited. It's your favourite group.

  B Guilty. You want to go to the concert.

  C Sad that it's on the same night. You don't know if you can go.

What's your score?

8–9: You're enthusiastic about life. You're sociable and love going out.

5–7: Sometimes you can be anxious and too cautious. You need to relax and enjoy yourself more with your friends.

3–4: You're very loyal to your friends, but you don't always do what you want. You should think about yourself a bit more.

2 Match the words with the photos above.

> grumpy competitive affectionate
> impatient excited

3 Complete the sentences with the words from the box.

> emotions grateful rewarded express
> conduct stressed sceptical

1 Sarah is getting very _____ about her exams; she's afraid that she's going to fail.

2 I'm always very _____ about what I read in newspapers and magazines. They often print things which are not true.

3 Scientists are preparing to _____ a series of experiments into the emotional life of animals.

4 Strong _____ such as joy and sadness are sometimes not easy to express.

5 I'm really _____ for your help with my science research project. I couldn't have done it without you.

6 When the circus animals perform a trick correctly, they are _____ by their trainer.

7 Most people agree that it's better to _____ your feelings rather than keeping them hidden.

CHATROOM

- Do the quiz results describe your personality correctly? Why/Why not?
- Which adjectives from this page would you use to describe your best friend?

5

Four-legged Friends

Friends – scientists and other researchers have conducted numerous experiments and come up with proof that we can't live without them. At their best, we can express all our emotions to our friends; whether we're feeling grumpy, stressed or fed up, we usually turn to true friends to cheer us up and get us through bad times. People being people, however, friends can also be competitive, impatient, and even downright disloyal! So, Fran Thomas, Teen Life's top reporter, has been doing research into another type of friend (the four-legged kind!) that is always loyal to us. Curious? Read on!

A ☐ When her poodle, Poopsie, died, Marge Cameron felt a depth of sadness and loneliness she'd never thought possible. Her daughter was anxious about her and insisted she get a new pet. Marge refused to discuss the issue. That was until she met Tiny. Sitting in the park one day, Marge failed to notice her wallet falling out of her bag. As she was walking home, she noticed she was being followed by a very excited little Chihuahua. In his mouth, he had a wallet. Marge was so shocked, and so grateful, she rewarded the little fellow by giving him a home.

B ☐ Joe, the cocker spaniel, belongs to the Mullins family. Today, he's being treated like royalty. He's just eaten a hamburger, and now he's eyeing a bowl of ice-cream with great enthusiasm. What's the special occasion? Joe is a hero. Last night, while the family slept in the upstairs bedrooms, their home caught fire. Joe knew something was wrong and began to bark, waking up his owners. Firemen believe that without Joe's super sense of smell, last night could have ended in tragedy.

C ☐ Everyone in elderly Mr Adams' building knows Ginger. A huge and very affectionate Great Dane, Ginger is known to be a fantastic but very sloppy kisser! Always on her best behaviour, Ginger is allowed to accompany Mr Adams wherever he goes. So imagine the neighbours' surprise when they saw Ginger running crazily around the building last month. On investigation, they found Mr Adams unconscious on the floor of his flat. When he came to, he explained that burglars had broken into his flat and frightened him so badly he'd fainted. Ginger, ferocious when necessary, had chased them out before they could take a thing!

D ☐ Before Tigger joined the Higgins family, the subject of getting a pet was hotly debated. Dad said getting a cat would teach the kids responsibility. Mum, somewhat sceptical, complained in frustration that she would probably be the only person learning the 'Responsibility Lesson'. Dad won, and Tigger arrived. It was love at first sight for Tigger and toddler, Hannah Higgins. Despite the frequent tail-pullings and eye-pokings, Tigger never left little Hannah's side. And that's exactly where he was when Hannah decided to descend the steep cellar stairs. His cries of panic brought Ms Higgins running; Hannah was saved, and Tigger … well, he had a lovely fish supper!

Reading

1 **Read the text and match the headings with the paragraphs. There is one heading you do not need.**

☐ Beware: guard dog
☐ A 'nose' for danger
☐ A pet is for life
☐ Babysitter on duty
☐ Feathered friend saves farmer
☐ Good things come in small packages

Reading Tip: matching headings to paragraphs

- Try and understand the gist of the text.
- Make sure the headings match the whole paragraph and not just one phrase or sentence.

E ☐ And, last but not least … here's the story of Rusty the Rooster. (Editor's note: No, he doesn't have four legs but we think he qualifies as one of man's best friends anyway!) Like all roosters, Rusty greets every dawn with a loud, enthusiastic 'COCK-A-DOODLE-DOO.' So why, thought Rusty's owner, Bill Tate, was 'that stupid bird' making so much noise in the middle of the night? Unaware of the danger he was in, he stumbled out of his front door into the farmyard. The earth began to shake and he nearly tripped over a fence knocked over by the tremors. As the walls of his house collapsed, Bill congratulated himself on owning 'the smartest bird' in the world.

2 Read the article again and choose the best answer (A, B, C or D).

Reading Tip: multiple-choice questions

- Read the question carefully and underline the key words.
- Look for synonyms of the keywords in the text. The correct answer might use words which are different from the word in the text, but mean the same thing.
- Read the options carefully and choose the best answer.

1 In the introduction, the writer says that friends
   A may be unnecessary according to experts.
   B don't always have to be human.
   C always make things worse for us.
   D rarely make us feel better about things.

2 Marge Cameron
   A had never had a pet before Tiny.
   B was lonely because she had no pet.
   C lived in a house quite close to the park.
   D considered getting a new pet fairly often.

3 In paragraph B, we learn that
   A the Mullins family are grateful to their pet.
   B Joe regularly gets special treats.
   C the fire broke out the day before a holiday.
   D the fire started on the second floor.

4 Mr Adams
   A lives in a house.
   B is an old man.
   C enjoys Ginger's kisses.
   D owns a small pet.

5 Ginger
   A shocked the neighbours by running out of her building.
   B scared her owner so that he blacked out from fright.
   C stopped the burglars from getting into her home.
   D prevented Mr Adams from being robbed.

6 Who was against the Higgins getting a cat?
   A Mr Higgins
   B the Higgins children
   C Ms Higgins
   D Hannah

7 What happened to Rusty's owner?
   A Rusty woke him up in the morning.
   B His house was slightly damaged.
   C He destroyed a fence in his garden.
   D He experienced an earthquake.

8 Where would we read this text?
   A in a magazine
   B in an encyclopaedia
   C in a children's book
   D in a school textbook

3 Find words or phrases in the text that mean the following.

1 very many (introduction)
2 unhappy or bored (introduction)
3 demanded that something should happen (paragraph A)
4 subject or topic (paragraph A)
5 the way a dog makes a sound (paragraph B)
6 discussed (paragraph D)

WebSearch

www.petshed.com/node/55
www.bestfriends.org

CHATROOM

- Do you know any stories about a pet helping or saving its owner?
- Do you believe that animals can sense things (like an earthquake) that humans can't?

Vocabulary

Word formation: words from the text

1 Complete the text with the correct form of the words in capitals. All the words are from the reading text on pages 6 and 7.

A happy home makes a happy cat, but if there is a feeling of ¹_____ in the air, then the cat will notice it and some alteration in its ²_____ may be observed. They tend to sleep more and will not show any of their usual ³_____ for their favourite games or toys. The best way to help a cat that's feeling sad is to talk to it. ⁴_____ say that cats like to hear the sound of a human voice. Direct eye contact should be avoided; for humans this is understood to be friendly, but ⁵_____ have revealed that they now have scientific ⁶_____ that direct eye contact with cats is regarded as threatening by cats. Of course, we don't yet fully understand the ⁷_____ of feline emotions, but increasing evidence suggests that, like us, they can feel joy, excitement and even ⁸_____ .

SAD
BEHAVE

ENTHUSIASTIC

SCIENCE

RESEARCH
PROVE

DEEP

LONELY

Word formation: nouns from adjectives

2 Complete the table with the correct noun form of the adjectives.

	Adjective	Nouns
-ty	loyal	1
-iness	lonely	2
-ion	frustrated	3
-dom	bored	4
-ity	creative	5
-ment	excited	6
-y	honest	7
-ence	impatient	8

3 Complete the sentences with the nouns from Exercise 2.

1 Alex couldn't hide his _____ when he won two tickets to see his favourite band in concert.

2 Do you ever get a feeling of _____ when your computer won't do what you want it to do?

3 The best quality a friend can have is _____ . They should always be there when you need them.

4 Oliver likes travelling on his own and doesn't mind the _____ of being away from family and friends.

5 When Adam took the money he found to the police station, the police offered him a reward for his _____ .

6 The Art teacher is very pleased with the _____ her students are showing in their work.

7 The instructor began to show his _____ after the students had made the same mistake for the fifth time.

8 I can't stand the _____ of waiting in a queue for hours.

Negative prefixes

4 Complete the sentences by adding the negative prefixes *in-*, *dis-*, *il-*, *im-* or *un-* to the adjectives.

1 Even though she always gets what she wants, she's _____ (grateful) and never says thank you.

2 Ben is _____ (decisive); he can't even decide whether he wants tea or coffee when we go to a café!

3 Liam is unwell; he's _____ (capable) of taking the exam today.

4 What you're saying is completely _____ (logical); if he is rich, then he wouldn't steal the money.

5 Alex is very _____ (mature). He behaves like a child.

6 Sarah's friends are having a surprise party for her; she's completely _____ (aware) of all the plans for the big day!

7 Emily is never _____ (loyal) to her friends. She always supports them.

Accidents and health

5 Match the pictures with the sentences.

1 He's got a bruise on his leg. ☐
2 I've got a rash on my arm. ☐
3 He's got a black eye. ☐
4 He's got a swollen thumb. ☐
5 She's got a bump on her head. ☐
6 She's been stung by a bee. ☐

6 **Choose the word that best completes the sentence.**

1 The doctor says I'm _____ good health; apart from a broken arm and black eye, of course!

   A with   B of   C in

2 Will's had an accident. He wasn't looking where he was going and he _____ over a tennis racquet.

   A tripped   B stepped   C walked

3 Luke was running in a long-distance race, but he _____ shortly before the end because he hadn't drunk enough water.

   A collided   B collapsed   C crashed

4 One of the football players has been _____ , so they've stopped the game.

   A injured   B wounded   C pained

5 I was _____ by a jelly fish when I was swimming in the sea.

   A burned   B bitten   C stung

6 I'm allergic to milk. If I drink it, I get _____ on my arms and face.

   A a burn   B a rash   C a bump

Back up your vocabulary

9 **Read the text and choose the best answer (A, B, C or D) for each gap.**

Phrasal verbs

7 **Match the phrasal verbs with their definitions.**

1 black out   A become happier
2 come to   B lose consciousness
3 cheer up   C go to someone for help
4 get through   D regain consciousness
5 turn to   E stop liking something
6 go off   F reach the end of a difficult time

8 **Complete the sentences with the correct form of the phrasal verbs from Exercise 7.**

1 When Sandra fell off her bike she hit her head and _____ for a few seconds.

2 I've got a bad headache. I don't know how I'll _____ the day.

3 Emily has _____ after the accident, but she doesn't remember what happened.

4 Nick always _____ his friends when he's worried about something.

5 I've always loved chocolate, but recently I've started to _____ it. I hardly ever eat it now.

6 _____! The exams are over now and we can enjoy the summer holidays.

Yes you can!

1 A going off   B turning to   C coming to   D seeing to
2 A health   B body   C outline   D fitness
3 A enthuse   B enthused   C enthusiastic D enthusiasm
4 A destroy   B wound   C damage   D injure
5 A break   B hit   C bump   D burn
6 A loneliness B lonely   C alone   D lonesome
7 A go off   B put off   C send off   D take off
8 A come to   B turn to   C get into   D get through

Nowadays there is a lot of media interest in keeping fit, changing what you eat or losing weight. More and more people are ¹_____ their doctors for advice. Most advise that thirty minutes of daily exercise is all that we need to stay in good ²_____ .

However, the truth is that not everybody shares such ³_____ for an early morning jog around the park. Also, if you haven't done any exercise for a long time you can easily ⁴_____ yourself and have to stop doing sport for a while. You will know what this is like if you've ever had a ⁵_____ on the head after a challenging game of football. Finally, although sport is often enjoyable, it can be very competitive, especially at school. Students who aren't good enough may not be accepted for the school team and this can produce feelings of ⁶_____ for those who feel they have been left out. It's hardly surprising that these students sometimes ⁷_____ sport completely.

Being active is important. It can help us ⁸_____ stressful times. However it should be fun too. So next time you go for a walk, invite a friend. Your friend will be grateful and so will your body!

CHATROOM

- What do you do when you're feeling anxious or worried?
- Have you ever been injured?

Grammar
Present tenses

present simple
*We usually **turn** to true friends …*
*Joe, the cocker spaniel, **belongs** to the Mullins family.*
present continuous
*Now he's **eyeing** a bowl of ice-cream with great enthusiasm.*
present perfect simple
*Researchers **have conducted** numerous experiments …*
present perfect continuous
*Fran Thomas, **has been doing** research into another type of friend.*
present passives
*Ginger **is allowed** to accompany Mr Adams.*
*Today, he's **being treated** like royalty.*

See **Grammar File**, page 156

1 Complete the email with the present simple or the present continuous.

New   Reply

Hi James,

Thanks for your email. I
[1]_____ (recover) well after the accident thanks, but I
[2]_____ (begin) to get very bored at home. The doctor
[3]_____ (not think) I can go back to school for another two weeks. The good thing is that my friends often [4]_____ (visit) me after school. This afternoon Max [5]_____ (come) with some Maths homework. I
[6]_____ (look forward) to seeing him, but I [7]_____ (not want) to get the homework!
Thanks for the photos. I
[8]_____ (try) to print them, but my computer [9]_____ (not work) at the moment. It's so frustrating!
[10] What _____ (you / do) on Saturday? I'm here if you want to come over.

Callum

2 Complete the dialogue with the present perfect simple or the present perfect continuous.

George: Hi Tom. You look a bit fed up. What [1]_____ (you / doing)?

Tom: Hi George. Nothing very exciting. I [2]_____ (revise) for my exams.

George: [3]_____ (they / finish / yet)?

Tom: Not quite. I [4]_____ (do) three, but I've got two more next week. I [5]_____ (not be able) to go out with friends because of them.

George: So that's why you [6]_____ (be) on MSN so much!

Tom: Yes. But the good news is, I [7]_____ (run) every day.

George: Every day? That's fantastic. [8]_____ (you / hear) that the school [9]_____ (organise) a race to raise money for charity? Why don't you enter it with me?

Tom: I will. Thanks, Ben. You [10]_____ (cheer up / me)!

© Randy Glasbergen, 1997.

PSYCHOLOGIST

GLASBERGEN

"My therapy is quite simple: I wag my tail and lick your face until you feel good about yourself again."

3 Rewrite parts of the article by replacing the underlined sections with the passive form. Use *by* if necessary.

Today educational professionals [1]are rewarding Maythorpe secondary school for its new fitness club. The school [2]is holding the fitness sessions during regular school hours. As well as aerobics and circuit training, the club [3]offers yoga and relaxation classes. Specialist tutors can offer support to students suffering from anxiety or exam nerves. With the correct techniques and a certain amount of practice students will discover that correct breathing [4]reduces stress and improves concentration. The club has impressed both parents and teachers alike, and school authorities [5]have also praised its 'positive atmosphere'.

1 Today Maythorpe secondary school _____ educational professionals for its new fitness club.
2 The fitness sessions _____ during regular school hours.
3 Yoga and relaxation classes _____ the club.
4 Students discover that stress _____ using the correct breathing techniques.
5 The club _____ for its 'positive atmosphere'.

Stative verbs

> *Firemen **believe** that without Joe's super sense of smell …*
> *Everyone in Mr Adam's building **knows** Ginger.*
> Some verbs can be used in both tenses but with a change of meaning.
> *I **think** he's got a black eye.*
> *I'm **thinking** about getting a job as a vet.*

See **Grammar File**, page 157

4 Complete the sentences with the correct form of the verbs from the box.

> seem   taste   believe   understand   hate   represent
> hope   need

1 Most animal-lovers agree that dogs _____ love and affection from their owners.
2 Julia _____ terribly excited about her audition for the school play. I hope she won't be disappointed.
3 The police _____ him. They know he's lying.
4 Don't eat that! It _____ very nice.
5 Samantha _____ getting up early, so she's a bit grumpy in the mornings!
6 What _____ (you) to do when you finish school?
7 A howl from a dog usually _____ pain or fear.
8 Can you explain this passage about animals' emotions? I _____ it.

5 Circle the correct option.

1 She **tends / is tending** to be rather insensitive to other people's emotional problems.
2 We **get / are getting** through this difficult time with the help of our friends and family.
3 Dogs **need / are needing** plenty of vigorous exercise every day.
4 The painting **represents / is representing** the difficulties of growing up in the twenty-first century.
5 I **think / am thinking** of getting a pet for my four-year-old daughter. Which animal would you recommend?
6 I **think / am thinking** that to be a teacher you need a lot of patience.

Back up your grammar

6 Choose the word or phrase that best completes the sentence.

1 The students _____ to be enjoying the new fitness classes.
   A they seem   C seems
   B seem   D are seeming
2 We'd better buy a drink because we _____ to bring our water bottles.
   A have forgotten   C forget
   B are forgetting   D are forgotten
3 Sam doesn't look well. He _____ a lot of late nights recently.
   A has   C is having
   B has been having   D has have
4 Paul has injured his leg playing football. He _____ to rest it for a few weeks.
   A is needed   C has needed
   B is needing   D needs
5 Rachel _____ some new medicine for her asthma.
   A is given   C gives
   B gave   D has been given
6 Adam is so competitive. He always _____ to win every single match he plays.
   A is wanting   C wants
   B has wanted   D is wanted
7 We _____ yoga for two months now and feel much fitter.
   A do   C have been doing
   B are done   D are doing
8 Jack's not here at the moment. He _____ for a run before dinner.
   A was gone   C has gone
   B is going   D has been
9 When the students finish the exam, they _____ to leave the classroom.
   A are allowed   C be allowed
   B allow   D are allowing
10 Melissa talks very clearly. I _____ everything she says.
   A am understood   C understand
   B am understanding   D understood

CHATROOM

Think of a famous person you admire or like. What is he or she like?

Listening

KlairyCrete95

My friend changed schools recently. Her new school sounds fantastic. I remember her as one of the shyest girls in class but now she's really confident.

Have any of your friends changed recently?

How are they different now?

More soon ... watch this space!

Listening 1

1 You will hear six short conversations. After you hear each one, you will be asked a question about what you heard. The answer choices are shown as pictures. Choose A, B or C.

Listening Tip: multiple-choice pictures

○ What is happening in each frame and how are they different from each other?

○ Think what the conversation or announcement might be about.

1

2

3

4
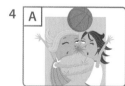

5

6
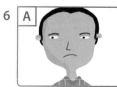

Listening 2

2 You will hear a radio interview with Sonia. Listen to the introduction and tick what the interview is about.

1 Sonia's journey through Europe.
2 Sonia's experience of living in another country.

Listening Tip: true or false

○ Read each statement first and underline the key words.

○ What words might you hear that relate to key words in the statement?

3 Now listen to the interview and decide if the statements are true or false.

1 Sonia wasn't worried about meeting new friends.
2 Sonia felt impatient and angry because she couldn't talk to the teachers.
3 The Italian students didn't want to practise their English vocabulary.
4 Sonia liked the fact that the Italian students showed what they were feeling.
5 English students are sociable.
6 It doesn't matter to Sonia what opinion other people have of her.
7 Sonia agrees that the experience was good.
8 Sonia's experience taught her about people in her own country.

CHATROOM

• How do you think a person feels when they are in a new school or town?
• How would you describe people in your town/country?

Speaking
Personal questions

1 Look at the photo. Tick (✓) what you most like talking about with your friends.

1 Plans for the evening ☐
2 Your exams ☐
3 Other friends ☐
4 Your teachers ☐
5 Your homework ☐
6 The news ☐
7 Shopping ☐
8 Your favourite music ☐

2 Match the questions with the topics from the box.

> friends   feelings   free-time   health
> my future   my personality

1 How do you feel when you've got an exam?
_____

2 Do you want to go to university?
_____

3 Are you a competitive person?
_____

4 What characteristics must a good friend have?
_____

5 Have you ever had a swollen ankle/a bad bruise/a black eye? What happened?
_____

6 What do you like doing at the weekends?
_____

3 Listen to some students answering the questions in Exercise 2. Match their answers with the questions.

A ____   B ____   C ____   D ____

4 Work with a partner. Ask and answer the questions in Exercise 2.

Speaking Tip: personal questions
Always try and give as much information as possible. Don't always use short sentences.

5 Tick the words that describe a good friend.

> competitive   honest   enthusiastic
> creative   sceptical   sensitive

6 Listen to Julia describe her friend, Antoni. Which words from Exercise 5 does she use?

7 Listen again and complete the sentences.

1 _____ we've been friends since we were five.
2 _____ , he's also very honest.
3 _____ about Antoni is he likes helping people.
4 Oh, and I _____ forgot.

8 Work in pairs to complete the task. When you have finished change roles. Use the Language Upload box to help you.

> **Student A:** You are going to describe somebody in your family. Think about words and structures you will use. You must talk for one minute. If you stop talking, Student B will ask a question.

> **Student B:** You are going to time Student A. If Student A stops talking before the minute is complete, ask the following questions:
> *What does (name of family member) do?*
> *What is (name of family member) doing now?*
> *What do you like about (name of family member)?*

9 Now talk for one minute about your best friend.

Language Upload

Introduce the subject
One of my best friends is …
I'd like to talk about …

Giving an opinion
I enjoy being with him because …
I suppose it's because …
I think that's important in a friend.
I think it's because …

Keeping the talk going
Let me see …   Well …
You see …   Oh and I nearly forgot …

Finishing
The best thing …   Above all …
Apart from that …   As well as that …
And last of all …

Writing: A Letter of Opinion
Before you write

1 Look at the photos and answer the questions.

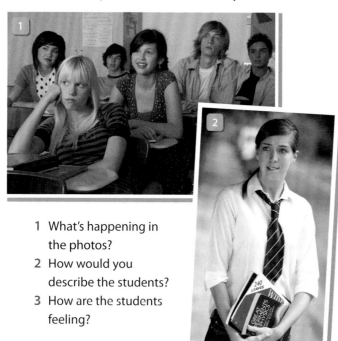

1 What's happening in the photos?
2 How would you describe the students?
3 How are the students feeling?

2 Read the newspaper article and underline the following points

1 why some teachers are worried
2 how Mike Harmer feels
3 why Mike thinks new students are good

More help for international students!

An increase in international students is causing concern for some teachers. They say schools should offer newcomers extra support to help them overcome their initial anxiety. However, Mike Harmer, a secondary school head, is excited about the situation. He believes international students can help us to learn about other cultures.

3 Does the information you have underlined give an opinion or a fact?

4 Now read a letter to the editor of the newspaper. Answer the questions.

1 What does the writer agree with?
2 What does the writer disagree with?
3 Is the style formal or informal? Why?
4 How does the writer start and end the letter?

Dear Sir or Madam,

I read your article about international students with interest. I have experience of this as I moved here four years ago from Russia. I'm a sociable person, but at first I found it very difficult to fit in.

Firstly, I couldn't agree more that international students feel anxious. But they get through that first, difficult stage by learning the language. They are usually enthusiastic and learn quickly. Furthermore, they are often glad to be at school and are keen to talk to other students. I honestly think Mike Harmer is right to be excited about the situation.

I also understand why teachers might be worried. However, I disagree that schools need to offer support. I think it's more important to encourage the students in the school to make contact with the international students. They could invite them to a sports club or help them with homework. I feel sure that international students would be grateful for it.

Lastly, I am convinced that if the new students find friends they can turn to, they will soon find happiness in their new school.

Yours faithfully,
Tatyana Solokova, 18

5 Find phrases in the letter the writer uses to give her opinion.

1 _____   4 _____
2 _____   5 _____
3 _____   6 _____

6 What words does the writer use to describe feelings or personality?

1 _____   5 _____
2 _____   6 _____
3 _____   7 _____
4 _____   8 _____

7 Complete the table with the phrases used by the writer in her letter.

1 introduce the first idea	1
2 add a contrasting idea	2
3 give extra information	3
4 introduce a final idea	4

8 Number the information in the order it appears in the letter.

- A Giving a first opinion and saying why ☐
- B Closing ☐
- C Reference to opposite view and explanation ☐
- D Confirmation of opinion ☐
- E Greeting ☐ 1
- F Introduction and reason for writing ☐

9 Read the Writing Checklist and find examples of each point in the model letter.

Time to write

10 Look at the picture and answer the questions.

1 Is the picture similar or different to your school?
2 Where do you go during break at school? Is it a nice area to be in? Why/Why not?

11 Work with a partner and decide if you agree or disagree with the following? Why?

1 Schools should spend money on equipment for classrooms and laboratories.
2 You can give students a nice place to sit in, but they won't be grateful for it.
3 If the outdoor area isn't safe, students could injure themselves.
4 Students need to relax. They should have attractive places to sit in.

12 Read the article and underline the key ideas.

More safe space for schools!

Head Teacher, Martin Dyers, believes that safe outdoor space is important for keeping students in good health, mentally and physically. 'They need somewhere they can exercise and be sociable,' he says. 'At the moment many schools have dangerous areas where students might trip or have an accident.'

Write a letter to the editor explaining your view. Write between 150 and 175 words.

Writing Checklist: A Letter of Opinion

1 Read the prompt carefully and underline key words and phrases.
2 Make notes of your opinions. (Things I agree with. Things I disagree with.)
3 Think of reasons to back up your opinion.
4 Explain *why* you are writing.
5 Give your first opinion and support it.
6 Give the opposite view.
7 Finally, confirm your opinion.

Does your letter include

1 a formal greeting and clear introduction?
2 relevant and interesting vocabulary?
3 one or two phrasal verbs?
4 stative verbs?
5 an agreement or disagreement with something?
6 a final opinion and a formal ending?

Memory Flash

Identifying yourself/reason for writing

I read the article about ... with interest.
I was interested in the article about ...
I have experience of this ...

Giving your first opinion

Firstly, I couldn't agree more that ...
First of all ...
To begin with ...

Supporting your opinion

Furthermore ...
In addition ...
Therefore ...
As a result of this ...

Referring to the opposite opinion

However ...
On the other hand ...

A final opinion

Finally ...
Lastly ...
Taking all of this into consideration ...

Vocabulary

1 Complete the article with the words from the box.

> insensitive   aware   loneliness   scientists
> excited   affectionate   behaviour

At a recent science exhibition, visitors were very ¹_____ by the arrival of a new robot. 'Heart Robot' was designed by a team of ²_____ who have been studying how humans react to a machine that seems ³_____ of what's happening around it. Left on its own, the ⁴_____ of the robot soon becomes obvious and big, sad eyes show it wants and needs company. This robot responds to noise and touch. Hugging it or being ⁵_____ with it makes it calm down. Aggressive ⁶_____ also produces the same reaction as in humans when they feel fear. Children's reactions to 'Heart Robot' are interesting. Some see it as a possible friend while the more ⁷_____ ones just want to frighten it.

2 Choose the correct answers.

1 'How do you know she's not well?' 'She's **gone off** / **turned to** her food.'
2 I'm **injured** / **under the weather** today. Nothing serious, but I think I'll go back to bed for a while.
3 A whole week of exams. How are we going to **get through** / **come to** them?
4 Amanda hasn't been feeling well for a while and **collapsed** / **tripped** on her way to work this morning.
5 Jack's finger is broken. The doctor says it will be **swollen** / **stung** for a few days.
6 Sam got **a black eye** / **a rash** after he ran into another player during the basketball match.
7 When Amy **turned to** / **came to** after her accident, she couldn't remember her name.

3 Complete the sentences with the correct noun form of the adjectives in capitals.

1 Melissa's friends respected her _____ and were glad she had decided to tell the truth. (HONEST)
2 Alex belonged to a large family and _____ wasn't something he had ever experienced. (LONELY)
3 The best way to deal with _____ on a long journey is to listen to lots of music. (BORED)
4 After all the _____ of her birthday party the last thing Amy could do was sleep. (EXCITED)
5 The company expects _____ from all of its workers. (LOYAL)

Grammar

4 Choose the correct answers.

1 **Have you decided** / **Do you decide** what you **do** / **'re doing** tonight?
2 Kate **is being interviewed** / **is interviewed** at the moment.
3 They **aren't** / **haven't been** this excited since their party.
4 It always **rains** / **is raining** on my birthday!
5 I **need** / **am needing** to know why you **are** / **are being** angry with me.

5 Complete the email with the correct form of the verbs.

> ✉ New   ✉ Reply
>
> Hi Cristina,
> Greetings from Warsaw! We ¹_____ (just / arrived) and I ²_____ (sit) in my hotel room. I ³_____ (travel) for two days, so it ⁴_____ (feel) good to be here at last.
> Warsaw is an amazing place! After dinner we ⁵_____ (go) on a tour of the city. Charlie Harris ⁶_____ (not come) with us. In fact he ⁷_____ (already / go) to bed! Typical Charlie! He ⁸_____ (complain) since we got here.
> I must go because dinner ⁹_____ (be served) now and I ¹⁰_____ (starve)!
> Love, Isabel

6 Complete the second sentence so that it has a similar meaning to the first. Use the word in capitals.

1 It's the first time I've visited Russia.
   NEVER
   I _____ Russia before
2 The doctor is examining John now.
   EXAMINED
   John _____ now.
3 The last time I saw Rachel was five years ago.
   FOR
   I _____ five years.
4 Helen always asks her sister for help.
   TURNS
   Helen always _____ her sister.
5 It looks as if the children have a rash.
   SEEM
   The children _____ a rash.
6 You look upset. Are your exams worrying you?
   ABOUT
   Are _____ your exams?
7 Nick started behaving badly a year ago.
   BEEN
   Nick _____ for a year.

I'd love to be famous. I could be a singer, a writer, a TV presenter or maybe an actor. How about you? Would you like to be famous? What would you like to be famous for?

2 That's Entertainment!

Vocabulary Starter
Entertainment

1 Read the text about a band. What do the highlighted words mean?

There are three of us in the band and I'm the lead guitarist. Last year we **released** our first album and it became an instant **hit**. We could hardly believe it when we reached number seven in the **charts**! There are ten **tracks** on the **album**, two of which have been released as **singles**. It took us six weeks to **record** the album in a studio in London. I'm not that talented at writing music, but I did write all the **lyrics**. I was always keen on writing and poetry at school. We've had loads of positive feedback about our music and people say that our **tunes** are really catchy. Now we want to play live **on stage** but we want to add a girl singer to the line-up. We're holding **auditions** at the moment, but haven't found anyone we like yet!

2 Complete the blog post with the words from the box.

cast   channels   episodes   programme   role   series

We haven't got a satellite so we can only get five ¹_____ on our TV. My favourite ²_____ was *Lost*, but it's finished now. There were six ³_____ altogether (I think the Americans call them seasons) and I watched all 121 ⁴_____ ! All the actors – the whole ⁵_____ – were perfect, but my favourite actor was Naveen Andrews who played the ⁶_____ of Sayid Jarrah.

3 Complete the puzzle to find out the name of a famous English dramatist.

1 Actors stand on this in the theatre.
2 With satellite you get hundreds of these on your TV.
3 A CD containing a number of songs.
4 One song from clue 3.
5 A part played by an actor in a film or play.
6 The words to a song.
7 The individual programmes in a TV series.
8 A set of television programmes with the same subject and characters.
9 A test to see if an actor is good enough.
10 Films are shown on a big one. A TV has a smaller one.
11 To make an album available for people to buy.

CELEBRITIES WE LOVE

A

HUGH LAURIE

Hugh Laurie started his career as a comedian and actor at Cambridge University. When he arrived, he was a keen rower like his father, who had won an Olympic gold medal in the 1948 Olympics. However, illness put a stop to his sports career and he turned to the stage. Twenty years of success at home in the UK finally led to him becoming a household name in the US too, when he starred in the role of Dr Gregory House in Fox Channel's award-winning TV series, *House*. There have already been over 100 episodes and it is a hugely popular show. Hugh Laurie is an extraordinarily talented entertainer who plays five musical instruments, is a best-selling novelist and has an American accent so good that the producer of *House* was convinced he was American when he saw his audition.

B

THE STROKES

The Strokes are a five-piece New York band who formed in 1998, although their lead singer, guitarist and drummer have been playing since they were at school together in Manhattan. Their debut album, *Is This It*, was a massive hit all over the world. It was released in the UK in the summer of 2001, but not until October in the USA. While they were waiting for the record to come out in their home country, the events of 9/11 took place which led to one track, a criticism of the New York police, being removed from the US version of the album. In 2009, the album, with its catchy tunes and clever lyrics, was voted the album of the decade by the influential rock magazine, the *NME*.

Reading

Logged in ✕

Durban45

I love reading about my favourite entertainers in magazines and books and on websites. I've just found a great website about the rapper Kanye West. It's so cool!

Who are your favourite performers? What do you know about their lives?

More soon ... watch this space.

1 You are going to read an article about five entertainers. Look at the photos and try to guess which area of the performing arts they are involved in. Then, read the text quickly to find out if you were right.

Reading Tip: multiple matching

- Skim the texts quickly.
- Underline a few key words in each text.
- Look at the key words in the answer sentences. Check to see if there are any synonyms for these in the underlined words.

2 For questions 1–10, choose from the people A–E. Some of the people may be chosen more than once. When more than one answer is required, these may be given in any order. There is an example at the beginning (0).

Who

didn't use to be so attractive to the opposite sex?	0 D
tried to do something they weren't very talented at?	1
didn't start performing as a schoolchild?	2
has sung about real life experiences?	3
was forced to change something due to the political situation?	4
achieved success earlier in life than anyone else?	5
used to do an activity that one of his/her parents had been good at?	6
had some problems at school?	7 8
was unsuccessful at first?	9
won an award for something they did several years earlier?	10

THE PERFORMERS THAT HAVE BROUGHT US HAPPINESS, TEARS AND LOTS OF FUN

CHARLOTTE CHURCH C

Charlotte Church can't remember a time when she wasn't singing. As a child, she used to sing in church (just a coincidence?!) and her debut album was released when she was just twelve years old. That record made her the youngest ever artist to reach Number One in the album charts. She also released four of the tracks as singles, reaching Number Two in the charts with one of them. Charlotte has also appeared on 'the big screen' in the 2003 film, *I'll Be There*. Fame, though, has brought some problems. As an attractive young woman, perhaps it's not surprising that Charlotte has often found herself the target of gossip columnists and her song, *Let's Be Alone*, comments on this phenomenon with lines such as, *'Why won't anyone leave us to be alone?'* and *'Why does the world love to hate us?'* We don't hate you, Charlotte – we're crazy about you!

D

Teen heartthrob Zac Efron had been performing for many years before he joined the cast of *High School Musical*. In fact, he made his first appearance on stage at the tender age of eleven. Girls didn't always think him so good-looking, though. Today he talks about how he was teased at school. 'Girls would laugh at the "huge gap" in my teeth'. Zac recently turned down the chance to star in a remake of the film *Footloose*. He was going to accept the role, but decided he didn't want to be in yet another musical. Instead, he has recently made two very different films in an attempt to mirror the career of his hero, Leonardo DiCaprio, who went from being a superstar in *Titanic* to a serious actor in films such as *Blood Diamond*. By the way, Zac is excellent in both of his serious film roles.

ZAC EFRON

GEORGE SAMPSON

E

In 2008, fourteen-year old dancer George Sampson appeared on the reality show *Britain's Got Talent*. A year before, he had auditioned for the 2007 show, but wasn't chosen to appear. That failure made him even more determined to succeed and in 2008, he not only passed the audition, but won the competition. He was delighted, but amazed. Since then, he has been very busy. He has appeared on stage in the musical, *Into the Hoods* and in a dance DVD. He even made a music CD but, as he isn't a singer, he wasn't very good and it wasn't very successful. He has also helped with an anti-bullying campaign run by the BBC after he revealed that at school he was a target of bullies himself. I'm sure no-one bullies him now!

3 **Replace the underlined words in the sentences with a word or phrase from the texts.**

1 It must be really difficult for <u>famous people</u> to have a normal life. (title)
2 The way you told that story really <u>made me believe</u> it was true. (text A)
3 What have you been doing over the past <u>ten years</u>? (text B)
4 The new Rihanna CD is not as good as her <u>first</u> album. (texts B and C)
5 Where does this <u>gossip newspaper writer</u> get all her information from? (text C)
6 I was a <u>person deliberately chosen to be attacked by</u> bullies. (text C)
7 Do you have to be perfect-looking to be <u>someone who lots of fans fall in love with</u>? (text D)
8 He's quite well-known, but he isn't <u>an incredibly famous person</u>. (text D)
9 The school is running an <u>organised effort to stop children being cruel to each other</u> which it hopes will create a safer and happier school environment. (text E)

WebSearch

http://www.fox.com/house
http://www.unrealitytv.co.uk

CHATROOM

Who is your favourite entertainer or celebrity? Choose two or three people and give reasons for your choices. What do you know about them?

Vocabulary

Word formation: words from the text

1 Complete the descriptions with the correct form of the words in capitals. All the words are from the reading texts on pages 18 and 19.

The most ¹_____ (SUCCESS) ²_____ (NOVEL) of the last decade is Stephenie Meyer, the writer of the *Twilight* series of books. She was voted one of *MSN Lifestyle's* most ³_____ (INFLUENCE) women. Despite her ⁴_____ (FAMOUS) and wealth, Stephenie remains unchanged by her star status.

The greatest ⁵_____ (COMEDY) of the last decade must be Ben Stiller. He has made twenty-eight films in ten years, although not all of them have been a success. But even a ⁶_____ (FAIL) can make money. *The Heartbreak Kid* received a lot of negative ⁷_____ (CRITICISE) in the press. In fact, it was voted the worst ⁸_____ (MAKE) of 2007 … but it still made $127 million!

Art

2 Match the highlighted words with the questions.

When people think of art, they usually imagine pleasant paintings done in **oils** or **watercolours** hanging in an **exhibition** at a **gallery**. Or perhaps a **portrait** or **landscape** taking pride of place in someone's home. However, add the adjective 'modern' and the image changes. **Sculptors** making controversial models out of different materials, artists exhibiting dead animals or piles of house bricks, **performance artists** sitting in a glass box for forty-four days. Are these really 'art' or just headline-grabbing publicity stunts?

Which word(s) is/are …
1 a place where you can see paintings?
2 a collection of pieces of art on show together?
3 a kind of painting?
4 a kind of artist?
5 something used to paint with?

Adjectives ending in -ed and -ing

3 Complete the conversations with the correct form of the words in capitals.

AMAZE/EXHAUST

Helen: Isn't the band just ¹_____ ?
Rob: Yes, I'm ²_____ they can still stand up at their age!
Helen: It must be really ³_____ to play for two hours non-stop.
Rob: I feel ⁴_____ just watching them. I need a drink and a rest!

DISAPPOINT/EXCITE

Jack: Stop complaining. I know you're ⁵_____ with the standard of the paintings, but you promised to come to the gallery with me. Wow! This is a really ⁶_____ painting.
Ed: No, it isn't. It's the most ⁷_____ painting we've seen so far. It's just black. How can you be ⁸_____ by a black square?

Phrasal verbs

4 Match the phrasal verbs with the correct meanings.

1	bring back	A	remember
2	come across	B	make you remember something
3	end up	C	result in
4	lead to	D	accept less than the best
5	look back on	E	reject
6	settle for	F	become available
7	stick to	G	keep doing an activity
8	turn down	H	to get to a state without intending to
9	come out	I	find by accident

5 Complete the dialogue with the correct form of the phrasal verbs from Exercise 4.

Matt: Wow. This old film ¹_____ memories. I saw it when it first ²_____ in 1997. Where did you find the video?
Paul: I ³_____ it in a second-hand book shop.
Matt: I love Molly Perkins. She's a great actress. She was offered the chance to go to Hollywood but she ⁴_____ it _____ . She wanted to be a serious actress and she ⁵_____ theatre work.
Paul: I wonder if she ever ⁶_____ her career and regrets it.
Matt: I doubt it. Hollywood actors all ⁷_____ the same way – rich and unhappy. Money and fame always ⁸_____ the same thing – big houses, good food, parties and exotic holidays. You forget who you really are and lose your talent.
Paul: I'd ⁹_____ that – a life of luxury in exchange for my talent.
Matt: That's because you haven't got any talent to lose!

Prepositions + nouns

6 Complete the sentences with *in, at* or *on.*

1 This is the first time they have appeared _____ **stage** together.
2 Did they film this scene in a studio or _____ **location**?
3 You can see *Britain's Got Talent* _____ the Fox **Channel**.
4 Tickets are available _____ **the box office** now.
5 I've never seen my name _____ **print** before.
6 Daniel usually paints _____ **oils** _____ **canvas**.
7 I love this book. It starts brilliantly _____ **page one** and gets better and better. There's a surprise _____ **chapter** three and you won't believe what happens _____ **the end**.
8 Mark Jacobson appears _____ **the role of** Detective Connors.

Collocations

7 Complete the sentences with the words from the box.

> face   fail   forget   form   get   reach   record   release

The optimist

Yes! I'm going to …
1 _____ a band.
2 _____ an album.
3 _____ the album.
4 _____ number one in the charts.

The pessimist

Oh no! I'm going to …
1 _____ the audition for the lead role.
2 only _____ a minor part in the play.
3 _____ the audience on the first night.
4 _____ my lines and never appear on stage again.

Word formation: nouns from verbs

8 Complete the sentences with the correct form of the words in capitals.

1 The world famous film _____ (PRODUCE), Matt Zeckerman, made a surprise _____ (APPEAR) at a local theatre.
2 Our school theatre group won the _____ (COMPETE) to find the best school play.
3 The new _____ (EXHIBIT) of modern art includes two new _____ (SCULPT) by Gustav Lehman.
4 Our final _____ (REHEARSE) for the play is on Friday and our first _____ (PERFORM) is on Saturday.
5 Out now! A new _____ (PUBLISH) filled with news of all the different forms of _____ (ENTERTAIN) you can see each week in Dublin.
6 The Vienna Orchestra is playing three new _____ (COMPOSE) by Stephanie Rose. The _____ (CONDUCT) of the orchestra is Stephanie's husband, Mario Pelc.

Back up your vocabulary

9 Read the text and think of the word which best fits each space. Use only one word in each space.

Legendary actor retires

Eric Matherson has decided to retire from the theatre after fifty-five years. Last night was the last time he will ever appear [1]_____ stage. That's his decision and I'm sure he will stick [2]_____ it. He has been offered a lot of money to appear [3]_____ the role of an ageing singer in a Hollywood comedy but he has [4]_____ that down as well. In interviews, Eric said that retirement would bring him more time to concentrate on his writing and art. While researching the life of Rembrandt for a play two years ago, Eric [5]_____ across an antique set of paints and brushes and has been painting ever since. He has already had one of his paintings shown at an [6]_____ of 'Art by Amateurs' at the National Gallery.

After news of his retirement became known, there was a rush for tickets at the [7]_____ office and all of the last week's shows were sold out. However, the BBC filmed one night's performance and will show it [8]_____ one of their channels next week.

CHATROOM

- What kinds of art do you like and dislike?
- What different skills do a stage performer and a film actor have to have? Which do you think is easier?

This is a fascinating piece of art. It represents the emptiness the artist feels

news
Thieves steal painting from frame in art gallery

Grammar
Past tenses

> **past simple**
> Hugh Laurie **started** his career as a comedian.
> **past continuous**
> While they **were waiting** for the record to come out, the events of 9/11 took place.
> **past perfect simple**
> A year before, he **had auditioned** for the 2007 show.
> **past perfect continuous**
> Zac Efron **had been performing** for many years before ...
> **used to / would**
> As a child, she **used to sing** in church.
> Girls **would laugh** at the 'huge gap' in my teeth.
> **past passives**
> Her debut album **was released** when she was 12.
> Brad Pitt **was being chased** by paparazzi when he crashed.

See **Grammar File**, pages 158 and 159

1 Complete the dialogue with the past simple or the present perfect simple.

Presenter: Welcome to *Your Quiz*, the radio quiz for teenagers where you choose the topic. Today's contestant has chosen to answer questions about George Clooney. First question. How many films ¹_____ (George / direct)?

Rose: He ²_____ (direct) three so far.

Presenter: Correct! His aunt was also a famous actress and singer before she died. How many films ³_____ (she / make)?

Rose: I don't know.

Presenter: She ⁴_____ (make) six before she died. ⁵_____ (they / work) together on TV or in film?

Rose: Yes they ⁶_____ (do).

Presenter: That's right! When ⁷_____ (George / first appear) on TV?

Rose: Was it in 1984?

Presenter: Very good. Now, how many times ⁸_____ (George / be) married?

Rose: Once. He ⁹_____ (be) married from 1989 until ... er ... 1992 or 3.

Presenter: 1993, yes to Talia Balsam. Now, what ¹⁰_____ (he / want) to do before he became an actor?

Rose: He ¹¹_____ (want) to be a baseball player.

Presenter: Max ¹²_____ (die) in 2006. Who was Max?

Rose: He was George's pig.

Presenter: Yes! You've scored five out of six. Well done!

2 Complete the dialogue with the past simple or the past continuous of the verbs from the box.

> he / ask   I / paint   I / talk   you / get   you / paint

Jenny: I had a strange day yesterday. I went to the harbour in the morning to paint.

Harry: ¹_____ when the storm came?

Jenny: Yes, I was. ²_____ the boats.

Harry: ³_____ everything packed up before it got wet?

Jenny: No, I didn't and I was really upset but later on, I was in the café and ⁴_____ to a man about what had happened. ⁵_____ me to show him the painting and he loved it. He loved the effect of the rainwater and he paid me $100 for it!

3 Complete the second sentence so that it means the same as the first. Use the past perfect simple or the past perfect continuous.

1 I waited at the cinema for ages before Brett arrived.
By the time Brett arrived at the cinema, _____ ages.

2 Steve started acting a long time before he appeared in his first film in 2008.
Steve didn't appear in a film until 2008, but _____ for a long time before that.

3 Someone borrowed the film we wanted from the DVD shop so we couldn't borrow it.
We went to the DVD shop, but someone _____ we wanted.

4 I used several ideas from other books when I wrote my novel and the publishers rejected it!
My novel was rejected by the publishers because _____ from other books.

4 Change the verb forms in the text about Harold Lloyd. Use *used to* (U) or *would* (W).

In the early days of Hollywood, stars ¹*did* (U) _____ everything by themselves. They ²*didn't have* (U)_____ stunt men to do the dangerous things. Harold Lloyd was one of the bravest actors. He ³*climbed* (W) _____ the side of buildings and jump off moving cars. In his films, Harold's character always ⁴*wore* (U)_____ glasses and the stories always ⁵*followed* (U)_____ the same pattern – the shy boy ⁶*fell* (W) _____ in love, he ⁷*had* (W)_____ some problem to overcome and, finally, he ⁸*won* (W)_____ the girl's heart. Audiences ⁹*loved* (U)_____ the sweet characters he played, but in real life, he wasn't shy at all. He was a clever, successful and stubborn businessman who ¹⁰*directed* (U)_____ and produce many of his own films.

Other structures with past forms

Future in the past
*He **was going to** accept the role, but decided …*
It's time / I'd rather
*It's **time we recorded** a new album.*
*I'd **rather we didn't go** to a modern art exhibition.*

See **Grammar File**, page 159

5 Write the plans using future in the past.

1 Kerry wanted to go to the beach. It rained, so she visited an art gallery.
Kerry wasn't going to visit an art gallery. She was going to go to the beach.
2 Danielle wanted to take a taxi. She didn't have enough money, so she took the bus.
3 David and Alison wanted to see a film. It was sold out. They saw a play.
4 Sean wanted to do a project about Dali. He couldn't find any information. He did a project about Picasso.

6 Read the situations and complete the sentences.

1 You are watching TV. It's late and you've got school in the morning. Your mum says:
'It's time you …'
2 Your friend suggests eating at a burger bar. You prefer Chinese food.
'I'd rather we …'
3 Your friend hasn't booked the concert tickets. You're worried they will be sold out.
'It's time you …'
4 You're going camping with some friends. They want to invite Liam but you don't like him.
'I'd rather you …'

Back up your grammar

7 Complete the text with the correct past form of the verbs in brackets.

Cartrain became famous in the art world in 2008 when he was sixteen years old, but he ¹_____ (paint) for four years before that. He ²_____ (use) to paint graffiti art near his home in East London.
   In 2007, the artist Damien Hirst, created a human skull out of platinum and diamonds, but using a real set of human teeth. While art critics ³_____ (congratulate) Hirst on his creation, Cartrain had an idea of his own. He used an image of the skull as the basis for a piece of his own artwork, which he then sold on the Internet. He made £200, but ⁴_____ (order) to give his artworks and the money to Hirst as he ⁵_____ (copy) the image illegally.
   The following year, Hirst had another exhibition, *Pharmacy*, which included a packet of pencils. While other visitors to the gallery ⁶_____ (look) at the exhibit, Cartrain took the pencils. He then made posters with them asking for his artworks back and he even signs his work with them now.

CHATROOM

Which TV programmes did you use to watch five years ago? What do you watch now? Have your tastes changed?

Listening

Listening 1

🔊 **1** You will hear someone talking about two organisations trying to
bring free theatre to people. Complete the sentences with a word
or short phrase.

Listening Tip: sentence completion

○ Before you listen, read the sentences carefully and find
clues to the kind of information that is missing.

○ Don't forget that you can write numbers in numerical form –
don't waste time writing out the words.

The letters TCG stand for Theatre ⬚ 1 .

The first free 'Night of Theatre' happened in only ⬚ 2 .

This year, theatres offered a total of ⬚ 3 .

The number of theatres offering free tickets this year is
⬚ 4 .

'A Night Less Ordinary' is organised by the ⬚ 5 .

You can't get a free ticket for the 'A Night Less Ordinary' scheme if
you are aged ⬚ 6 or above.

The 'A Night Less Ordinary' scheme aims to give away 618,000
tickets over a period of ⬚ 7 .

Young people tend to prefer going to either the cinema or
⬚ 8 to going to the theatre.

Another Arts Council idea is to give every school student five hours
a week of ⬚ 9 .

You can get tickets from the theatre ⬚ 10 .

Listening 2

🔊 **2** You will hear five people talking about
free events they have attended. For each
speaker choose the correct heading
(A–F). There is one extra heading which
you don't need to use.

Listening Tip: multiple matching

○ During the first listening, make notes
about key information that each
speaker gives.

○ Even if you think you are right, listen
carefully to check when the recording
is played for a second time.

Speaker 1 ⬚

Speaker 2 ⬚

Speaker 3 ⬚

Speaker 4 ⬚

Speaker 5 ⬚

A Celebrating our culture in a different
country.
B Amazing experience a long way from
home.
C A choice of plays in the park.
D We travel there every year.
E A different film free each day.
F Inspired by a star of stage and screen.

WebSearch

http://www.alianait.ca/
http://www.publictheater.org/
http://www.tcg.org/

Speaking
Comparing two photographs

1 Look at the two pictures of teenagers watching films in two different places and answer the questions.

1. Where are the young people in each photo?
2. How are they feeling? Why do you think this might be?
3. What are the advantages and disadvantages of each place?

2 You will hear someone talking about these photos. How many of your ideas does he mention?

3 Listen again and number the points below in the correct order.

- A short description of the first photo. ☐
- A short summing up showing the speaker's own opinion. ☐
- A very brief overall comment about what is shown in the two photos. ☐
- Advantages and disadvantages of each photo. ☐
- A short description of the second photo. ☐

Speaking Tip: timing

- For a one-minute description, try describing the first photo in fifteen seconds, the second in another fifteen and the follow up question in the final thirty seconds.

4 Look at the two pictures and read the task.

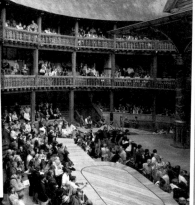

Compare the two photos of people at the theatre. Which theatre would you prefer to visit and why?

5 Now work with a partner and answer these questions.

1. What are the main differences between the two photos?
2. Are there any similarities?
3. Do you think that different kinds of plays are performed in each place?
4. Which theatre would you prefer to visit?
5. What might affect your decision? (cost, comfort, sound, view, weather, standard of acting, other?)

6 Now do the task while your partner times you for one minute. Then swap roles. Use the Language Upload box to help you.

Speaking Tip: comparing photographs

- Listen carefully to the question. It does not *always* mention advantages and disadvantages of the different photos.
- If neither picture is attractive for you, be honest but give good reasons for your answer.

Language Upload

Describing photos

In the first photo I can see / there are …
Both photos show …
They look bored/excited/interested
It looks boring/exciting/interesting
They look/seem as if they are …
Perhaps/Maybe/They might be …

Comparing the photos

There are several similarities.
There are several advantages to …
The main similarity/difference is that …
In the first photo … whereas in the second

Stating your opinion

In my opinion …
As far as I'm concerned …
Overall I (would) prefer to …
I'm not very keen on either picture to be honest …
However, if I had to choose between the two places, I would choose …

Writing: A Discursive Essay

Before you write

1 Look at the pictures. Do you think they reflect the life of a celebrity? Why?

2 List the advantages and disadvantages of being famous.

3 Read the extract from a magazine and the task and tick the things you have to do.

1 Describe Lisa Fairview.
2 Talk about the advantages and disadvantages of being famous.
3 Say why you want to be famous.
4 Give your opinion of Lisa Fairview's view.
5 Explain why you agree or disagree.

Entertainment **today**

Last night, Lisa Fairview, the singer and actress, attacked paparazzi who were waiting for her outside a nightclub. Lisa had been celebrating the success of her latest single with friends, but lost her temper when photographers stopped her as she was getting into a taxi. At a press conference this morning, Lisa told reporters that fame 'only looks good to those who haven't got it'.

Lisa said, 'fame only looks good to those who haven't got it'. Discuss the advantages and disadvantages of being famous and decide whether you agree with Lisa or not. Give reasons for your answer. Write between 120 and 180 words.

4 Now read the model essay. How many of your ideas from Exercise 2 were mentioned?

> Many people are obsessed with becoming famous. Some succeed by uploading videos to Youtube or appearing on reality TV. But, do those who manage to become famous enjoy their new life?
>
> There are many advantages to being famous. The most obvious is that you are given better treatment in places such as restaurants or when travelling. **In addition**, your fame allows you to experience new things. For example, you may be offered tickets to top sporting events or invited to parties.
>
> **However**, there are problems connected with fame. You are a public figure **so** people believe they have the right to know what you are doing all the time. **Moreover**, some people will try to discover things about your past or even spread lies about you.
>
> **All in all**, I think the benefits of being famous are outweighed by the disadvantages. **In my opinion**, fame looks good **because** the public see the smiling faces of celebrities, but they don't know how those celebrities are feeling on the inside.

5 Look at the essay on fame and match the paragraph headings with the correct paragraphs. Which two paragraphs could be written in reverse order?

A Advantages of fame.
B Summary and writer's opinion.
C Introduction.
D Disadvantages of fame.

6 Match the words highlighted in the text with the correct linking expression.

Addition: _____ , _____   Contrast: _____
Reasons: _____   Result: _____
Giving opinions: _____   Summarising: _____

7 Rewrite these sentences from the text using an expression from the box. Sometimes, more than one answer may be possible.

> as far as I'm concerned   as well as this
> overall   though   what's more

1 **In addition**, your fame allows you to experience new things.
_____

2 **However**, there are problems associated with fame.
_____

3 **Moreover**, some people will even try to find out things about your past or even spread lies about you.
_____

4 **All in all**, I think the benefits of being famous are outweighed by the disadvantages.
_____

5 **In my opinion**, fame looks good because the public see the smiling faces of celebrities but they don't know how those celebrities are feeling on the inside.
_____

8 Read the article and the task.

Daily News

Schoolgirl's nightmare after talent show appearance

Emily Prince, aged 15, was delighted when she appeared on a TV talent show but, since then, things have changed. People who used to be her friends now talk about her behind her back. Emily now says, 'School children shouldn't enter TV talent shows. It only brings misery.'

"I can't sing or dance, but I can remove bandaids very slowly without flinching!"

Emily doesn't think that school children should enter TV talent shows. Do you agree with her or not? What are the advantages and disadvantages of entering talent contests while still at school? Give reasons for your answer. Write between 120–180 words.

9 Look at these ideas for the essay. Are the points advantages (A) or disadvantages (D)?

- Other students will be jealous of you.
- It can give you confidence.
- You may be seen by a producer or director.
- You might not have time for studies.
- Real friends will be happy for you.
- It's difficult to fail in front of others.

10 Look at some items of vocabulary that you might be able to use in your essay. Decide which would be useful for you and which not. There is no right answer, you can use as many or as few words as you like.

jealousy	neglect	stage	supportive
immature	true friend	competition	revision
homework	in public	humiliation	
career	classmates		

11 Decide what your own opinion is and why.

12 Write a plan of your essay similar to that in Exercise 5.

13 Write your essay. Use the Writing Checklist and Memory Flash to help you.

Writing Checklist: A Discursive Essay

Does the essay include

1 a word derived from a key word in the question?

2 a question which the writer answers later in the text?

3 topic sentences which clearly tell the reader what the paragraph is about?

4 passive verbs?

5 words to give emphasis such as 'in fact', 'even', 'actually', etc?

6 examples to back up an argument?

7 a number of items showing a good range of vocabulary for this level?

8 appropriately formal language with full forms of words NOT contractions?

Memory Flash

Addition: As well as, In addition, Moreover, What's more, Furthermore

Contrast: However, Although, Despite, In spite of, On the other hand

Reasons: Because, Because of, Due to (the fact that)

Result: So, Therefore, That's why

Giving opinions: In my opinion, As far as I'm concerned

Introducing examples: For example, For instance

Summarising: To sum up, All in all, Overall, In conclusion

Vocabulary

1 Choose the word that best completes the sentence.

1 We went to a(n) _____ of modern art.
   A rehearsal   C exhibition
   B audition   D sculpture

2 I started laughing when one of the actors forgot his _____ .
   A role   C part
   B lines   D turn

3 While we were walking around the town, we came _____ a lovely little café.
   A up   C through
   B across   D over

4 We couldn't decide what to do, so we ended _____ renting a DVD.
   A up   C out
   B off   D over

5 Despite bad reviews, the film did well at the _____ .
   A location   C screen
   B studio   D box office

6 I applied for a summer job at a recording studio but they _____ me down.
   A pushed   C put
   B turned   D ran

2 Complete the article about Demi Lovato with the words from the box.

> album   charts   compositions   location
> reached   recorded   release
> role   series

Demi Lovato is an actress and singer from Texas in the USA. She is best known for starring in the film *Camp Rock* in the ¹_____ of Mitchie Torres, a fourteen-year-old who dreams of becoming a singer. The film also starred the Jonas Brothers and was filmed on ²_____ in Canada. Demi, though, had been acting for a long time before that. Her first TV appearances were in the TV ³_____ *Barney and Friends* when she was just six years old. Demi likes writing songs and some of her own ⁴_____ were used on that show. She also ⁵_____ three of the songs from *Camp Rock*. The following year, she released her debut ⁶_____, *Don't Forget*, which ⁷_____ Number Two in the American ⁸_____ . Her second album, *Here We Go Again*, did even better and got to Number One in its first week of ⁹_____ .

Grammar

3 Complete the second sentence so that it has a similar meaning to the first. Use the word in capitals.

1 The theatre director invited us to meet the actors.
   WERE
   We _____ the actors by the theatre director.

2 When I was young, we went to the theatre every Christmas.
   WOULD
   When I was young, _____ theatre every Christmas.

3 What music did you listen to when you were a child?
   USE
   What music _____ to when you were a child?

4 I had planned to check what was on at the cinema but I didn't have time.
   GOING
   I _____ what was on at the cinema, but I didn't have time.

5 I got the tickets after a three-hour queue.
   QUEUEING
   When I got the tickets, _____ three hours.

4 Read the article about Ronald K. Brown and think of the word which best fits each space. Use only one word in each space.

When Ronald K. Brown left school in 1983, he ¹_____ already appeared in several school musicals. Dance had always ²_____ his passion and he ³_____ dance around the house at a very early age.

He began studying dance seriously in the summer of 1983. He was ⁴_____ to start college that September but, in the end, he went to the Mary Anthony Dance Studio instead.

While he ⁵_____ studying with the dancer Jennifer Muller, he formed the *Evidence Dance Company*.

He ⁶_____ now written over 100 pieces and won many awards. In the autumn of 2006, fifty artists ⁷_____ given the United States Artists Rose Fellowship and Brown was one of only four choreographers to receive this honour.

It hasn't always been easy for his company. Before 2002 the dancers used ⁸_____ work without pay. Now the company is becoming known around the world.

I want a job where I can travel around the world and meet different people. What about you? What do you dream of doing when you leave school?

3 Sweet Success!

Vocabulary Starter
Jobs and work

1 Match the jobs with the photos.

> fitness instructor   make-up artist   newsreader
> architect   paramedic   lorry driver

2 Who am I? Do the quiz and match the person with the jobs in Exercise 1.

Who am I?

① It's exciting when there's an important story and I'm the one who tells the public.

② I like seeing people change their lives through regular exercise and good diet.

③ I love designing houses.

④ I get actors ready for stage or TV.

⑤ I get a lot of satisfaction from saving peoples' lives.

⑥ I put the radio on and enjoy watching the scenery as I drive past.

3 Are the sentences to do with *money*, *hours* or *benefits*?

1 Four weeks **paid holiday**.   *money*
2 Good opportunities for **overtime**.
3 Friendly **working environment**.
4 30% **staff discount** on clothing.
5 We offer **flexible hours**.
6 We're recruiting for two **full-time** posts.
7 Salary **negotiable** depending on age and experience.
8 Salary: beginning at £35,000 with a generous **annual bonus**.

4 Unscramble the letters to find the words.

1 You have one of these to see if you are right for a job.   ivterwine _____
2 A job or profession that you have trained for.   earerc _____
3 Money you receive every month from your job.   ysalra _____
4 A room with a desk, computer, telephone, etc.   cofief _____
5 A document with spaces to write information.   romf _____
6 Extra money, like a reward for good work.   obusn _____
7 This group of people all work for an organisation.   ftasf _____
8 A well-known firm or 'name' which makes clothes.   blela _____

CHATROOM

- Which do you think is more important – money, the hours you work or job satisfaction?
- Can you name two dangerous jobs and two boring jobs?

Reading

MeiPeking96

I've just downloaded a podcast about jobs for the future. It says that we won't need so many sales assistants as people will shop online.

What do you think?

Which jobs will be more important in the future?

More soon ... watch this space!

1 You're going to read six advertisements related to jobs and work. Read the advertisements (1–6) and match them with the statements (A–F).

A I've always wanted to be a fitness instructor because I like keeping fit. I can help people change their lives for the better!

B I was top of the class in Maths at school so being an accountant is the perfect job for me.

C I'm really into clothes, so I love being a sales assistant in a clothes shop. The discount is great too!

D One day I'm going to be a chef with my own restaurant. Until then I want to get as much experience as possible.

E Being a firefighter is dangerous but rewarding. It's the best job ever!

F I love being a lorry driver. I'm in a different place every day.

1 Teenrags

Keep up with the fashion and earn good money too!

We are a large department store that has taken over the **Teenrags** clothing label. We are looking for four part-time sales assistants who can make **Teenrags** the best label on the high street. You will deal with customers, come up with ideas for the shop window and work at the checkout.

Hours: 9 a.m.–1 p.m. or 2 p.m.–6 p.m. with good opportunity for overtime at weekends. Full training will be given.

Benefits: Four weeks paid holiday. Friendly working environment. 30 percent staff discount on clothing.

Salary: £7 per hour

To apply, please send your CV to

admin@teenrags.com

2 New training courses start next week!

BFS

Bristol Fire Service is recruiting two full-time firefighters. Applications are invited from strong, fit people who can work well in challenging situations. A four-month training course will be held in London and special clothing will be provided. You will already have passed secondary school exams. Perhaps you're going to graduate soon. Final interviews are going to be held in November.

Benefits: Plenty of job satisfaction. Private medical insurance.

Salary: approx £19,000 per annum.

Download your application form from our website today. www.fireservice.co.uk/recruitment

3 Flexibility and freedom!

Earn up to £34,000 per annum. Large haulage company is looking for long-distance lorry drivers for our warehouses in the UK and abroad. We offer flexible hours so that you decide when you work and how much you work. Thanks to new technology our trucks are as easy to drive as a small car. Drivers must be able to use their own initiative and have some mechanical knowledge.

We're interviewing next week so call us now on 0865 875 345. The faster you apply, the sooner your career starts moving.

4 Help us to help them!

The *Health Club* is looking for qualified fitness instructors to join its team. You will work out individual health and fitness programmes when new members arrive. You will also have been trained to carry out fitness tests and offer advice on nutrition and lifestyle. We need someone who can take responsibility for evening and weekend shifts as those are our busiest times. The successful applicant must also have good communication skills.

Salary £10,000–£16,000 per annum depending on experience. Free membership of the *Health Club* pool and gym as soon as you start working for us!

Join our creative kitchen

Successful, new restaurant is now busier than ever! That's why we're going to take on two full-time chefs. You will be working under pressure in a busy environment and will be expected to turn out exciting menus and quality food. This is a fantastic opportunity for the right person with proven experience and lots of creativity. If you are as good a leader as you are a team player then we need to hear from you.

Salary: negotiable depending on experience. Degree in catering essential.

To apply for this job please contact anna@countryhallhotel.info

Do you think numbers are boring?

We don't and that's why we're one of the biggest accountancy firms in Europe. We're looking for an accountant who speaks French to manage a large team in our head office in Switzerland. You will have an eye for detail and will have already shown successful leadership qualities.

Salary: £35,000 with a generous annual bonus. If you have the right qualifications, apply online at www.Hamleysaccountants.com.

HAMLEYS ACCOUNTANTS

---

2 Read the advertisements again and choose the correct answer.

Reading Tip: multiple-choice matching questions

- Don't waste time. If you can't answer a question, go on to the next one.
- Even if you're not sure, answer all the questions!

1 Which jobs offer the opportunity to see other parts of the world?
   A 2 and 3   B 3 and 6   C 3 and 5   D 5 and 6

2 Which job does **not** mention any benefits?
   A 1   B 3   C 5   D 6

3 Which job offers an extra financial benefit?
   A 2   B 3   C 4   D 6

4 Which advert wants you to email details of your education and past jobs?
   A 1   B 2   C 3   D 5

5 Which advert has a plan to help you if you're ill?
   A 1   B 2   C 3   D 5

6 For which job does it help to know how things work?
   A 1   B 3   C 4   D 5

7 Which job requires you to work after 6 pm and on Saturdays and Sundays?
   A 1   B 4   C 5   D 6

8 In which jobs can you work more hours if you want to?
   A 1 and 3   B 1 and 5   C 2 and 3   D 3 and 5

9 Which job is only part-time?
   A 1   B 3   C 5   D 6

10 Which jobs offer more money to someone with more experience?
   A 3 and 4   B 4 and 5   C 4 and 6   D 5 and 6

3 Find words or phrases in the text that mean the following.

1 someone who buys things from a shop or company (advert 1)
2 a document listing your education, qualifications and experience (advert 1)
3 the place in a shop where you pay (advert 1)
4 a programme where you pay money and get paid if you are ill (advert 2)
5 the business of carrying things by road or rail (advert 3)
6 having knowledge, experience and skills for a job (advert 4)
7 the food you eat and the way it affects your health (advert 4)
8 shown to be good (advert 5)
9 the job of providing and serving food and drinks (advert 5)
10 more than the usual amount (advert 6)

CHATROOM

- Who do you know with an interesting or exciting job?
- What do they do?

WebSearch

http://www.bbctraining.com
http://www.youngentrepreneur.com
http://gotajob.com

Vocabulary
Word formation: words from the text

1 Complete the text with the correct form of the words in capitals. All the words are from the reading texts on pages 30 and 31.

It means everything to me!

I hope to be a sports teacher one day. I think it's a job that will give me the ¹_____ (SATISFY) of seeing people learn skills that they will keep for life. First I have to get the right ²_____ (QUALIFY) for the job. There aren't many university places, so I want to make sure I hand in my ³_____ (APPLY) early. This summer I'm going to a ⁴_____ (RECRUIT) day for sports teachers. I'll be able to learn more about the course and meet the ⁵_____ (SUCCEED) students who've already found jobs. The university courses offer ⁶_____ (FLEXIBLE), so if I'm not happy I'll be able to change my course.

I need a good level of ⁷_____ (FIT) before I can start the course. That's easy for me because I play basketball and I'm captain of the school team. That means I have to make sure that the other ⁸_____ (PLAY) turn up for the games and training. I enjoy the ⁹_____ (RESPONSIBLE) and I think it's something I do well. Doing sport also gives me the ¹⁰_____ (FREE) to go out at the weekends and meet new people.

Work

2 Complete the sentences with the words from the box.

> journalist   surgeon   plumber   comedian

1 That's the _____ who performed the operation on my knee.
2 Mark's looking for work as a _____ on TV. He's been telling jokes since he was a child.
3 We'll have to call a _____ because we haven't got any water in the kitchen.
4 When the prime minister came out of his house, a _____ was waiting to ask him questions.

Compound nouns

3 Match the pairs of words to make compound nouns for jobs.

1	lorry	A	instructor
2	make-up	B	fighter
3	social	C	assistant
4	fitness	D	agent
5	fire	E	warden
6	estate	F	driver
7	sales	G	artist
8	traffic	H	worker

Workplaces

4 Choose the correct answer.

1 We're selling the house so we've contacted an estate **agency** / **office** and they'll come and take some photos.
2 We're still waiting for our TV to be delivered. Apparently it won't be leaving the **company** / **warehouse** until next week!
3 Jack works as a firefighter; when on duty at night he has to sleep in the **station** / **factory** in case he's called out to a fire.
4 Every year the **head office** / **factory** produces thousands of cars that are sold all over the world.
5 I'm really not happy about my new computer. I'm going to write a letter of complaint to the **head office** / **factory**.
6 My car has been at the **clinic** / **garage** for two days. The mechanics are looking at the brakes.
7 We are a family **business** / **factory** that offers financial advice.
8 Sandersons is a famous **advertising agency** / **department store** that sells everything from shoes to kitchen cookers.

"I always give 110% to my job.
40% on Monday, 30% on Tuesday, 20% on Wednesday, 15% on Thursday, and 5% on Friday."

Education

5 Complete the email with the words from the box.

> qualifications   experience   revise   degree
> passed   graduate   training

New   Reply

Hi Ben,

I've just found out that I ¹_____ all my exams, so in September I'm going to do a ²_____ at university. I want to study medicine. After I ³_____ I hope to become a surgeon. What about you? Do you still want to be a paramedic? Your exams sound difficult, but if you have the right ⁴_____ you'll have a better chance of getting a good job.

This afternoon I've got an interview for a job at the swimming pool during the summer. The advert says that I don't need any previous ⁵_____ because full ⁶_____ will be given. I hope I get the job. I can't quite believe I don't have to ⁷_____ for any more exams!

Love, Lucy

Collocations

6 Complete the adverts and notes with the verbs from the box.

have   apply   manage   send   be   attend

Bar staff wanted. ¹_____
your CV to
admin@ barbobo.com

We would like to thank you for
your application. Please let us
know if you can ²_____ an
interview on Monday 12th January.

vulput ma reuis ans acm

Shop Manager: Wanted
Smart person who can ³_____
a small team. Call: 0945 8756 333

Wanted
Mechanic for city centre workshop.
Call us NOW if you ⁴_____
mechanical knowledge and can
⁵_____ a good team player.

Wanted
Chef with good leadership skills.
Please ⁶_____ online at
www.jobsforchefs.com
to feugiatio comm llgn

Phrasal verbs

7 Match the phrasal verbs with their definitions.

1 keep up with
2 take over
3 deal with
4 come up with
5 take on
6 count on
7 work out
8 turn out

A start to employ someone
B produce
C depend on someone
D calculate something
E know the latest information about something
F get control of a business or job
G manage a difficult situation
H think of an idea or plan

8 Complete the sentences with the correct form of the phrasal verbs from Exercise 7.

1 We visited a chocolate factory. It's incredible how quickly they can _____ thousands of chocolates.
2 Have you heard the news? The sports centre Activa has been sold. It's been _____ and the new owners are offering great discounts to students.
3 The best thing about my job is _____ the customers. I enjoy helping them choose the right product.
4 You can _____ me if you're looking for people to do over-time. I need the extra money.
5 Dan's very creative. He always _____ great ideas for our advertising campaigns.
6 Rachel works in a clothes shop so she has no problem _____ the latest fashions.
7 The shop is doing very badly. The manager is trying to _____ a way to attract new customers.
8 I'm going for an interview at The Bay Café. They _____ new staff for the summer.

Back up your vocabulary

9 Read the text and choose the best answer (A, B, C or D) for each gap.

Jobs for the future

What will you be doing in ten years' time? Perhaps you will be a doctor or an estate ¹_____ . If you're lucky you'll be in a job that you've chosen and that you like. However, you may find that firms of the future will be asking for ²_____ that don't exist at the moment.

Space tourism, for example, is rapidly becoming a reality. If tourists begin to travel into space, then travel companies will need tour guides. If this is a job that you think you would like to ³_____ for, you'll be pleased to know that a university in America is offering a ⁴_____ in Science that includes space exploration. Working with robots will also be a possibility. Could you ⁵_____ a team of robot workers who can work day and night shifts without stopping?

There will be big changes in the working world. Experts say that the more we shop online, the less we'll need friendly sales ⁶_____ in shops to ⁷_____ advice. The fact is that the working world is changing and we need to do what we can to ⁸_____ up with those changes and secure a job in the future.

1 A officer   C agent
   B clerk   D assistant
2 A exams   C experiences
   B results   D qualifications
3 A apply   C attend
   B assist   D supply
4 A subject   C grade
   B exam   D degree
5 A check   C manage
   B cope   D deal
6 A clerks   C workers
   B helpers   D assistants
7 A offer   C have
   B use   D make
8 A turn   C keep
   B come   D count

Grammar
Future forms

present simple for future use
*New training courses **start** next week!*
present continuous for future use
*We're **interviewing** next week so call us now.*
future simple
*You **will deal** with customers.*
future continuous
*You **will be working** under pressure.*
going to
*That's why we're **going to take on** two full-time chefs.*
future perfect
*You **will** already **have passed** secondary school exams.*
future passive
*Full training **will be given**.*
*Final interviews **are going to be held** in November.*
*You **will** also **have been trained** to carry out fitness tests.*
future time clauses
*You **will work out** individual fitness programmes when new members **arrive**.*
*Free membership of the Health Club pool as soon as you **start** working for us!*

See **Grammar File**, page 160

1 Complete the dialogue with the correct form of the present simple, present continuous or *will*.

Adam: Where are you going, Emily?
Emily: I've got an interview for a summer job. It ¹_____ (start) at nine o'clock, so I can't stop.
Adam: That's OK. What ²_____ (you / do) this afternoon?
Emily: I don't know yet. I ³_____ (call) you later.
Adam: Fine. I ⁴_____ (play) basketball until 1 pm, but after that I ⁵_____ (not do) anything.
Emily: OK. I was hoping to go to the cinema.
Adam: Great! We can get the bus that ⁶_____ (leave) at two o'clock. Do you think that ⁷_____ (you / be) back by then?
Emily: I hope so! I don't think the interview ⁸_____ (take) more than half an hour.
Adam: Good luck with the interview!

2 Complete the short dialogues with the correct *going to* or *will* form of the verbs.

1 **A:** What are you doing on the computer?
   B: I'm writing my CV. The supermarket is taking on more people. I _____ (apply) for a job there!
2 **A:** I'm sorry but I can't work today, I don't feel well.
   B: That's OK. Sandra says she _____ (take) over for you.
3 **A:** Did you phone the estate agency about the job?
   B: Yes, I did. I _____ (see) the manager this afternoon.
4 **A:** Oh no! The bus is late and my interview starts in ten minutes.
   B: Don't worry. I _____ (take) you in my car.
5 **A:** Has Anna decided what she wants to do after school?
   B: Oh yes, she can't wait. She _____ (do) a degree in English at university.

3 Complete the postcard with the present simple, the future simple, the future continuous or the future perfect simple.

Hi Max,

Here I am on a tour of our European offices. By the time you get this postcard of Prague I ¹_____ (arrive) in Rome. The meetings are going well and everybody is very friendly. Tonight I ²_____ (fly) on to Milan. I'm quite tired but I think I ³_____ (be able) to sleep on the journey. I probably ⁴_____ (not arrive) at the hotel until after midnight. I ⁵_____ (email) you on Monday from my hotel room. Don't try calling me during the day because I ⁶_____ (work) in the warehouse all day. Anyway, everything's going well but I ⁷_____ (be) glad to get home. How are your exams going this week? Just think — you ⁸_____ (finish) by the time I get back!

See you soon,
Amanda

4 Complete the second sentence so that it has a similar meaning to the first. Use *by* when necessary.

1 I hope the university will accept me on the Business Management course.
I hope _____ the University on its Business Management course.

2 Thousands of cars will have been produced by the factory before the end of the year.
The factory _____ thousands of cars before the end of the year.

3 The head office is going to select applicants to attend a training course.
Applicants _____ the head office to attend a training course.

4 The staff won't be allowed to work flexible hours.
The manager _____ the staff to work flexible hours.

5 More social workers are going to be trained by the government.
The government _____ more social workers.

5 Choose the correct answer.

Anna: Hi Lucy, look at this advert. The beach café is looking for staff. ¹**As soon as / Until** I finish my exams I'm going to apply.

Lucy: But it says you can't work there ²**until / after** you're eighteen.

Anna: Oh no! That's really annoying. What are you going to do ³**by the time / when** the summer holidays start?

Lucy: Well, I usually help my mum's friends. I look after their children ⁴**when / until** they come home from work.

Anna: That's a great idea. I think I'll put an advert in the local shop ⁵**before / the moment** everybody else has the same idea.

Lucy: You don't need to! My aunt starts a new job next week. You could look after my cousin ⁶**while / until** she's working.

Anna: Great! Give me her number and I'll phone her ⁷**the moment / by the time** I get home!

Comparatives, superlatives and quantifiers

comparatives
*Successful, new restaurant is now **busier** than ever.*
*Thanks to new technology our trucks are **as easy** to drive **as** a small car.*
superlatives
*We're one of **the biggest** accountancy firms in Europe.*
*… sales assistants who can make Teenrags **the best** label on the high street.*
***The faster** you apply, **the sooner** your career starts moving.*
quantifiers
*Drivers must have **some** mechanical knowledge.*
***Plenty of** job satisfaction.*
*A fantastic opportunity for the right person with proven experience and **lots of** creativity.*

See **Grammar File**, page 161

6 Choose the correct answer.

After school I did a catering course. It was much ¹*most difficult / more difficult* than other courses I'd done and I had to take ²*lots of / much* exams. In the end I got ³*the better / the best* mark in the class. Now I'm a chef in ⁴*the most famous / more famous* restaurant in town! It's always full of customers – I've even cooked for ⁵*a few / little* famous actors. The more they enjoy their meal, the ⁶*the happiest / the happier* I feel.

Back up your grammar

7 Read the article and think of the word which best fits each space. Use only one word in each space.

Most people have an idea of what they want to do ¹_____ the time they leave school. During their final school year they will have ²_____ advised of the options that are available to them. Some students will choose careers that offer plenty ³_____ job satisfaction while others will look for jobs that offer a high salary.

But what do you do if you ⁴_____ already become successful before you leave school? For example, look at the actress, Emma Watson, who plays Hermione in the *Harry Potter* films. Emma has already made ten films and it is hoped that she will ⁵_____ appearing on cinema screens for many years to come. However, Emma has decided that she is ⁶_____ to study. She knows that fame isn't permanent and wants to lead as normal a life ⁷_____ possible.

CHATROOM

What will you be doing in five years' time / in ten years' time?

Listening

Listening 1

1 You will hear eight short conversations. Choose the best answer, A, B or C.

Listening Tip: multiple-choice questions

- Read the questions carefully.
- The tone of the speaker's voice can help you listen for the correct information.
- Remember the words in the questions probably won't be the words that you hear.

1 A young man is talking about a course he wants to do. Why does he want to do it?
  A He wants a better-paid job.
  B He wants a more interesting job.
  C His friends suggested that he do it.

2 You overhear a student talking about somewhere she visited on a school trip. Where did she go?
  A a factory
  B a clothes shop
  C a department store

3 You hear a girl talking about a summer job. Where did she work?
  A in a restaurant
  B in a family
  C in a school

4 You will hear a man and a woman talking. What does the woman want to do?
  A apply for a job
  B buy a house
  C arrange an interview

5 You hear two people talking. What is the relationship between them?
  A school friends
  B university tutor and student
  C school teacher and pupil

6 Listen to a man talking on the radio about someone he met a few years ago. Who was the person?
  A a theatre manager
  B a make-up artist
  C a dress designer

7 Listen to two people talking. Where are they?
  A in a university
  B in a health club
  C in a fire station

8 Listen to a radio announcement about a TV programme. What is the programme about?
  A changing careers
  B training to be a DJ
  C nightclubs in Edinburgh

Listening 2

2 You will hear a radio announcement about a careers event. Listen and complete the table.

Listening Tip: table completion

Look at the information in the table before you begin. Try and guess what you are listening for.

Making the Right Choice	
Venue:	Manchester University
Date:	Saturday, March ¹_____
Time:	9 am – ²_____
First presentation	
Stella Matthews ³_____ two years ago. Now manager of ⁴_____ . She is ⁵_____ years old.	
Second presentation	
Will Evans enjoyed travelling before becoming a ⁶_____ . In the next ⁷_____ he will be working in ⁸_____ , Spain, Italy and ⁹_____ .	
After lunch	
Mark Hamilton will offer advice on training courses ranging from catering to ¹⁰_____ .	
Between 4 pm and ¹¹_____ meet make-up artists, ¹²_____ and others.	
Information and booking details	
Refreshments:	Coffee and tea are free. Price of sandwiches is ¹³_____
Admission:	¹⁴_____
Reservations:	Book online at www. ¹⁵_____

WebSearch

http://www.youngbiz.com
http://video.success.com

Speaking
Making a choice

1 Imagine you are going to do a course during the holidays. Look at pictures 1 and 2. What courses do you think they show?

2 Listen to someone asking about one of the courses. Note down the information about the course.

- What type of course is it?
- What will I learn on this course?
- Who is the course for?
- Do I need any special skills or qualifications?
- When is the course?
- How long does it last?
- How much does it cost?

3 Work in pairs.

Student A: ask the questions from Exercise 2 to find out about the second course.
Student B: turn to page 125 for the information you need to answer the questions.

4 Listen to someone choosing a course. Which course does she choose and why?

5 Now say which course you would choose. Explain why, using the phrases in the Language Upload box to help you.

6 Now find out about two more courses.

Student A: look at the information about the courses on page 125.
Student B: ask the questions from Exercise 2 to find out about the courses.

7 When you have information about both courses, explain which one you would choose and why. Use the phrases from the Language Upload box to help you.

Speaking Tip: making a choice

When you explain your choice, support it with information that you have learned from asking the questions.

Language Upload

Making comparisons

I think that the … course is … than the … course because …
I prefer doing … to …
I like being … more than …

Making a decision

I've chosen to apply for the … course because …
I'm going to opt for the … course

Giving reasons

I think it's a good course for me because …
This really appeals to me because …

Reasons for not choosing something

I'm not sure I'd like the course … because …

Writing: A Report
Before you write

1 You want some experience of working in another country. Which of the jobs in the photos would you prefer to do and why?

2 A group of foreign students is looking for work in your town over the summer. Read the report to their group leader Nicola Pinter and write the headings in the correct place.

> Facts about the town   Conclusion
> Introduction   Suggested workplaces

To: Nicola Pinter
From: Matthew Harrison
Date: 30 April 2011
Subject: Work placements

1 _____
The purpose of this report is to recommend the best places for your students to work during the summer.

2 _____
This is a small, tourist town. Many foreign students are employed during the summer. Your students might prefer to work in a hotel or restaurant or they could find employment working at a summer camp with children. I would like to suggest two work places that are particularly interesting:

3 _____
The Grand Hotel is a large, family-run hotel. It is very popular with families and is known for its friendly working environment. Excellent training is given to all new employees and uniforms and accommodation are also provided.
KoolKids is an international summer camp that organises activities for children from all over Europe. It needs young people to teach sports and crafts. They will also help children with any problems they experience while away from home.

4 _____
To conclude, I can strongly recommend the hotel and the summer camp as places to work. They are both excellent companies. I am sure your students would have a positive experience.

3 Underline a phrase in the report that:

1 introduces the report
2 presents information to the reader
3 makes a suggestion
4 offers a final recommendation

4 Put the phrases in the correct place in the chart.

> I can highly recommend …
> Many young people are employed by this company.
> This report is intended to …
> In conclusion, I would recommend … because …
> I suggest that …
> The aim of this report is …
> The town has many small businesses.
> May I also suggest that …?

Introduction
1 _____
2 _____
Presenting information
3 _____
4 _____
Suggestions
5 _____
6 _____
Final recommendations
7 _____
8 _____

5 Look at the passive sentences from the report. Why is the passive used here?

Many foreign students are employed during the summer. Excellent training is given …

6 Rewrite the sentences in a more impersonal style.

1 They interview a lot of foreign students.

_____

2 They have offered their workers language classes.

_____

3 They could offer flexible hours.

_____

4 They will provide excellent training.

_____

5 The training course motivates the staff.

_____

Time to write

7 Read the task and write some facts about the camp. You can use your own ideas.

You work at Koolkids. Mr Dixon, the manager, wants to take on some foreign students this summer. You have been asked to write a report recommending the skills and qualifications the students will need to have.

It's international

_____

_____

_____

_____

8 Tick the skills or qualifications you think a student needs to work at Koolkids. Add two more ideas of your own.

a degree ☐
secondary school education ☐
be a team player ☐
good communication skills ☐
good written skills ☐

_____

_____

9 Choose the best heading for each section of your report. Explain your choices.

1 Aim / Introduction
2 All about Koolkids / Facts about Koolkids
3 Suggested skills and qualifications / Suggested activities
4 Conclusion / My opinion

10 Complete the information for the beginning of your report.

To:
From:
Date:
Subject:

11 Now write your report. Write between 120 and 180 words. Use the Writing Checklist and Memory Flash to help you.

Writing Tip: a report

- Read the question and underline what you have to do.
- Make a plan.
- Start with a clear introduction.
- Present the facts.
- List two or three suggestions.
- Finish with your recommendations.

Writing Checklist: A Report

1 Have you used the correct layout at the beginning of the report? Date:, To:, From:, Subject:
2 Is it clear at the beginning what the report is about?
3 Have you got clear headings at the beginning of each section?
4 Have you used formal language, e.g. passive tenses?
5 Have you presented information for the report?
6 Are your ideas easy to understand?
7 Is it obvious where you have made a suggestion or recommendation?
8 Have you used vocabulary from this unit?

Memory Flash

The purpose/aim of this report is to …
This report aims to …
This report is intended to …
I would like to suggest that …
I suggest that …
I strongly/highly recommend that …
In my opinion, the best … would be …
To conclude …
In conclusion …

Vocabulary

1 Choose the correct answer.

1 People think you just have to look attractive to be on TV, but **journalists** / **newsreaders** often have to write the stories, too.

2 When Adrian was rushed into hospital the **paramedic** / **surgeon** was waiting to operate on him.

3 I've always been interested in buildings, but I had no idea that one day I would be an **architect** / **accountant** and design them.

4 You need to be fit, but the best skill a **fitness instructor** / **firefighter** can have is knowing how to cope in a stressful situation.

5 A good **chef** / **make-up artist** has to understand colour on a plate. You wouldn't serve something that didn't look attractive.

6 A lot of cars were badly parked. When the **lorry driver** / **traffic warden** came, he wrote tickets and put them on the windscreens.

7 When there was a problem with water in the house, we phoned the **estate agent** / **plumber** who came and fixed it.

8 We will be able to look at houses for sale at the **accountant's** / **estate agent's**.

2 Complete the advert with the words from the box.

> managing   attend   full-time   turn out   degree
> head office   graduated   paid   apply

An international publishing company is looking for experienced journalists. Ideally you will have ¹_____ from university with a ²_____ in English or Media Studies. You will have excellent written skills and will be able to ³_____ exciting articles at top speed. You will also be ⁴_____ a team of talented writers and photographers and will be expected to ⁵_____ regular meetings in London. This is a ⁶_____ post and there will be plenty of opportunities for overtime. Five weeks ⁷_____ holiday will be offered to the successful applicant. If you are interested, please ⁸_____ online at www.lookpublications.co.uk or send your CV to the address below.
Interviews will be held next week at our ⁹_____ .

Look Publications plc, 121 Mill Lane, London, W1

Grammar

3 Complete the second sentence so that it has a similar meaning to the first. Use the word in capitals.

1 Your job is more exciting than mine.
AS
My job _____ yours.

2 There isn't a better place than this to work.
THE
This _____ to work.

3 The factory wasn't as big as I expected.
THAN
The factory _____ I expected.

4 They're going to open a new department store here.
BE
A new department store _____ here.

5 They will employ a lot of young people during the summer.
EMPLOYED
A lot of young people _____ during the summer.

6 The company didn't offer any professional training.
WAS
No professional training _____ by the company.

4 Choose the word or phrase that best completes the sentence.

1 _____ you hear about the job, call me.
A While   C As soon as
B By the time   D Until

2 'Have you finished writing your CV yet?'
'No, but I _____ it by dinner time.'
A will have finished   C will be finishing
B have finished   D finish

3 'How did Ben's interview go?'
'I've no idea. I'll call him when I _____ home.'
A will get   C am getting
B get   D am going to get

4 The family business _____ by an international company next year.
A will be taken over   C will take over
B is taking over   D is taken over

5 'Look at the time. I'm late for the interview.'
'Don't worry. I _____ you there.'
A drive   C will drive
B am going to drive   D will have driven

6 This is _____ result I've ever had!
A the best   C as good as
B a better   D the good

I love watching extreme sports on the TV or playing extreme sports computer games, but I'm not brave enough to try them for real. I go skiing in the winter in Las Leñas in the Andes, but I haven't tried snowboarding. What about you? Are you a risk-taker or do you prefer being safe?

4 Extreme!

Vocabulary Starter
Activities, equipment and dangers

1 Match the words in the box with the pictures.

> bungee jumping   face guard   goal
> helmet   hockey stick   ironing   snowkiting
> ledge   ski lift   ski run   snowboarding   kit
> spectators   vacuuming

2 Read the sentences. Can you guess what the underlined words mean?

1 If you want to ski, you need to find a <u>slope</u> to go down.
2 When a ball moves along the ground, it <u>rolls</u>.
3 I stepped awkwardly on a loose stone and <u>twisted</u> my ankle.
4 When Bob fell down the stairs his legs were badly <u>bruised</u>, but he didn't break any bones.
5 Only a real <u>thrill-seeker</u> would try snowboarding <u>off-piste</u>.

3 Ask and answer the questions. Use words from Exercises 1 and 2 to answer them.

> A What do you do if your carpet is dirty?
> How do skiers get to the top of the ski run?
> What do hockey players use to hit the ball?
> What might you get if you fall over?
> What can pull you along on skis on a windy day?

> B What do you wear when playing a team sport?
> What do you do with clothes when they're clean and dry?
> Who watches a sporting event?
> What could happen to your ankle if you don't wear good walking boots?

CHATROOM

- Do you have to wear a PE kit at school? If so, what is it like? If not, what do you wear?
- Who does the ironing and vacuuming in your house?

Reading

Rubén01BuenosAires

I love finding out about bizarre sports. The best thing I've seen is bossaball in Ecuador. It's a mix of football, volleyball, trampolining and gymnastics!

What about you?

Have you heard about any strange sports or crazy events?

More soon ... watch this space!

1 Read the text quickly and choose the correct answer.

The text is from
A a website advertising sports holidays.
B a magazine article on risky leisure time activities.
C a newspaper article about recent sporting events.

2 Read the tip and the missing sentences. Underline the words in each sentence which will help you to link it to the text.

Reading Tip: missing sentences

- Look for a word in the missing sentences which links to a part of the text. For example,
- **pronouns:** *he, we, them,* etc.
- **linkers:** *That's why, Despite this, In addition, For example,* etc.
- **determiners:** *this, that, these, those.*
- **other words:** *others, prefer, would rather,* etc.

A For example, you could try the Irish sport of hurling.
B Most of them don't realise how dangerous the event is.
C We've got an idea that will allow you to do both at the same time.
D Others believe that the only activities worth doing are those which involve some real danger.
E However, snowy fields are just as good if the ice isn't thick enough.
F But that is just one example.
G Today's winter sports adrenaline junkies prefer heli-skiing or snowkiting.
H This is an event that is held every year in Britain.

3 Now read the text again and match the sentences A–H with the gaps. There is one extra sentence that you do not need to use.

Thrills, danger and ...

When you are choosing a sport or hobby to take up, what influences your decision? Some people may wish to avoid excessive risk. ☐1 So,
5 what activities could you do and how risky are they?
The risk-takers among us enjoy
10 participating in extreme sports, but what is fashionable changes every year.
15 Snowboarding and bungee jumping are just too well-known these days. ☐2
The first requires a helicopter to fly you to the top of a mountain, far from the ski lifts and slopes full of ordinary
20 people. You then leap out and ski down the crisp, white snow. Of course, you're skiing off-piste without marked runs and you don't know whether you're going to go off the edge of the mountain or start an avalanche, but that's the whole idea. Snowkiting is just what you would expect.
25 The skier or snowboarder is pulled along by a large kite which is blown by the wind. On a windy day, you can go so fast that you think you are on the steepest of slopes. The best thing about it is that you aren't dependent on the crowded ski lifts and queues of the typical ski resort.
30 Frozen lakes are the most popular surface. ☐3 Experts are able to do jumps and even somersaults.
Perhaps you're not quite brave enough to try extreme sports, yet. After all, it isn't unreasonable to prefer to return home unharmed after a day's activity. How would
35 you like to try an exciting, traditional sport? ☐4 It is often said to be the fastest ball sport in the world. It looks like hockey, with players using a stick to hit a ball into a goal, but the rules allow players to hook each other's sticks with their own
40 as well as pushing each other as they go for the ball. With
45 the ball travelling so quickly, injuries are

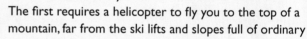

common and, last year, all players at every level of the game were forced to wear face masks and helmets while playing. 50

OK, so you'd rather not play hurling. Perhaps you want to take part in an activity that doesn't require so much energy 55 and is less likely to cause physical pain? Maybe you don't have enough time to do sports because 60 you have too much housework to do? 5 ☐ Extreme ironing! Not only does it involve ironing, but also a sport 65 or activity of your choice. For those who like heights, you can set your ironing board up on a rocky ledge high above the ground. For the more athletic, you can try ironing while cycling, waterskiing or even underwater. The sport 70 started up in the late 1990s and today silly people the world over take part in competitions and can even win awards! And when you've finished the ironing, you can start on extreme vacuuming!

Finally, how about this for a risky activity? Cheese 75 rolling. 6 ☐ Well, almost every year. In 1998, the police stopped it because there had been too many injuries the year before. In 2009, two hundred people took part and 10,000 spectators watched the event. There were fifty-eight injuries and eleven people had to be taken 80 to hospital. It's a simple sport in which a large, round cheese is rolled down a very steep hill and participants race after it to try to catch up with it. The only problem is that it is such a steep hill that contestants are 85 soon falling down, twisting ankles, getting bruised and hurting their backs. 7 ☐ 90 Neither did one poor spectator who was knocked down by the giant lump of cheese 95 itself!

4 Check your answers. Write the sentences you chose next to these summaries of the text which appears before each gap. Do they link correctly?

1 Some people avoid excessive risk.
2 Risk takers think that snowboarding and bungee jumping aren't fashionable enough.
3 The best place for snowkiting is on a frozen lake.
4 Would you like to try a traditional sport?
5 You may not have time to do sports and housework.
6 Cheese rolling is a risky activity.
7 Some contestants were injured.

5 Find these words or phrases in the completed text and choose the definition which is closest in meaning.

1 excessive (line 4)
   A too much   B not enough   C any
2 participating in (lines 10 and 11)
   A avoiding   B paying for   C taking part in
3 adrenaline junkies (line 17)
   A people addicted to excitement
   B people who hate taking risks
   C people who used to go bungee jumping
4 requires (line 18)
   A produces   B needs   C affects
5 somersaults (line 31)
   A races
   B 360° turns in the air
   C dangerous falls
6 housework (line 62)
   A work people bring home to do in the evening
   B jobs such as ironing, cooking, etc.
   C work done to a house, for example building
7 steep (line 84)
   A almost flat
   B going up and down
   C at a high angle

CHATROOM

What do you think of the activities in the text? Work with a friend and say which you would most like to do and watch and which you would least like to do and watch.

WebSearch

http://www.cheese-rolling.co.uk
http://www.bossaballsports.com

Vocabulary

Word formation: words from the text

1 Complete the text with the correct form of the words in capitals. All the words are from the reading text on pages 42 and 43.

Wherever you travel these days, you seem to come across young people running, climbing and jumping through city streets. They are taking part in the sport of 'parkour' which has become very ¹_____(FASHION) in the last year or two. It's not a relaxing ²_____ (ACTIVE) and anyone who wants to participate must be very ³_____(ATHLETE) and strong, both mentally and physically.

It is not a new sport. Georges Hebert, a physical education teacher in France, combined ⁴_____(TRADITION) sports such as running, walking and jumping into a new 'natural method'. This was before the First World War and his method became the standard training system used by the French army.

The more dramatic moves look very dangerous, especially to those who are afraid of heights. In fact, in the real world, ⁵_____ (EXCESS) risks aren't taken and most of the moves are ground-based.

The main philosophy of 'parkour' is that it is a way to train the mind. It's an individual activity and the people involved are ⁶_____ (PARTICIPATE), not ⁷_____(CONTEST). There is no ⁸_____(COMPETE) between them; no winners, no losers and no medals.

Sports and equipment

2 Complete the chart with the sports and activities.

athletics   ice-hockey   rugby   cricket
jogging   snowboarding   baseball   golf
snowkiting   surfing   boxing   gymnastics
martial arts   wakeboarding   cards
hockey   painting   windsurfing

individual activities	individual or pair against other individuals or pairs	team sports

3 Match the words in the box with the pictures. What sports use these pieces of equipment?

bat   board   club   net   pads   racquet
shuttlecock   wetsuit

Verbs for sports

4 Complete the sentences with the correct form of *do, play* or *go*.

1 My parents often _____ jogging. They love it.
2 Do you _____ rugby at your school?
3 I don't know whether to _____ cards or not.
4 _____ martial arts is good for the mind as well as the body.
5 Dad has _____ surfing today. I hope he's alright!
6 I like the summer because we _____ athletics in our school PE lessons.

Phrasal verbs

5 Choose the correct definition for the underlined words.

1 When you are choosing a sport or hobby to <u>take up</u>, what influences your decision?
   start doing / watch / research
2 The referee <u>sent off</u> one player from each team.
   shouted at / warned / told to leave the pitch
3 They try to <u>catch up with</u> the rolling cheese.
   reach / go past / throw
4 I went jogging with my friends but I couldn't <u>keep up with</u> them.
   agree on a route with / afford the same equipment as / go as fast as
5 I managed to <u>get through to</u> the third round in the badminton competition.
   reach / watch / go past
6 I started to <u>speed up</u> when I should have <u>slowed down</u>.
   go slower / go faster / get tired
   gone less fast / rested / stopped
7 The match was <u>called off</u> because of the bad weather.
   late / arranged / cancelled

6 Complete the second sentence so that it has a similar meaning to the first. Use the word in capitals and verbs from Exercise 5 in your answer.

1 If you can't go as fast as me, I won't wait for you.
WITH
If you can't _____ , I won't wait for you.

2 You can't cancel the game now. Our supporters have travelled hundreds of miles to get here.
OFF
It's wrong to _____ now when our supporters have travelled so far to see it.

3 Did you know that Steve has started playing rugby?
UP
Did you know that Steve _____ rugby?

4 You should reduce your speed before you have an accident.
DOWN
If you don't _____ , you're going to have an accident.

5 Why did you tell me to leave the field? I didn't do anything wrong.
OFF
Why _____ ? I didn't do anything wrong.

6 If our team manages to reach the second round, I'll be amazed.
TO
I'll be amazed if our team manages to _____ second round.

7 You'll have to go faster if you want to win this race.
UP
The only way you're going to win is if you _____ .

Word formation: adjective prefixes

7 Complete the adjectives with the correct prefix. Some prefixes can go with more than one adjective.

> dis- il- in- inter- ir- over- under- sub-

1 ___confident
2 ___standard
3 ___legal
4 ___national
5 ___paid
6 ___qualified
7 ___rational
8 ___experienced

8 Complete the sentences with words from Exercise 7.

1 This slope can be a problem for _____ snowboarders.

2 Using martial arts outside the gym is often _____ .

3 My fear of snowkiting is not _____ . It's a very dangerous sport.

4 The golfer was _____ for moving the ball with his hand.

5 Ricky was _____ and didn't train hard enough for his fight.

6 Compared to other sports stars, who earn millions of pounds, cricketers are _____ .

7 One of the biggest dangers for amateur sports enthusiasts is that of _____ equipment.

8 _____ sports events like the Olympics bring people of the world together.

Back up your vocabulary

9 Complete the dialogues with one word from the box in each gap. There are four extra words.

> bat catch disqualified illegal
> inexperienced keep overconfident pads
> sent off stick substandard

1 A: How was the chess tournament?
B: I was _____ because I forgot to switch my mobile phone off.

2 A: You're fitter than me, so I'll leave now on my bike and you can leave in about half an hour.
B: I should _____ up with you in about an hour.

3 A: Stop waving that hockey _____ in the air.
B: Don't worry, we're all wearing helmets.

4 A: Why don't you go to the gym anymore?
B: They overcharged and had _____ equipment.

5 A: All these _____ snowboarders annoy me. Why can't they use a different slope?
B: You weren't always an expert, were you?

6 A: Right everybody, concentrate. The biggest danger we face today is being _____ .
B: Don't worry boss. We know what we've got to do.

7 A: Be careful. He throws the ball hard and fast.
B: So? I'm wearing a helmet, face guard, gloves and _____ on my legs and arms. I'll be OK.

> **CHATROOM**
> • What sport or activity would you like to take up? Why?
> • What sporting equipment have you got at home?

Grammar

too, enough, so/such, few/little

> **too**
>
> Snowboarding and bungee jumping are just **too well-known** these days.
> Maybe you have **too much housework** to do.
> There had been **too many injuries** the year before.
>
> **not … enough**
>
> Perhaps you're **not** quite **brave enough** to try extreme sports, yet.
>
> **so / such**
>
> On a windy day, you can go **so fast** that you think you are on the steepest of slopes.
> It is **such a steep hill** that contestants are soon falling down.
>
> **few / little**
>
> There were **too few ski lifts** operating and the queues were terrible.
> I have **too little knowledge** of extreme sports to give you advice about which one to take up.

See **Grammar File**, page 162

IS THIS SLOPE STEEP ENOUGH FOR YOU?

1 Complete the sentences with the phrases from the box.

> not brave enough   not thick enough to
> so fast that   so scared that   such a safe
> too many times   too much   too unfit to

1 I'm sorry, I can't come and watch you play. I've got _____ work to do.
2 That ice is _____ skate on.
3 I'm _____ to do a parachute jump.
4 I've been hit _____ to think it's safe to play cricket without pads.
5 Jason's _____ he can't move.
6 I'm _____ run in a marathon.
7 This is _____ race-track that even inexperienced drivers can drive on it.
8 This game is _____ I can't keep up with the action.

2 Complete the second sentence so that it has a similar meaning to the first. Use the word in capitals.

1 Dave is too inexperienced to ride a horse on his own.
ENOUGH
Dave _____ ride a horse on his own.
2 It's dangerous to cycle here because there are too many cars.
TRAFFIC
It's dangerous to cycle here because _____ .
3 This ski run is so exciting that I'm coming back next week.
SUCH
This _____ ski run that I'm coming back next week.
4 The children showed such a lot of enthusiasm for the idea that we took them to the army training course.
ENTHUSIASTIC
The children _____ about the idea that we took them to the army training course.
5 I can't play cards because I've got too much ironing to do.
CLOTHES
I can't play cards because I've got _____ iron.
6 I haven't got enough time to play golf.
BUSY
I'm _____ play golf.

3 Choose the correct answer.

1 The club has **such a / such** substandard equipment that it's not worth using it.
2 There's too **little / few** information about the dangers of diving.
3 I'm making so **many / much** progress with my training that I've been chosen for the school team.
4 I've had too **many / much** bad experiences on the slopes to go snowboarding without a helmet.
5 Parents shouldn't give their children too **much / many** freedom.
6 Unfortunately, you have too **little / few** skills to be a sports instructor.
7 Too **many / much** courage can be a dangerous thing.
8 How did you get so **much / many** gymnastics medals?

Inversion, So do I / Neither do I

> **not only … but also**
>
> **Not only does** it involve ironing, **but also** a sport or activity of your choice.
>
> **so do I / Neither do I**
>
> Some of you may think that snowkiting is too dangerous. **So do I!**
> Most of them didn't realise how dangerous the event was. **Neither did** one poor spectator.

See **Grammar File**, page 163

4 Choose the correct answer.

1 Not only _____ my leg three times, I've also broken my arm.

  A I have broken B have I broken C I broke

2 Not only _____ dangerous, but it's also bad for the environment.

  A is it   B it is   C does it

3 Not only _____ his own life, but he also risks other people's.

  A he risks   B he does risk C does he risk

4 Not only _____ collecting stamps, but I also collect coins.

  A I enjoy   B do I enjoy   C I do enjoy

5 Not only _____ badly, but he also got sent off.

  A did he play B he played   C he did play

5 Match the sentences (1–10) with the correct responses (A–J).

1 We went camping during the holidays.
2 I can't understand why people play chess.
3 I'd love to try heli-skiing.
4 I don't like jogging.
5 I've got a K2 Jibpan snowboard.
6 I'm not a fast runner.
7 I play for the school volleyball team.
8 I would never do anything too risky.
9 I can windsurf.
10 My paintings are awful.

A Neither do I.
B Can you? I've never tried.
C Have you? I've got a Flow Team one.
D So did I.
E Wouldn't you? I'd love to.
F Neither can I.
G So would I.
H Do you? That's great.
I So are mine.
J Neither am I.

6 Respond to the statements. Use So … or Neither … .

I go jogging every morning before school.
So do I.

1 I never wear a helmet when I go cycling.

_____

2 I'd rather play computer games than real sports.

_____

3 I always warm up before playing sports.

_____

4 I've never been sailing.

_____

5 My skis are really old.

_____

6 I can swim well.

_____

Back up your grammar

7 Read the article and think of the word which best fits each space. Use only one word in each space.

Dangers on and off the pitch

Football can be dangerous. However, it isn't only opponents who can cause injuries.

In the World Cup Final, 1982, Marco Tardelli was [1]_____ excited after scoring a goal that he ran to the corner of the pitch and punched the flag. Unfortunately, he was a little bit [2]_____ excited and he hit the flag so hard that it bounced back and hit him in the face. So [3]_____ a flag that Thierry Henry hit in 2000 when he was playing for Arsenal against Chelsea. I guess he wasn't old [4]_____ to remember what had happened eighteen years earlier!

Steve Morrow was even more badly hurt in 1993 when he jumped onto the back of one of his teammates in celebration. Not [5]_____ did he fall off and make a fool of himself, [6]_____ he also hurt himself badly. So [7]_____ Shaun Goater, who celebrated a goal by kicking an advertising board, which broke his foot. He obviously didn't realise that he could kick so hard and [8]_____ did Manchester United manager, Alex Ferguson, when he kicked a football boot in the dressing room which hit David Beckham in the eye!

In the 1970s Manchester United were [9]_____ a bad team that their goalkeeper, Alex Stepney, spent most of his time shouting at them until he shouted so much [10]_____ he dislocated his jaw!

CHATROOM

Talk about sports or activities you don't like playing or don't want to try and use the grammar points on these pages to give your reasons.

Listening

Listening 1

1 What activities can you see in the photos? Do you do any of them?

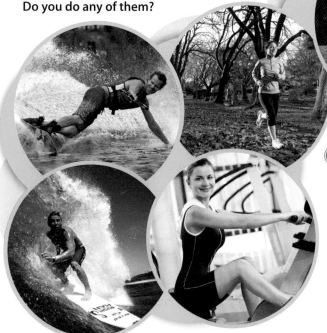

2 You are going to listen to three different conversations. For each conversation, choose the correct answers to the questions.

Listening Tip: multiple-choice questions

Listen carefully to what is said and try to work out why the other two options are wrong.

1 Steve is
   A going running.
   B working out.
   C doing a martial art.

2 Stephanie
   A does a different activity to Steve.
   B does the same activity as Steve.
   C doesn't do any activity.

3 Jeff and Sylvie are
   A playing a sport against each other.
   B playing a sport against a different couple.
   C having a training session.

4 Jeff knows Tom and Barbara because
   A they went to school together.
   B he lives near them.
   C he is their tennis trainer.

5 Penelope is about to go
   A snowkiting.
   B windsurfing.
   C swimming.

6 Greg will
   A watch her from the beach.
   B follow her on a boat.
   C follow her on his board.

Listening 2

3 You will hear someone talking about a cave diving training course. Decide whether the statements below are true (T), false (F) or if there is no information (NI).

Listening Tip: true, false, no information

○ Read through the statements carefully so that you know exactly what you are listening out for.
○ Make notes while listening.

1 The trainer knows that not everyone will pass the course.

2 The dangers of cave diving have been exaggerated.

3 The trainer invented the slogan 'The Good Divers Are Living'.

4 Students will spend the first half of the course in the classroom.

5 Divers always need a rope.

6 There are often air supply problems during dives.

7 Dives must stop as soon as a diver loses one source of light.

8 Trainees will learn how to see and listen out for problems in caves.

WebSearch

http://www.cavediving.com/
http://www.alpherosardinia.net/

Logged in

RubénO1BuenosAires

I don't understand cave diving. Diving in the ocean sounds great. You see fish and coral. But diving in a dark, dirty cave? You can't see anything.

Are there any sports or activities that you just don't understand why people do?

More soon ... watch this space!

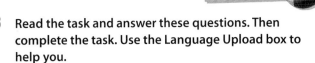

Speaking
Reaching a decision

1 Work with a partner and answer these questions.

   1 What after-school activities can you do at your school?

   2 How popular are they?

   3 What activities would you like your school to offer that it doesn't?

> **Speaking Tip:** reaching a decision
> - Discuss each idea in turn rather than looking for the best ideas straight away.
> - If you can't agree on a final answer, it doesn't matter as long as you say this.

2 You will hear two pairs of students starting the task below. Which pair approaches it better? Why?

> A school wants to offer more after-school activities to its students (aged between 13 and 16). It doesn't want to offer anything dangerous or which needs expensive equipment. Look at the ideas and discuss which three you think would be most suitable.

Wall climbing

Computer games **Photography**

New School Clubs

Film-making **Martial arts**

3 You will hear the first pair doing more of the task. Which two activities do they talk about and what do they think about them?

4 Listen again and tick the phrases from the Language Upload box that you hear.

5 Now do the whole task with a partner.

6 Read the task and answer these questions. Then complete the task. Use the Language Upload box to help you.

   1 Will the guides know where to go? What will this mean you won't need?

   2 What piece of equipment would climbers need that walkers don't need?

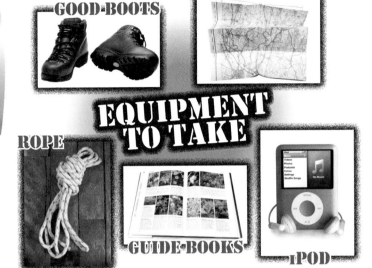

GOOD BOOTS **MAPS**

ROPE **EQUIPMENT TO TAKE**

GUIDE BOOKS **iPOD**

> You are going on a mountain walk with a group. You have been told that the ground will be rocky but not dangerous and there won't be any climbing. Guides will lead you but you should bring everything you might need. You can fit three of the items above into your bag. Decide together which you would take and why.

Language Upload

Asking your partner

What do you think?
Do you agree?

Agreeing

I agree. / That's true.
That's a good idea/point.

Disagreeing politely

I'm sorry, but I disagree.
I see what you mean, but …
To be honest, I don't think you're right.
I see your point, but …

Interrupting

Can I just say something here?
May I interrupt for a minute?

Summarising

So, we've agreed on …
Well, we'll just have to agree to disagree.

Writing: A Letter of Complaint
Before you write

1 Before you read the letter, answer these questions.

   1 Have you ever had to complain about anything? What was it?

   2 What sort of equipment would you expect to find in a good sports centre?

2 Read the advert and the task and answer the questions.

   1 What was the main problem with the equipment?

   2 What was wrong with the trainers?

   3 Why couldn't the writer complain to the manager?

Look at the advertisement for a new sports centre and the handwritten notes giving details of why you are unhappy. Write a letter complaining about the gym. Write between 120 and 180 words in an appropriate style.

Dear Sir or Madam,

I am writing to complain about your sports centre which I joined last month.

According to your advertisement, the gym in the centre offers lots of equipment as well as expert trainers. Although it does have equipment, it is so substandard that it is impossible or dangerous to use. In addition, the trainers were not experts, but inexperienced youngsters.

To make matters worse, the club is often closed without any explanation, especially in the mornings before school. On top of everything, when I tried to express my dissatisfaction, I was unable to find the manager who, I was told, was too busy to talk to me. Not only did I waste my money but I also lost a month of training.

I hope to receive a full refund of my fees as I have been unable to make use of the gym as I had expected. I look forward to your reply.

Yours faithfully,

Mark Dobson

3 Read the model letter. How has the writer rephrased these words or phrases from the notes?

   1 poor quality   -   <u>substandard</u>

   2 not experts   -   _____

   3 no reason given   -   _____

   4 complain   -   _____

4 Find more formal equivalents of these words in the letter.

advert	-	<u>advertisement</u>
it's	-	_____
I couldn't	-	_____
someone told me	-	_____
to get	-	_____

5 Match the phrases with the correct paragraphs.

Para 1: Reason for writing

Para 2: What was promised / the main complaint(s)

Para 3: Further complaints

Para 4: What the writer wants and why / A polite finish

A To make matters worse …

B According to your advertisement …

C On top of everything …

D I look forward to hearing from you …

E I am writing to complain about …

F In addition …

G I hope to receive … as …

6 Use the phrases from Exercise 5 to expand these notes into full sentences.

   1 Reason for writing – skis bought online

      I am writing to complain about some skis I bought from you on the Internet.

   2 What was promised / skis – sent the same day. Took 2 months.
      According … .

   3 Further problems – not new, scratched, sent emails and phoned. No response.
      To make … . On top … .

   4 What the writer wants – refund for skis, payment for having to rent skis on holiday. Shouldn't have had this expense
      I hope … as … .

   5 Polite ending
      I look … .

7 Look at the Writing Checklist. Find and underline examples of the eight points in the model letter. They may appear in more than one paragraph.

Time to write

8 Look at the poster, notes and the task and answer the questions using your imagination.

1 Only one sport was offered. Which one?

2 How many people did you have to share with?

3 In what way were the organisers rude?

4 What do you want from the company?

9 Rewrite the words and phrases from the poster and notes. Use these ideas.

> choice available   fast food   impolite
> my own   not…enough

1 a range of sports offered   *a choice of sports is available*

2 private room

3 takeaways

4 too small

5 rude

10 Write your letter. Use the Writing Checklist and Memory Flash to help you.

only one

had to share

Summer Sports Camp for 15–18 year olds

Two week camp in beautiful countryside
A range of sports offered
Private rooms
All meals included in the price
Evening activities
Only €450

too small — had to get takeaways

organisers rude when I complained

Look at the advertisement for a summer sports camp you went to and the handwritten notes giving details of why you are unhappy. Write a letter complaining about the camp. Write between 120 and 180 words in an appropriate style.

Writing Checklist: A Letter of Complaint

Does the letter of complaint include

1 the correct way of starting and finishing a formal letter?

2 all the handwritten points on the task?

3 set phrases to start each paragraph?

4 a polite ending?

5 addition linking words?

6 contrast linking words?

7 vocabulary which shows you can rephrase the task in your own words?

8 formal language?

Memory Flash

Opening: Dear Sir/Madam
Opening paragraph: (Reason for writing)
I am writing to complain about …
Second paragraph: (What was promised / main complaints)
According to your (advertisement) …
Third paragraph: (Further complaints)
To make matters worse …
Fourth paragraph: (What you want and why)
I hope to receive … as …
Closing sentence: (Polite finish)
I look forward to hearing from you.
Contrast linkers: Although, However, Despite, In spite of, Even though
Addition linkers and phrases: What's more, In addition, On top of everything, Not only … but also, To make matters worse …

Vocabulary

1 **Choose the word that best completes the sentence.**

1 Does anyone in your class _____ athletics?
   A go   B do   C play

2 We'll never get _____ to the final against so many good teams.
   A through B along   C over

3 The ball is very hard, which is why we wear _____ on our legs.
   A guards   B nets   C pads

4 You can't play on the team if you haven't got your basketball _____ .
   A uniform B kit   C outfit

5 You're holding your tennis _____ wrongly.
   A racquet B bat   C stick

6 I can't believe you were _____ for cheating.
   A qualified B unqualified
   C disqualified

2 **Use the same word to complete both sentences.**

1 A In tennis, you have to hit the ball over the _____ to your opponent's side of the court.
   B The ball hit the _____ .

2 A I'd like to _____ up golf when I retire.
   B Do you want to _____ part in a chess competition at school?

3 A Try to keep _____ with the rest of the runners, Toby.
   B Don't forget to warm _____ before you jump in the pool.

4 A An _____ player is one who plays for their country.
   B The Olympic Games is the biggest _____ sports event.

5 A What is the proper way to hold a golf _____?
   B Are you a member of a sports _____?

6 A I was sent _____ for kicking a player on the other team.
   B The game was called _____ because so many players were ill.

Grammar

3 **Choose the sentence which is closest in meaning to the original.**

1 Despite its size, the pool is too crowded today to do any serious swimming.
   A The pool isn't big enough to swim seriously in. ☐
   B There are so many people in the pool that it is impossible to swim seriously. ☐

2 I'm too scared to surf or water ski.
   A I'm too scared to surf, so I can't water ski. ☐
   B Not only am I not brave enough to surf, but I'm also too scared to water ski. ☐

3 I don't like dangerous sports and neither does my brother.
   A Both my brother and I dislike dangerous sports. ☐
   B I don't like dangerous sports, but my brother does. ☐

4 There aren't many people here because it's not safe to swim.
   A This is such a dangerous place to swim that it's almost empty. ☐
   B There are so few people here that it's dangerous to swim. ☐

5 We tried surfing, but the waves were too small.
   A The waves were so small that we couldn't surf. ☐
   B The waves weren't small enough for us to try surfing. ☐

4 **Read the text and choose the best answer (A, B or C) for each gap.**

Is cheerleading a sport? 'No', you cry! It's ¹_____ easy to be a sport. That's what you think and ²_____ do many others.

The *All-Star Cheerleading* league started up in 1987. There were ³_____ different teams, all with their own rules and ideas. The competition was intense. Not only ⁴_____ the teams try to perform ordinary routines better than their competitors, but they also created their own secret routines to try to impress the judges. There was ⁵_____ a determined effort to win that safety rules were ignored.

There were too many unqualified coaches and too ⁶_____ experienced cheerleaders. Now things have changed. Not only ⁷_____ judges check the quality of moves, but they also make sure no illegal moves are made.

Cheerleading is still very dangerous, though. The human pyramid is ⁸_____ dangerous that many schools have banned it. The danger doesn't seem to put people off doing the sport, though. Last year, not only ⁹_____ 65 percent of all high school girls' sports injuries caused by cheerleading, ¹⁰_____ also, 67 percent of all college girls' sports injuries came from the activity.

	A	B	C
1	too	so	such
2	also	so	neither
3	too much	not enough	too many
4	do	were	did
5	too	such	so
6	little	small	few
7	do	are	did
8	such	too	so
9	do	were	did
10	but	and	so

I couldn't live without my computer. I use it to keep in touch with friends, upload my photos and surf the Net for my homework. What about you? What do you enjoy doing on the computer? Have you ever lost an important file on the computer?

5 Cool Computing!

Vocabulary Starter
Computers

1 Match the sentences with the words from the box.

> file   software   mouse   cable   bug
> database   keyboard   hardware

1 A system for storing large amounts of information.
2 A plastic tube with wires inside it.
3 Another name for computer programs.
4 Information on a computer that you store under a particular name.
5 Computer machinery and equipment.
6 A mistake in a computer program that stops it working correctly.
7 A small object that you move with your hand.
8 You press this with your fingers to make letters and numbers appear on the screen.

2 The words in bold are in the wrong sentences. Put them in the correct sentence.

1 Marios **crashed** a fantastic game from the Internet; you have to find the hidden treasure.
2 If your printer isn't working, check that it is **deleted** to the computer.
3 If companies don't **post** their clients' personal information, criminals could use it to hack into their bank accounts.
4 Sandra wrote a long email then accidentally **connected** it when she hit the wrong key.
5 When I'm working on the computer, I **key in** my work every ten minutes so that I don't lose it.
6 I was looking at my summer holiday photos when the computer **downloaded** and I lost them all.
7 Now **protect** these numbers and letters, that's your password, in order to log on to the site.
8 You can **save** a comment about the school canteen on our new school website.

3 Replace the underlined words in the sentences with words from the box.

> damaged   concerned   troubleshooter
> convince   glitch   query

1 Excuse me, I've got a <u>question</u> about my phone bill.
2 I'm <u>worried</u> about my computer; when I play games on it for a long time, it gets really hot.
3 I love my laptop. You'll never <u>persuade</u> me to buy a desktop computer; I need something portable.
4 Emily's firm is having a few problems but she's a <u>person who can solve them</u>. I'm sure things will improve with her help.
5 The computer is working very slowly. I think there must be a <u>fault</u> in the operating system.
6 I think I <u>caused some harm to</u> my laptop when I dropped it on the floor.

CHATROOM
- How often do you use the Internet?
- What's your favourite Internet site? Why?

Reading

Logged in

MagdaMadrid94

When there's something wrong with my laptop I have to get my friend, Dan to look at it. He can always sort things out.

What problems do you sometimes have with your computer?

More soon ... watch this space!

1 Read the article and complete the sentences.

1 When Jimmy saw the _____ he realised there was a problem.
2 The company executives gave Jimmy _____ when they discovered he had been right.
3 Money had been put into _____ for Jimmy Jones.
4 Mr Jones hurried to _____ after he had spoken to the bank manager.
5 It took Jimmy and the engineers _____ to solve the problem.
6 One day Jimmy might become _____ .

Teen hacker saves the day!

1

School boy Jimmy Jones knew something was wrong as soon as his dad proudly showed him the new firewall software his company had installed for a local bank. Despite the fact that no-one believed him, fifteen-year-old Jimmy proved them all wrong and won himself a £1000 reward from grateful executives at his father's software company.

2

'I could see a glitch in it straightaway,' said Jimmy. 'A firewall is a specialised defence system for a computer network. If it doesn't work properly, unauthorised users can gain access to all the information on the database. I should have said something to Dad at the time, but he was too tired to talk about it, so I went upstairs to my own computer and played the part of a hacker. After only a few attempts I found I could access private files on the bank's database.'

3

The next morning, Jimmy's dad, Ian Jones, arrived at work to a phone call from a very concerned bank manager. 'He told me that overnight someone called Jimmy Jones had opened a new account and deposited one million 'galleons' into it – the money used in the Harry Potter books,' said Mr Jones. 'Realising the implications of what Jimmy had done, I had to act fast. I tried to convince the client there must have been a dreadful mistake and raced round to Jimmy's school.'

4

Jimmy was allowed time off school and sat down with some of the country's top software engineers to sort out the failure in the software system. Within a few hours they were able to find a solution and Mr Jones called the bank with the good news. He realised that without Jimmy's intervention they might not have found the problem until it was too late. 'Important data could have been wiped off the system,' said Mr Jones.

5

Regarding the payment for his good work, Jimmy received some real money to put into his bank account and is the subject of articles being written in the computing media. 'I am so proud of him,' said Mr Jones. 'He could make a great troubleshooter for the company when he leaves school.'

Help Desk Horror Stories

Technicians who answer queries from computer users have compiled a list of their funniest stories. The collection, published in a leading computing magazine, shows how baffled some people are by new technology. Often, computer terminology that many of us now take for granted is puzzling for new users. One technician advised an elderly customer to put his CD back in the drive and close the drawer. The customer was heard putting the phone down and closing the desk drawer.

A frequent query is when users are confronted with the command, 'Press Any Key'. Technicians say it should be 'Press Return Key' because too many people ask where the 'Any' key is! Using printers is also a source of frustration and can be the reason for many of the calls. One caller told a technician there was a message on the screen that the computer 'couldn't find the printer'. The user had turned the computer screen to face the printer but said the computer 'still couldn't see it'. Another customer with a printer problem was asked if her PC was running under Windows. 'No, my desk is next to the door and nowhere near the window,' was her response. 'But that must be the problem because the man sitting next to me is under a window and his printer is working fine!'

Then there was the technician who asked a customer what type of computer he had. 'A white one,' was the answer. The same customer had another concern. 'I must get another computer,' he insisted. 'You see, this one doesn't have the latest version of the Internet on it.'

One customer complained that his keyboard wasn't working. He had taken it apart to clean it and had soaked it for a day in hot water. When he put it together again the squeaky clean keys wouldn't work. And finally, a caller complained that her mouse was hard to control with the dust cover on. The cover was the plastic bag the mouse was wrapped in.

Unfortunately, some of the most desperate calls are from people who have damaged their computers and lost potentially useful data. An accountant who thought he'd catch up on some work in the bath dropped his laptop and was horrified to see bubbles coming out of his hard drive. And a student who had just saved a copy of a 5000-word assignment cracked the screen of her laptop when it fell off the back of her moped. In both cases, the users had backed up and technicians managed to retrieve their files. 'The problem is,' say the technicians, 'too many people think they can carry out their own repairs. They take the computer apart, put it back together and get into a rage when it doesn't work. They should log off, cool off and call us – the experts.'

---

2 Read the online news report and answer the questions.

> **Reading Tip:** open questions
>
> Read the questions carefully. The answers will be a word, a phrase or a number.

1 Which 'drawer' should the elderly customer have closed?
_____

2 What frustrates a lot of the callers?
_____

3 Where was the computer screen when it 'still couldn't see the printer'?
_____

4 What did the customer with the white computer think he needed?
_____

5 How had the man with the faulty keyboard tried to clean it?
_____

6 What had prevented one user's mouse from working well?
_____

7 What had the girl done shortly before she damaged her laptop?
_____

8 How do people often feel when they can't fix their computer themselves?
_____

3 Match the highlighted words in the texts with their meanings.

1 another word for 'worry'
2 action that interrupts a process so you can control it yourself
3 put something into water and left it
4 something that is given to someone for doing well
5 an order or instruction given to a computer
6 to calm down after being angry
7 TV, newspapers, radio and magazines
8 put money into a bank account

CHATROOM
- Do you get angry or frustrated if your computer goes wrong?
- Have you ever taken your computer to an expert to be fixed?

WebSearch

www.wikihow.com
www.fwd.five.tv

Vocabulary

Word formation: words from the text

1 Complete the text with the correct form of the words in capitals. All the words are from the reading texts on pages 54 and 55.

What's new for schools?

Digital ¹_____ (TECHNICAL) have been demonstrating the latest gadgets for schools at a technology show. Students especially enjoyed the demonstration of a new 3D ²_____ (PRINT). Imagine a machine that can create your own computer design in plastic! It's the perfect ³_____ (SOLVE) for that challenging Art ⁴_____ (ASSIGN).
New interactive whiteboards with web cams have already been installed in a number of classrooms. They could have huge ⁵_____ (IMPLY) for many students who will be able to participate in classes in other schools around the world.
⁶_____ (UNFORTUNATE) not all teachers gave such a positive ⁷_____ (RESPOND). Some blame computer ⁸_____ (FAIL) as a major cause of disruption in class.

Computer equipment

2 Choose the correct word to complete the dialogue.

> wireless   hard drive   modem   disk
> battery   screen   netbook

Max: Can I have a look at your new computer, Alice?
Alice: Yes, of course. It's brilliant. It's called a ¹_____ . It's smaller than a laptop but it does all the same things and it's got a 500 gigabyte ²_____ .
Max: That's fantastic. Has it got a ³_____ Internet connection?
Alice: Yes, it has. It's got an internal ⁴_____ which is great because I don't have loads of cables across my desk.
Max: Have you got your photos on it?
Alice: Of course. Here are some from the party last night. Do you want them?
Max: That would be great. Can you put them on a ⁵_____ for me?
Alice: Sure, there are loads of them.
Max: Just a minute, Alice. The ⁶_____ has gone blank! What's happened?
Alice: Oh, don't worry. It's just the ⁷_____ . I've been using it for hours. I'll have to plug the netbook in to the mains electricity.

Verbs related to computers

3 Choose the correct answer.

1 My computer is running very slowly. I think I'll **restart** / **download** it and see if that helps.
2 Anna's computer was damaged when she dropped it on the floor and she's **missed** / **lost** all her files.
3 To **insert** / **run** the program for the first time you have to put the CD into the drawer and follow the instructions.
4 Here's the CD with the new software. **Click on** / **Insert** it in the disk drive and the installation wizard will start up automatically.
5 Wow! You've got *Rihanna's* new album. If I give you a CD, can you **burn** / **run** a copy for me?
6 **Surf** / **Click on** the link to find out more information about the school drama club.
7 Our teacher has told us to **surf** / **restart** the Internet for our Art project. I'm looking for information about Salvador Dalí.
8 Please **unplug** / **store** the laptop from the mains electricity and put it away in its case.

4 Match the phrasal verbs with the definitions.

1 back up   A delete information or files
2 log on   B join different parts to make a
3 wipe off   machine or model
4 take apart   C disconnect from the Internet
5 log off   D separate into different parts
6 put something   E save information or files
  together   F connect to the Internet

5 Complete the blog with the correct form of the phrasal verbs from Exercise 4.

I've been trying to ¹_____ to a website about the ancient Romans to get some information for my school History assignment, but my computer keeps crashing. I usually ²_____ my work on a memory stick every evening, but today I've done it three times already because I'm terrified of losing all the work I've completed so far. One girl in my class, Emily, lost five pages of her homework after her brother accidentally ³_____ the file _____ the system. He then ⁴_____ the computer _____ to fix it, but he ended up with hundreds of small pieces. A computer expert finally ⁵_____ it _____, but Emily had to do her homework again. Anyway it's time to ⁶_____ because I've been wasting my time writing this blog instead of completing my homework!

Minor disasters

6 Match the pictures with the verbs in the box.

> crack   crush   spill   drop   scratch   rip

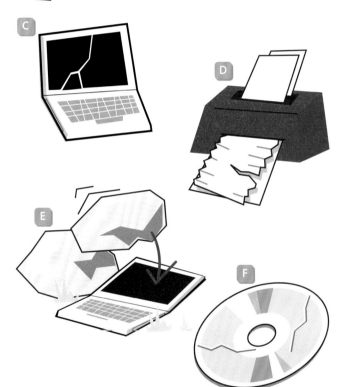

7 Complete the sentences with the correct form of the verbs from Exercise 6.

1 The DVD was so badly _____ that we couldn't watch the film. The picture just jumped around on the screen.

2 Keep your glass away from the computer. You might _____ water on the keyboard.

3 I _____ the TV on my foot while I was carrying it into the living room. It really hurts!

4 My iPod® fell out of my bag and the screen has _____ . Now there's a line down the middle of it.

5 When Julian had finished with the can of lemonade he _____ it and threw it in the bin.

6 I couldn't get the paper out of the printer and when I pulled it, it _____ .

8 Match the sentence halves.

1 I can't use my computer because there's something
2 When I inserted the CD it started to
3 The keyboard felt warm because the computer
4 All of a sudden the computer screen
5 How annoying! The printer isn't working
6 The information in the system was destroyed
7 Jack tried to restart the computer after

A make a funny noise.
B went blank.
C it crashed.
D was overheating.
E by a virus.
F properly and I need to print something.
G wrong with it.

Back up your vocabulary

9 Choose the word or phrase that best completes the sentence.

1 Do you know which _____ connects the computer to the printer?
   A battery   C cable
   B modem   D screen

2 There's a problem with the _____ so you won't be able to connect to the Internet.
   A USB drive   C scanner
   B modem   D mouse

3 Emily was worried about the exam although her friends tried to _____ her she would do well.
   A convince   C blame
   B protect   D concern

4 Before I turn off the computer, I always _____ my work so that I know it's safe.
   A back up   C take apart
   B log off   D wipe off

5 Be careful with that new book. Look, you've already _____ the first page!
   A cracked   C crushed
   B dropped   D ripped

6 I've just _____ a PDF file about how to use my new digital camera.
   A surfed   C made
   B downloaded   D run

CHATROOM

• Have you or someone you know ever had a mishap or accident with your iPod or MP3 player? What happened?
• What's your favourite gadget: mobile phone, computer, MP3 player or iPod? Why?

Grammar
Modal verbs (1)

obligation and necessity
I **must** get another computer.
I **had to** act fast.

prohibition
Users **mustn't** try and fix the problem themselves.

lack of necessity
You **don't have to** read the whole file – just the first page.
I **don't need to** save my work – my computer does it automatically.
But Mr Jones **needn't have been** concerned.

deduction
That **must** be the problem.
There **must have been** a dreadful mistake.

ability
People think they **can** carry out their own repairs.
The computer **couldn't** find the printer.
Technicians **managed to** retrieve their files.
Within a few hours they **were able to** find a solution.

See **Grammar File**, pages 164 and 165

CAN'T YOU DO ANYTHING RIGHT?

GLASBERGEN

Copyright 2003 by Randy Glasbergen. www.glasbergen.com

1   Choose the correct answer.

1 Adam wants a laptop but his parents have told him that he **has to wait** / **could wait** until his birthday.

2 You **mustn't** / **don't have to** take your iPod to the swimming pool. You might drop it in the water.

3 Phoebe **can** / **must** turn off her mobile phone in class. It's the same rule for everybody.

4 You **couldn't** / **don't need to** switch off the computer. It will switch itself off.

5 I can't find my MP3 player. I **can't have** / **must have** left it at Anna's house.

6 **Can** / **Must** the printer copy 3D designs too?

7 In the end we **managed to** / **could** save the data but from now on I'll always back up my work.

2   Complete the sentences with the correct form of the verbs in brackets.

1 I didn't think I would have enough money for a new computer. But I _____ (not need / worry) because I found one in the sale.

2 Our computer is so slow. We _____ _____ (ought to / take) it to the repair shop.

3 Ben's eyes are red. He _____ (must / look) at the screen for too long.

4 The printer isn't working. It _____ _____ (might / run out) of ink.

5 I didn't do very well in the exam. I _____ _____ (shouldn't / go) to bed so late.

6 We didn't know why it _____ (not able to / print) until we discovered it wasn't switched on.

7 Over the past few months I _____ _____ (manage to / upload) all the photos from my camera.

3   Complete the dialogue with the words in the box.

should   couldn't   had to   needn't have   can't
must   managed to   have to   could have

Sylvia: Look at this magazine article, Tom. A school in America has given each student a laptop.

Tom: Wow, that [1]_____ be really exciting. I've never had my own computer.

Sylvia: It says the students still [2]_____ _____ use paper and pen for Maths.

Tom: That's because you [3]_____ work out mathematical problems on the screen. I think we [4]_____ have laptops in our schools, don't you?

Sylvia: Yes, you're right. We haven't got enough computers at our school.

Tom: I [5]_____ finish some work last week because all the computers were busy.

Sylvia: So what did you do?

Tom: I [6]_____ do it during my lunch break when a computer was free.

Sylvia: That's really annoying but you [7]_____ _____ done that. You [8]_____ _____ borrowed my new laptop.

Tom: Thanks. By the way, have you [9]_____ _____ download those photos I sent you?

Sylvia: Yes, I have. They were really funny, especially the one of me falling in the river!

Modal verbs (2)

> **possibility**
> *He says he **could** apply for other jobs ...*
> *Who knows what he **might** do in the future.*
> *It **may** take months to sort it out.*
> *They**'ll probably** unplug the computer, take it apart, then put it together again.*

See **Grammar File**, pages 164 and 165 ≫

4 Match the sentences.

1 You're doing a lot of copies.
2 The laptop feels very hot.
3 Naomi wants to work with computers.
4 You need to do your homework.
5 There's a new website about crazy gadgets.
6 Can you burn a copy of this CD?

A I might look at it later.
B You could start it after dinner.
C She might get a job with that new IT company.
D I may need it for the party.
E It'll cool down in a minute.
F The printer might run out of paper.

5 Tick (✓) the sentences that describe a possibility.

1 They can repair the laptop this evening. ☐
2 Let's call Sandra. She might be at home. ☐
3 Let's speak to the manager. He might give us a discount. ☐
4 I think Jack can sing really well. ☐
5 Do you think we could do it again? ☐
6 Students may use the computers during the day. ☐
7 It's a long way. You could take my bike. ☐
8 Laptops might come down in price. ☐

6 Write complete sentences. Use the modal verbs in brackets.

1 Olivia / go / concert / this evening (might)
   _____

2 we / download / photos? (could)
   _____

3 careful! you / delete / files / if / you / not be careful (can)
   _____

4 they / give / laptops / to every student (might not)
   _____

5 all classrooms / have web cams / one day? (will)
   _____

6 she / be happy / her results / when / she / see / them (may not)
   _____

Back up your grammar

7 Complete the second sentence so that it has a similar meaning to the first using the word given.

1 I expect you were angry when your computer crashed.
   been
   You _____ angry when your computer crashed.

2 Sandra regrets not having saved her homework.
   ought
   Sandra _____ her homework.

3 We couldn't install the program.
   able
   We _____ install the program.

4 There's a possibility that the computer has overheated.
   might
   The computer _____ overheated.

5 All students are obliged to switch off their mobile phones in class.
   must
   Mobile phones _____ in class.

6 Perhaps I'll call you when I get home.
   may
   I _____ you when I get home.

7 Students are not permitted to use Facebook during school hours.
   mustn't
   Students _____ during school hours.

8 It wasn't a good idea for Peter to have a drink when he was on the computer.
   shouldn't
   Peter _____ a drink when he was on the computer.

CHATROOM

- What equipment would you like to have at school?
- What subjects do you use computers for at school?

"We rarely back up our data. We prefer not to keep a permanent record of everything that goes wrong around here."

Listening

I've just been chatting online to my friend Bernat. He lives in the same road as me, but we often talk on MSN or text each other.

How often do you text your friends or chat online?

MagdaMadrid94

Listening 1

1 You will hear six short conversations. Choose the correct picture, A, B or C.

Listening Tip: multiple-choice pictures

- If you're listening for prices or numbers, make sure you listen to all of the information.
- You might hear some numbers that you don't need.

1

2

3
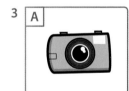 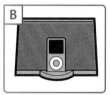 

4

5
  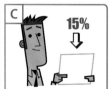

6
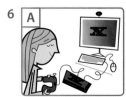  

Listening 2

2 You will hear an interview with Liam Hearne. He and a group of school friends have just won a prize for their website called Teenbiz.com. After each section you will hear two to three questions. Choose A, B or C.

Listening: multiple-choice questions

- You will **hear** the questions, but not be able to read them on the page. Be prepared to take notes while you listen.
- Write down any important words you hear such as places, names, dates, numbers, etc.

1 A twelve months ago
  B eighteen months ago
  C six months ago

2 A his IT teacher
  B other teenagers
  C a student at his school

3 A one in three   B one in four
  C one in five

4 A weekly   B daily
  C monthly

5 A It's exciting.   B It's factual.
  C It's always new.

6 A sports events
  B festival guide
  C cinema listings

7 A new software
  B photography
  C music

8 A Liam
  B the website team
  C the website designers

9 A two   B three
  C five

10 A a designer   B a writer
   C a student

11 A old computer games
   B new equipment
   C extra people

CHATROOM
- What are your favourite websites?
- Do you like shopping online? What do you buy online?

Speaking

Role play

1 Look at the photo. Where is he? What can you buy in this type of shop?

2 You want to buy a new laptop. Tick (✓) what is most important to you.

What colour it is. ☐
How much it costs. ☐
Whether it's in good condition. ☐
What make it is. ☐
Whether it's easy to use. ☐

3 Listen to Sylvia, who has just bought a new computer. What is the problem with it?

4 Listen again and tick the expressions in the Language Upload box that are used.

5 Listen to the sentences. Does the intonation go up or down at the end? Practise saying the sentences.

1 There's a problem with the mouse. up / down
2 Would it be possible to have a
   different make? up / down
3 We could try and repair it for you. up / down
4 Do you have the receipt? up / down
5 I'm sorry to hear about that. up / down

6 Work in pairs. Student A is a shop assistant. Student B is a customer. Read the role cards.

Student A: You are a shop assistant. Find out what the problem is. Offer to replace the item. If the customer refuses, offer a refund. Begin the role play by saying. 'Hello Sir/Madam. Can I help you?'

Student B:

The situation

You are in a computer shop. You bought a netbook two weeks ago but it isn't working properly. You are quite angry. Your partner is the shop assistant.

Your goal

Explain the problem. Ask for your money back.

7 Now practise your role play. Use the prompts.

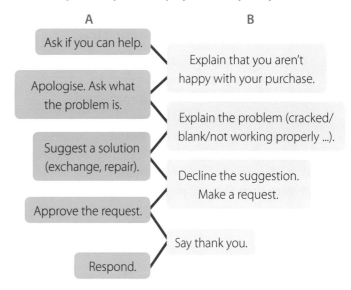

A — Ask if you can help.

B — Explain that you aren't happy with your purchase.

A — Apologise. Ask what the problem is.

B — Explain the problem (cracked/blank/not working properly ...).

A — Suggest a solution (exchange, repair).

B — Decline the suggestion. Make a request.

A — Approve the request.

B — Say thank you.

A — Respond.

8 Now change roles. Do another role play on page 125.

Speaking Tip: role play

• Read the situation carefully and get ideas.
• When you reply or give information, support your ideas with reasons and opinions.

Language Upload

Offering help

Would you like any help?
Can I help you?

Apologising

I'm sorry to hear that.
Oh, I'm sorry about that.

Asking about the problem

What's the matter with it?
What do you think the problem is?

Suggesting a solution

Would you like us to try and repair it for you?
We could try and repair it for you.

Declining an idea

I'm not sure about that.
I'm not too keen on that idea.

Making a request

Could I exchange it for another one?
Would it be possible to have a refund?

Approving a request

Yes, that's no problem at all.
Of course.

Writing: An Informal Email
Before you write

1 Read Andy's email to Becky and the notes Becky has made. Tick (✓) the information that is true.

1 Andy has already decided what to do with the prize money. ☐

2 Andy wants Becky to suggest some good places for cameras and laptops. ☐

3 Becky must explain why he should save some money. ☐

4 Andy wants to meet on Saturday. ☐

5 Becky isn't free on Saturday. ☐

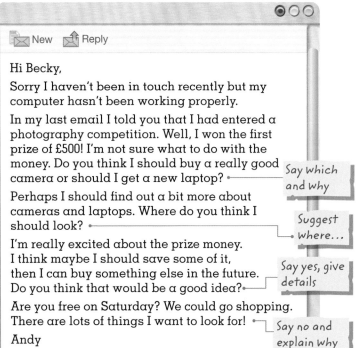

New Reply

Hi Becky,

Sorry I haven't been in touch recently but my computer hasn't been working properly.

In my last email I told you that I had entered a photography competition. Well, I won the first prize of £500! I'm not sure what to do with the money. Do you think I should buy a really good camera or should I get a new laptop? • ——— *Say which and why*

Perhaps I should find out a bit more about cameras and laptops. Where do you think I should look? • ——— *Suggest where...*

I'm really excited about the prize money. I think maybe I should save some of it, then I can buy something else in the future. Do you think that would be a good idea? • ——— *Say yes, give details*

Are you free on Saturday? We could go shopping. There are lots of things I want to look for! • ——— *Say no and explain why*

Andy

2 Read Becky's email to Andy. Underline Becky's answers to Andy's questions.

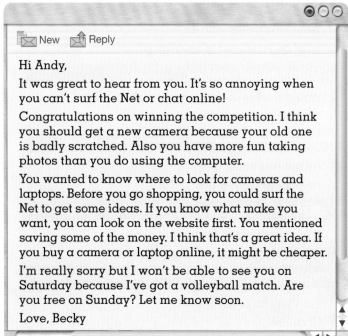

New Reply

Hi Andy,

It was great to hear from you. It's so annoying when you can't surf the Net or chat online!

Congratulations on winning the competition. I think you should get a new camera because your old one is badly scratched. Also you have more fun taking photos than you do using the computer.

You wanted to know where to look for cameras and laptops. Before you go shopping, you could surf the Net to get some ideas. If you know what make you want, you can look on the website first. You mentioned saving some of the money. I think that's a great idea. If you buy a camera or laptop online, it might be cheaper.

I'm really sorry but I won't be able to see you on Saturday because I've got a volleyball match. Are you free on Sunday? Let me know soon.

Love, Becky

3 Read the email again and complete the sentences.

1 Becky thinks Andy should buy _____ because _____ .

2 Before he goes shopping Becky suggests that Andy _____ .

3 Andy might save money if _____ .

4 Becky is sorry she can't see Andy on Saturday, but _____ .

4 Put the information in Becky's email in order.

Ideas and suggestions ☐	Finish ☐	
Reference to Andy's email ☐	Greeting ☐	
Reaction to Andy's news ☐	Plans to meet ☐	

5 Complete the table with examples of informal vocabulary or style from Becky's email.

	Formal	Informal
1	Dear Sir	
2	I was pleased to receive your news.	
3	I'd like to suggest that you ...	
4	Would Sunday be convenient for you?	
5	I would be grateful if you would let me know soon.	
6	Yours sincerely	

6 Rewrite the short email in an informal style.

New Reply

Dear Jo,

I was pleased to receive your news about your exams. I'd like to suggest that you have a party to celebrate. Would Sunday be convenient for you? I could help with the food. I would be grateful if you would let me know soon.

Yours sincerely,

Max

Writing Tip: an informal email

- Make a plan.
- Begin your letter with a simple greeting and a general comment.
- Paragraph 1 should comment on the email/ letter you received.
- Paragraphs 2 and 3 should give suggestions, recommendations, details etc.
- The final paragraph should answer the last question and ask the reader to do something.

Writing Checklist: An Informal Email

Does your email
1 answer all the questions?
2 have the correct informal style?
3 start and finish correctly?
4 include computer vocabulary from this unit?
5 use phrases from the Memory Flash box?

Memory Flash

Time to write

7 Read the task and the email. Think of your own suggestions and explanations for each of the notes.

You receive the following email from Patrick and have made notes. Write your reply. Write between 120 and 150 words.

○○○

✉ New ⬆ Reply

It was great to see you at my birthday party. I had a fantastic time.

Did I tell you that I've been saving up my money? Well, I got some from my parents for my birthday as well, and now I want to buy something. I can't decide whether I should get a TV for my bedroom or a laptop to replace the one I dropped down the stairs. What do you think I should do? — *Say which and why*

I'm not sure where I should buy a TV or laptop from, but you love shopping. Perhaps you could suggest some good places? — *Suggest where...*

How will I find out about the TV or laptop before I buy it? If I don't find out enough information, I might buy the wrong one! — *Offer advice, give details*

Are you free to meet after school on Friday? I could show you the photos from the party. — *Say no and explain why*

Let me know soon.

Patrick

◀▶

Starting the email
Thanks for your news. It was great to hear from you.
It was great to hear your news.
Sorry I haven't been in touch for ages, but ...

Giving news
By the way, did you know that ...?
You'll never guess what happened to me last week/ yesterday! I ...
I might have already told you, but ...

Responding to questions
You mentioned that ...
You asked me about ...
You wanted to know ...

Saying no to an arrangement
I'm really sorry, but ...

Finishing an email
Let me know soon.
Hope to hear from you soon.
Write soon.
Take care.
Love,

Vocabulary

1 Complete the email with the correct form of the words from the box.

> crash   make a funny noise   drop   restart
> download   keyboard   go blank   save

New   **Reply**

Sorry I didn't reply to your email earlier. I've been trying to ¹_____ the pictures you sent me, but last week I ²_____ my new laptop on the kitchen floor and now it ³_____ every five minutes. I think there's a problem with the ⁴_____ because whenever I press the letter 't' the screen ⁵_____ . It also ⁶_____ that keeps getting louder and louder. If I try to ⁷_____ it, it tells me there's an error in the system. I have to keep ⁸_____ what I'm doing so that I don't lose anything. At least I can still send emails!

Melissa

---

2 Choose the correct answers.

1 When you finish, make sure you **log off** / **back up** your homework so that you don't lose it.

2 James **ripped** / **cracked** the letter when he tried to pull it out of his bag.

3 Will you **log on** / **log off** now please? It's time you stopped using the computer.

4 Jack's got all the right pieces to make the model, but he doesn't know how to **back it up** / **put it together**.

5 Alice's boss wasn't happy when she **spilled** / **crushed** the coffee on the printer.

3 Choose the correct word or phrase.

1 The _____ contains the names and addresses of all the people who work here.
   A hardware   C database
   B software   D keyboard

2 Take this computer game and tell me if you can _____ it on your laptop.
   A run   C surf
   B click on   D delete

3 The _____ will only last for another hour, so you'd better hurry up and find the cable.
   A battery   C modem
   B USB drive   D screen

4 You should buy a case for your iPod so that you don't _____ the screen.
   A scratch   C drop
   B crash   D spill

Grammar

4 Choose the word or phrase that best completes the sentence.

1 They worked all night, but they _____ solve the problem.
   A couldn't have   C didn't have to
   B mightn't   D weren't able to

2 Jack _____ cracked the screen if he'd been more careful with his computer.
   A mightn't have   C couldn't have
   B will have   D could have

3 I'm not busy tonight, so I _____ help you with your assignment if you like.
   A need to   C can
   B have to   D must

4 You're playing on the computer again when you _____ doing your homework.
   A should   C might
   B ought to be   D could have be

5 There's Adam's mobile phone. He _____ left it here after the class.
   A had   C must
   B must have   D might be

6 If you'd backed up your work, you _____ worried about losing the data.
   A needn't have   C mustn't have
   B couldn't have   D can't have

5 Choose the correct answers.

On the news the other night, it said that one in five school pupils see their computer as a friend. 'They ¹*may* / *must* be mad!' said my brother. 'A computer is just a machine. It ²*can't* / *needn't* be a friend'.

I know what he means, but in some ways a computer is like a friend. When I get home from school, I ³*must* / *might* log on for an hour or so and chat to friends. It's not that I ⁴*mustn't* / *couldn't* live without it, but that I don't want to live without it. Sometimes I know I ⁵*might* / *should* spend less time on the computer, but it helps me relax. Last night for example, I ⁶*could have* / *should have* talked for hours to my friends, but my dad kept saying, 'You ⁷*must* / *may* spend less time on the computer.' He gets really angry about it. I know he's probably right, but I think that he ⁸*might have been* / *needn't have been* the same when he was my age ... if he'd had a computer!

The most important relationships in my life are with my parents, my older brother and my best friend. How close are you to your parents, brothers and sisters and other family members? Who are your best friends?

6 Use Your Imagination

Vocabulary Starter
Friends, family and relationships

1 Match the halves of the idiomatic phrases.

1	to keep	A	hard to get
2	to lose	B	the courage
3	to pluck up	C	on a date
4	to go	D	the clock back
5	to play	E	touch with
6	to go through	F	in touch with
7	to make	G	a fresh start
8	to turn	H	a difficult time

2 Complete the sentences with the words from the box.

> anniversary blind divorced engaged gap
> opposites proposed regrets relationship
> reunion separated tongue twins

1 My parents were _____ for two years before they finally got _____ last year.

2 Neil _____ to Cathy and she said 'Yes' so now they're _____ . The wedding is in May.

3 All the people I was at school with are having a _____ next Saturday. I can't believe it's fifteen years since I saw them all!

4 I don't have many _____ , but I do wish I'd asked Jackie out before Ron did.

5 Mick and Sam are _____ , but they don't look at all alike.

6 What can I buy my parents for their twentieth wedding _____?

7 I get quite _____-tied when I meet someone who I'm attracted to.

8 Some people say that _____ attract, but I think it's better to have plenty of things in common.

9 There's a five-year age _____ between my parents.

10 I met a really cool boy on a _____ date organised by my cousin. Unfortunately, it didn't develop into a long term _____.

3 Which phrases from Exercises 1 and 2 are shown in the pictures?

CHATROOM

- If you could turn the clock back, what would you change and why?
- Would you ever agree to go on a blind date?

Reading

1 Read the text and match the people with the facts.

1 Melanie	A	Mike was engaged to her.
2 Sue	B	He used to go out with Emily.
3 Keith Miller	C	Mike went on a date with her.
4 Andy	D	She is Melanie's sister.
5 Julie	E	He was Mike's best friend.
6 Emily	F	She is married to Andy.

2 Read the text again and choose the correct answer, A, B, C or D.

1 From what Mike says about himself when he was young, we know that
   A he was unattractive to the opposite sex.
   B he found it difficult to talk to girls.
   C he never had any girlfriends.
   D he wasn't interested in girls.

2 The reason he didn't ask Emily out was that
   A he didn't like her character.
   B she wasn't as attractive as Melanie.
   C he felt that he was too young for her.
   D she talked too much.

3 His friends suggested that he should
   A not talk when he was with Emily.
   B show Emily that he was interested in her.
   C talk to Emily about things she was interested in.
   D be rude to Emily.

4 Mike moved when he was sixteen because
   A his mum was forced to leave the family home.
   B he left his dad to move in with his mum.
   C he wanted more freedom.
   D his mum no longer wanted to stay in the same place.

5 What can we say about Mike's engagement?
   A It lasted for three weeks.
   B It was an unhappy time for both of them.
   C It didn't work due to their characters.
   D Neither Mike nor Sue could be blamed for it finishing.

Regrets,

1 When I was younger, I was known as the good-looking but shy kid of the neighbourhood. I was the tongue-tied, slightly immature boy whose shyness prevented him from getting to know any members of the opposite sex he was interested in
5 (and there were lots)! Actually, that's not entirely true. I once plucked up the courage to ask a girl called Melanie out on a date and we had a disastrous trip to the old Roxy cinema! I actually always preferred her older sister, Emily, but she was three years older than me and the age gap was just too great
10 for a boy like me who was lacking in confidence. She always seemed so chatty – in fact she never stopped talking! Anyway, my friends advised me to play hard to get and keep silent in her presence. At least I didn't have to think of interesting topics to chat about. She probably wondered why I always
15 ignored her! It wasn't rudeness but mistaken tactics designed to make her interested in me! Needless to say, it didn't work!

I left the area when I was sixteen after my mum and dad got divorced – just after their twentieth anniversary! I wish my mum had stayed in our old house because I didn't want
20 to move. I know she went through a difficult time with my dad

6 The reason for his and Keith's nickname was their
   A close friendship.
   B looks.
   C family relationship.
   D character.

7 The reason Mike isn't as close to people at college as he was to Keith is because
   A they aren't as friendly.
   B they didn't get to know each other as children.
   C he doesn't like them so much.
   D they have to share a room.

8 Which is the most accurate statement?
   A Mike only has negative memories from his childhood.
   B Mike never wants to return to his old neighbourhood.
   C Mike would be happy if he had the chance to relive his childhood.
   D Mike is glad that his childhood is over.

Reading Tip: multiple-choice questions

• Try answering the question without looking at the answer options. Then choose the answer option which is nearest in meaning to the answer you found on your own.

• Confirm your choice by checking that the other answer options are wrong.

relationships and a reunion ...

before they separated and they hadn't had a happy marriage. She wanted to move so that she could make a fresh start. When we moved, I had a lot more freedom because my father wasn't around and I did some foolish things. I even got engaged to a
25 girl named Sue! I met her on a blind date and we had similar characters so we started going out. I proposed after three weeks! It didn't last – luckily. If I had married her, I wouldn't be happy now. Neither would she! It was nobody's fault – we were just too young. Anyway, I passed my exams and got a place at university
30 to study Economics. I moved out of my mum's house with a new feeling of optimism about life and here I am – I love student life and I'm having a great time.

I lost touch with most of my old friends. We drifted apart, especially during my engagement when I stopped sending
35 emails for a few months. The only person I've kept in touch with is Keith Miller. They called us the terrible twins because we were inseparable at school, although we certainly weren't related and we looked nothing like each other! I liked him because he was so different from me and he needed someone quiet like me to
40 calm him down. Well, you know the old saying that 'opposites

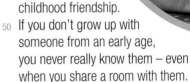

attract'. If only I had a friend like that here. There are some great people here
45 and I have made a lot of friends, but it's not quite the same as a childhood friendship.
50 If you don't grow up with someone from an early age, you never really know them – even when you share a room with them.

Anyway, my roommate here told me about a social
55 networking site that he uses. I used to laugh at people with their two hundred plus online 'friends', but the number of people who use the site is unbelievable – almost everyone I know is a member. Of course I signed up, and then I bombarded them all with 'friends' requests and I'll try to keep
60 in touch this time. I read that Emily's ex-boyfriend, Andy, got married to a girl called Julie. Well, I guess he's her ex. If they hadn't split up, I don't think he would have got married to someone else!

Looking back, it was an enjoyable childhood. There was
65 a lot of frustration and boredom but, if I could turn the clock back, I'd love to go back and experience it all again. I often try to imagine what it would have been like if I had been a different kind of person. There are a few things I regret doing and many things I regret not doing!
70 But, now, I'm going back! We're having a reunion at Keith's house, on March 15th. I'll be there unless something unavoidable comes up. I told him that I'll only come as long as he invites all of the old gang – even the few who aren't online. He promised to do his best. I hope Emily will be there!

CAN I ASK YOU FOR A DATE?

OF COURSE. JUNE 18TH 1759.

CHATROOM

- Think about somebody who has moved away from your school or area. Do you miss him/her? Why?
- Is there anything you regret doing? Why?

WebSearch

www.facebook.com
www.myspace.com
www.blogger.com

3 **Match these words from the text with the correct meanings.**

1	prevented (line 3)	A	being without
2	disastrous (line 7)	B	happens unexpectedly
3	lacking in (line 10)	C	methods
4	chatty (line 11)	D	paid no attention to
5	ignored (line 15)	E	stopped
6	tactics (line 15)	F	terrible
7	bombarded (line 59)	G	talkative
8	comes up (line 72)	H	sent out a lot of information at one time

Vocabulary

Word formation: words from the text

1 Complete the sentences with the correct form of the words in capitals. All the words are from the reading text on page 67.

I was chatting to a guy on the Internet last night. He was nice, but some of the things he said about himself were pretty ¹_____ (BELIEVE)!

I suffer from terrible ²_____ (SHY). I had a ³_____ (DISASTER) time at a party I went to last week. I didn't speak to a single person all night!

Jackie and Peter are ⁴_____ (SEPARATE). They've been together for three years now and they are almost never apart. I wouldn't be surprised if they announced their ⁵_____ (ENGAGE) soon.

My brother is older than me although you wouldn't know it. He's ⁶_____ (MATURE) and loves playing silly tricks on his friends. I must admit that his company is quite ⁷_____ (ENJOY) – he's great fun to be with.

The thing I can't stand is ⁸_____ (RUDE). My last boyfriend was rude to everyone; my friends, bus drivers, waiters … I was ⁹_____ (FOOL) to ever go out with him. Now I don't have a boyfriend and I'm enjoying my ¹⁰_____ (FREE).

Family and friends

2 Match the people with the descriptions.

> spouse   online friend   roommate   sibling
> mother-in-law/father-in-law (in-laws)
> fiancée/fiancé   widow/widower   close friend
> bachelor   ex-boyfriend/girlfriend

A you share a room with him/her _____

B you used to go out with him/her _____

C you keep in touch on the Internet _____

D this man isn't married _____

E this person has lost his/her husband/wife _____

F a very good friend _____

G a brother or sister _____

H a husband or wife _____

I your husband or wife's parents _____

J you are engaged to him/her _____

3 Complete the email with words from Exercise 2.

New   Reply

Hi Mike,

This is a photo of me and my ¹_____ , Rebecca. Yes, I'm engaged and getting married next year! The couple behind her are her parents – my future ²_____ ! It'll be a quiet wedding. Neither of us have got any ³_____ , although Leo Davies was such a ⁴_____ that he was like a brother to me. I'm going to invite a few old school friends, but Rebecca says definitely no ⁵_____ ! She thinks people you meet on the Internet aren't really friends at all.

Hope all is well with you and you're enjoying life as a ⁶_____ . Unless you haven't updated your profile and you're actually married?! See you at the reunion.

Jason

Collocations

4 Complete the sentences with the words from the box.

> arranged   black   double   fresh
> generation   maiden   opposite

1 Are you shy when you talk to a member of the _____ sex?

2 I won't keep in touch with my school friends after I go to university; I want to make a _____ start.

3 When Amina grows up she'll have an _____ marriage with a man her parents choose for her.

4 My mother's _____ name was Pigg. She was very happy to change it when she married!

5 Liam and I are going on a _____ date with two girls from our class.

6 Uncle Stan is the _____ sheep of our family. He's never had a proper job and refuses to marry.

7 The _____ gap means that teenagers and parents often have a lot of trouble understanding each other.

Phrasal verbs

5 Choose the correct word to complete the phrasal verbs.

1 I'd really like to <u>ask</u> Marie **off / on / out**, but I don't know how to approach her.

2 I need more freedom now that I'm eighteen, so I'm going to <u>move</u> **off / along / out** of the family home.

3 I can't believe that Cheryl and Ashley have <u>split</u> **up / out / off**.

4 It's important that everyone in the class <u>gets</u> **in / on / off** well with each other.

5 I'm only allowed to <u>stay</u> **on / up / off** until ten o'clock on school nights.

6 Mark's parents <u>threw</u> him **off / down / out** when he got into trouble with the police.

7 You can only <u>stay</u> **out / off / through** until eight o'clock because you've got to do your homework.

8 Will your mum <u>tell</u> you **off / out / over** if you are late home tonight?

Word formation: noun suffixes

6 Complete the sentences with the correct form of the words in capitals. Use the suffixes from the box. Make any other changes to the words necessary.

> -hood   -dom   -ship   -ism   -ful

1 What are your happiest memories from your _____? CHILD

2 _____ is no excuse for bad behaviour. BORE

3 _____ is good for men who never want to grow up! BACHELOR

4 After making a clean start, he woke up with a feeling of _____. OPTIMIST

5 This is a nice, quiet _____ to live in. NEIGHBOUR

6 I know we're only fifteen, but you can't say this isn't a serious _____. RELATION

7 How much _____ do your parents give you? FREE

8 I've got lots of online friends, but only a _____ of close friends. HAND

9 We allow your brother to stay out late because he's older than you. It's not _____. FAVOURITE

10 I dislike _____ , so I got annoyed when Mr Lee said that girls couldn't play football. SEX

11 If you lie to James, you will spoil your _____ because he will never trust you again. FRIEND

7 Complete the text with words from Exercise 6.

Despite the hours of [1]_____ with nothing to do, my [2]_____ years were a great time. Our [3]_____ was really great for young people. We were jealous of the children who lived in the city centre, but in fact, we were given a lot more [4]_____ than they were. Well, we boys were. There was quite a lot of [5]_____ in those days; the girls were expected to do the housework, while we could enjoy our free time. When I was eighteen, I had my first serious [6]_____ and five years later, we got married. I always wanted to get married – [7]_____ wasn't for me. Now we have children of our own. My only worry is with my in-laws. They seem to prefer our daughter to our son. The [8]_____ they show her is quite obvious and sometimes my son asks why he doesn't get treated the same.

Back up your vocabulary

8 Complete the second sentence so that it has a similar meaning to the first using the word given.

1 Ben's mum was angry with him because he broke the window.
off
Ben's mum _____ for breaking the window.

2 I finished my relationship with my girlfriend because I had to revise for my exams.
up
I _____ my girlfriend because I had to revise for my exams.

3 All my best friends are girls, but I'm a boy
opposite
All my best friends _____ sex.

4 I can't believe that your parents forced you to leave home.
threw
I can't believe that your parents
_____.

5 Why don't you and I and our two girlfriends all go out together?
double
Why don't we _____ date?

Grammar
Conditionals

> zero conditional
> If you **don't grow up** with someone from an early age, you never really **know** them.
> first conditional
> If you **tell** me everything on the phone, we**'ll have** nothing to talk about when we meet.
> second conditional
> If I **could turn** the clock back, I**'d love** to go back.
> third conditional
> If they **hadn't split up**, I don't think he **would have got married** to someone else!
> mixed conditionals (2nd and 3rd)
> If I **had married** her, I **wouldn't be** happy now.
> unless, as long as, provided that, on condition that, suppose
> I'll be there **unless** something unavoidable comes up.
> I'll only come **as long as** he invites all of the old gang.
> I'll find out more at the reunion, **provided that** my shyness doesn't come back!
> We'll invite you to the wedding **on condition that** you don't cause any trouble!
> **Suppose** no one asks you to the end of year ball, what will you do?

See **Grammar File**, page 166 ≫

1 Complete the second sentence so that it has a similar meaning to the first.

1 You didn't have a good time because you didn't take Cathy to the party.
If you _____ to the party, you _____ a good time.

2 They'll only come if we pay for the taxi.
As _____ for the taxi, they'll come.

3 Don't share too much information online if you don't know the other person.
Don't share too much information online unless _____ .

4 We'll go to the cinema provided that I can get some money from my parents.
We'll go to the cinema on _____ some money from my parents.

5 People always feel better after a good night's sleep.
If people _____ good night's sleep, they _____ .

6 The only reason Lisa won't go out with me is that she still loves Ed.
If Lisa didn't _____ with me.

7 I only managed to get to university because I didn't go out when I was a teenager.
If I _____ out when I was a teenager, I _____ at university now.

---

2 Read the article and think of the word which best fits each space. Use only one word in each space.

Write your own alternate history ... and win a prize!

Alternate history is a kind of science fiction in which some historical event happens differently to reality and the plot of the story looks at the differences this would have made to the world. It's fantasy and, [1]_____ we build a time machine which can change history, we [2]_____ never know how accurate the authors' ideas are. However, as [3]_____ as the writers make the plot believable, there will always be people who enjoy reading the stories.

The earliest example of such a story was *Ab Urbe Condita* by Livy. In this, Livy asks what would [4]_____ happened if Alexander the Great [5]_____ gone West instead of East. Another famous example was Louis Geoffroy's look at Napoleon. In this he says that, [6]_____ Napoleon had defeated Russia in 1812, he would have [7]_____ able to defeat England. If that had happened, [8]_____ we all be speaking French now?

What we're asking is this – if you could change history, what [9]_____ you change and how do you think it would affect our lives today? Just to make it slightly more difficult, we [10]_____ only accept your ideas on [11]_____ that they do not involve the result of a war. A prize goes to the best idea! Remember, if [12]_____ don't enter the competition, you won't win!

Wishes

> wishes about the present or future
> *If only / I wish I **knew** how to talk to girls.*
> wishes about the past / regrets
> *If only / I wish my mum **had stayed** in our old house.*

See **Grammar File**, page 167

3 Complete the boy's wishes with the correct form of the verbs in brackets.

I wish …

1 I / not be / so shy

_____

2 I / can / talk to girls

_____

3 I / have / more fashionable clothes

_____

4 I / stay / at home

_____

If only …

5 I / not have to / leave at ten o'clock

_____

6 my mum / not be coming / to pick me up

_____

7 I / meet / her earlier

_____

8 tonight / can last forever

_____

4 Complete the dialogue with the correct form of the verbs in brackets.

John: I've got a date with Olivia this evening. I wish I ¹_____ (not be) so nervous. What will I do if I can't think of anything to say to her?

Ben: Play the 'film wishes' game.

John: What's that?

Ben: You think of a film and make wishes about what one of the characters might have said. The other person has to guess the film. For example, I wish my brother ²_____ (be) still alive. I wish I ³_____ (can) walk. If only they ⁴_____ (not destroy) the big tree. I wish Tsu'tey ⁵_____ (will) trust me.

John: *Avatar.*

Ben: Very good. You have a go.

John: Hmm. I wish I ⁶_____ (not take) this job. If only the monkey ⁷_____ (not steal) my instructions. I wish it ⁸_____ (be) morning so I could go home … er …

Ben: *Night at the Museum.*

John: Yes. Are you sure this will work?

Ben: Of course it will. It's a brilliant plan.

Back up your grammar

5 Choose the word or phrase that best completes the sentence.

1 If we _____ in such a hurry, I'd buy you a cola.
   A weren't   B hadn't been   C wouldn't be   D won't be

2 You can't go out on Friday night _____ you've finished all your homework.
   A if   B as long as   C unless   D provided that

3 I wish I _____ an only child. I get lonely sometimes.
   A am not   B hadn't been   C wouldn't be   D wasn't

4 If someone _____ help, they usually ask their family, not friends.
   A will need   B needs   C would need   D needed

5 I wish I _____ that girl for her name and phone number.
   A had asked   B asked   C would ask   D ask

6 _____ she says 'No', how will I feel?
   A As long as   B Unless   C Suppose   D Provided that

7 If my sister hadn't got married last Saturday, I _____ missed Sarah's party.
   A didn't   B won't   C wouldn't   D wouldn't have

8 Of course she didn't turn up. If she _____ up, I wouldn't be here now, would I?
   A turned   B had turned   C would turn   D turns

> **CHATROOM**
> • Imagine a genie offered you three wishes. What would you wish for?
> • What 'alternate history' story would interest you most? Why?

Listening

Listening 1

🔊 **1** You will hear an interview with a behavioural scientist about online relationships. Choose A, B or C.

> **Listening Tip: multiple-choice questions**
>
> Don't panic if you miss a question – go on to the next one.

1 The research into non-human primates' interaction patterns was carried out
  A by Robin Dunbar.
  B before Robin Dunbar looked at human relationships.
  C after Robin Dunbar started his research.

2 The true 'Dunbar's number'
  A is unknown.
  B is less than the number usually stated.
  C was changed because it was found to be wrong.

3 When Dunbar looked at the history of human interaction he found
  A one example of the significance of the number 150.
  B two examples of the significance of the number 150.
  C many examples of the significance of the number 150.

4 Dunbar's number is
  A accepted by most people.
  B accepted by everyone.
  C one of several possible numbers.

5 Swedish tax authorities have
  A tried to employ people who know and get on with each other.
  B moved their offices to areas where communities are very close.
  C limited the number of people working in their offices.

6 Dunbar has found that the number of 'real' online friends a person has
  A is unaffected by the total number of their online friends.
  B is related to the total number of their online friends.
  C is completely random.

Listening 2

🔊 **2** You will hear five people talking about things that have gone wrong on dates. For each speaker choose the correct problem (A–F). There is one extra problem which you don't need to use.

> **Listening Tip: multiple matching**
>
> Think of what each problem in the list could be about. Even if your ideas are not exactly right, it will prepare you for what you are about to hear.

Speaker 1 ☐

Speaker 2 ☐

Speaker 3 ☐

Speaker 4 ☐

Speaker 5 ☐

A He/She said the wrong thing.

B He/She reacted in the wrong way.

C He/She was unable to find someone.

D He/She forgot something important.

E He/She lost something.

F He/She was bored.

Yes, yes, I love listening to your stories of the school football team. Honestly!

Listening 3

🔊 **3** You will hear a recording from a news broadcast. Listen to the whole recording once. Then you will hear the recording again with pauses for you to write what you hear. Make sure you spell the words correctly.

Speaking
Presenting a topic

1 Look at the choice of speaking topics from an exam. Which one would you choose? Why?

A The advantages and disadvantages of online friendships.

B Is the generation gap a bad thing?

C What do you like about your best friend and why do you think he/she likes you?

2 Read the notes and match them with the correct topic from Exercise 1.

1 It causes arguments – for example over clothes.
2 I learn a lot from him.
3 I make him laugh.
4 People think they have got friends, but haven't really.
5 It helps teenagers to be independent.
6 You can chat anytime, even when you're not allowed to go out.

3 Listen to a student talking about the first topic, online friendships. What advantages and disadvantages does he mention?

4 Listen again and tick the phrases in the Language Upload box that are used.

5 Complete the notes about the other two topics with your own ideas.

Is the generation gap a bad thing?

Yes	No
• It causes arguments, for example over clothes.	• It helps teenagers to be independent.
•	•
•	•

What do you like about your best friend and why do you think he/she likes you?

I like my friend because ...	He/she likes me because ...
•	•
•	•
•	•

6 Choose one of the two topics from Exercise 5 and present it to the class. Try to talk for about one and a half minutes. Use the Language Upload box to help you.

Speaking Tip: speaking clearly

Try to think about what you are going to say and to organise your thoughts before you start speaking.

7 Work with a partner to answer these questions.

The generation gap

1 Has there always been a generation gap or is it a modern phenomenon?

2 Should parents try to control their teenage children's behaviour? Why/Why not?

3 Who or what is the biggest influence on teenagers' tastes?

Your best friend

1 How do you think your friendship will change in the future?

2 Do you prefer being with one friend or a group of friends? Why?

Language Upload

Giving your opinion

In my opinion, …
As far as I'm concerned, …
Personally, I believe …

Sequencing points

Firstly, Secondly, Lastly, Finally,
The next point/reason/advantage/disadvantage is …
As I said …
Another point/reason/factor is …

Personalising your talk

In my experience, …   I remember …
That has happened to me.

Giving examples

For example, …   As an example, …   For one thing, …

Adding points

In addition, …   Moreover, …   Furthermore, …

Contrasting points

However, …   But …   Even though, …

Writing: A Story

Before you write

1 Answer these questions.

1 Describe a story you have read and enjoyed. What made it enjoyable?
2 Describe a story that you didn't enjoy. What didn't you like about it?
3 Look at these ideas and decide whether they are important or not.

realistic plot

interesting and varied vocabulary

dramatic dialogue

a variety of structures

detailed descriptions of characters and places

2 Read the two stories. Which one do you think is better? Why?

> Write a story which ends with the sentence, 'If I had known, I would never have gone with him.'
> Write between 120 and 180 words.

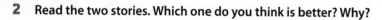

1   There was one boy at school, who I
    had liked for ages. His name was William.
    Unfortunately, he had a girlfriend called Jane.
    One day, they had an argument in the middle
5   of the school canteen. Jane stood up and
    walked out of the room.
        A few days later, I was sitting on my own
    when William appeared by my side and asked
    me to a party. I said 'Yes', and went to tell my
10 friends.
        I took ages to get ready. I brushed my hair
    and put on make-up. When we arrived at the
    party, Jane was standing there looking at me.
    She asked William to go to another room with
15 her. He left me. Later I found out that he had
    never stopped loving her and had only asked
    me to make her jealous. If I had known, I
    would never have gone with him.

1   There was a boy at school, who I had
    fancied for ages. William was tall and
    handsome with long, wavy hair. Unfortunately,
    he had an attractive, fun girlfriend called
5   Jane. One day, they had a huge argument
    in the middle of the school canteen. Suddenly,
    Jane stood up, and angrily stormed out of
    the room.
        A few days later, I was sitting quietly
10 on my own in the playground when William
    appeared by my side and asked me to a
    party. Blushing, I mumbled, 'Yes', and ran
    off excitedly to tell my friends.
        I took ages to get ready. I carefully
15 brushed my hair and nervously put on make-
    up, which I wasn't used to at all. When we
    arrived at the party, Jane was standing there
    staring suspiciously at me. She persuaded
    William to go to another room with her. He
20 left me without a second glance. Later I found
    out that he had never stopped loving her and
    had only invited me to make her jealous. If I
    had known, I would never have gone with him.

3 Put the parts of the story in the order they appear.

A The main body of the story. Developing the plot.
B An introduction of the main characters.
C A conclusion showing consequences or people's feelings and reactions.
D Setting the scene for the plot – the time and place that the story starts.

4 Read the stories again and answer the questions.

1 What do you know about William and Jane from the *first story / second story*?
2 What do we know about the writer's feelings in the *first story / second story*?
3 How did the writer prepare for the party in the *first story / second story*?

5 Look at these words from the first story. How have they been expressed in the second story?

had liked (line 2) _____
walked out (line 6) _____
said (line 9) _____
went (line 9) _____
looking at (line 13) _____
asked (line 14) _____
asked (line 16) _____

6 Add an adjective or an adverb to complete each sentence. Then use your imagination to complete the sentences.

1 She left home and moved into a _____ one-bedroom flat, where …
2 He was _____ and _____ with dark brown hair which …
3 She slammed the door _____ behind her and rushed out of the house, where …
4 They were walking along the _____ street without speaking, when …
5 She was a _____ beautiful woman who …

7 Complete the table with the verbs from the box.

expect   gaze   glance   imagine
race   reply   stammer   stare   stroll
wander   whisper   wonder

Ways of walking	Ways of speaking

Ways of thinking	Ways of looking

Time to write

8 Look at the task and choose the best idea for a plot.

Write a story which begins with the sentence, 'Alan knew it was time to get up, but he wished that he didn't have to.' Write between 120 and 180 words.

A It's the day of an important exam.
B He is nervous on the morning of his first date.
C He has just split up with his girlfriend and will have to face her in school.

9 Write notes using your own imagination.

1 What does Alan look like?
2 What is his character like?
3 Who else is important in the story? Describe them.
4 How does Alan feel in the morning? Do his feelings change during the day?
5 How does the story end? Happily? Sadly?

10 Write your story using the Writing Checklist and Memory Flash to help you. Remember to make a plan before you begin.

Writing Checklist: A Story

Does your story include

1 an attention-grabbing opening sentence?
2 adverbs of manner?
3 adjectives to describe people and feelings?
4 extra information in relative clauses?
5 a range of vocabulary to avoid repetition?
6 a variety of verbs which give exact information, for example, *whisper, crawl, wonder*?
7 a realistic plot which uses the given sentence naturally?
8 a range of narrative tenses (past simple, past continuous, past perfect)?

Memory Flash

Remember!
There are no set phrases that can be used in a story. You need to use vocabulary which is suitable for the story you are writing.

Adverbs and adjectives
stunningly beautiful, terribly shy, incredibly embarrassed

Adverbs of manner
carefully, politely, stupidly, sadly

Useful verbs
whisper, stammer, wonder, imagine, stare, glance

Narrative tenses
While he was waiting, he saw …
He had already been there for …,
They had been waiting …

Vocabulary

1 Complete the sentences with the correct form of the words in capitals.

1 Monika and Harry only invited a _____ of close friends to their wedding. (HAND)

2 You both need to be more tolerant if you want to improve your _____. (RELATION)

3 No-one goes out at night in this _____ ; it's too dangerous. (NEIGHBOUR)

4 His behaviour was _____ ; I've never seen somebody go so crazy! (BELIEVE)

5 I never got into trouble during my _____. (CHILD)

2 Read the blog and think of the word which best fits each space. Use only one word in each space.

When I got married, I wanted to make a fresh ¹_____, which is why I was happy to change my surname. I'm now Janet Conway, which sounds much better than my ²_____ name which was Janet Johnson.

For a long time, I was considered to be the black ³_____ of my family. I didn't want to go to university and I didn't want to work. My father often used to say that he would throw me ⁴_____. I did move out in the end, but only to a flat two streets away. I loved it. I could stay out all night and there was nobody waiting to tell me ⁵_____ when I got home late.

Now, I get ⁶_____ well with my mum, but there's still a problem with my dad. Sometimes, I'd like to ⁷_____ the clock back and try to make things right, but I'm not sure it would be possible.

Grammar

3 Complete the dialogue with the correct form of the verbs.

Genie: I am the Genie of the Lamp. I will give you three wishes.

Andy: A genie – wow! I wish I ¹_____ (remember) to bring my camera. Hey, what's this?

Genie: It's your camera. You wished for it.

Sarah: I wish you ²_____ (think) before speaking!

Genie: Your wish is my command! From now on your friend will always think before speaking.

Andy: Oh no! Now we only have one wish left. If only I ³_____ (can) come up with an idea!

Sarah: I've got it! Genie, we wish we ⁴_____ (not meet) you yet and could start all over again.

Genie: I am the Genie of the Lamp. I will give you three wishes.

Andy: Hey, it worked. Well done, Sarah! I wish I ⁵_____ (be) as clever as you are! Aaah! What have I said? I didn't mean it, Genie! I wish I ⁶_____ (never / say) that!

Sarah: Shut up! You've wasted two of our three wishes!

Andy: Oh no, not again! Why don't we try your idea again?

Sarah: Yes, but suppose it ⁷_____ (not work). Let's just ask for some money.

Andy: Good idea. I wish I ⁸_____ (think) of that!

Sarah: Oh no!

4 Choose the word or phrase that best completes the quotation.

1 'Nothing will work unless you _____.' **Maya Angelou**

   A will do   B do   C would

2 'Americans _____ with anything provided it doesn't block traffic.' **Dan Rather**

   A will put up   B had put up   C would have put up

3 'If you _____ practise, you _____ deserve to win.' **Andre Agassi**

   A don't / don't   B don't / wouldn't   C wouldn't / won't

4 'If only we _____ pull out our brain and use only our eyes.' **Pablo Picasso**

   A can   B could   C could have

5 'If General Motors had kept up with technology like the computer industry, we _____ driving $25 cars.' **Bill Gates**

   A will all be   B have all been   C would all be

I love using the Internet to catch up with friends. I usually stay in touch with them on Facebook, but sometimes I text or email them. It's quick and easy. What about you? How do you keep up with the latest gossip from friends?

7 Let's Communic8!

2 Do the quiz and test your knowledge.

I ♥ communication

true false

1 A **chain email** is an electronic message that asks you to send it to multiple people. ☐ ☐

2 **Networking** is a way of talking to other people to share information or make friends. ☐ ☐

3 **Spam** contains important information and you should save it for future use. ☐ ☐

4 A **podcast** is a TV programme that can be downloaded from the Internet. ☐ ☐

5 **Instant messaging** is a conversation with one or more people using the Internet. ☐ ☐

6 **Snail mail** is usually faster than email. ☐ ☐

3 Match the verbs with the definitions.

1 secretly listen to other people's conversations   A overhear
2 give an opinion   B comment
3 become red in the face with embarrassment   C display
4 hear what people are saying by chance   D interact
5 talk to people and do things with them   E browse
6 look through a book or magazine   F blush
7 show information   G eavesdrop

Vocabulary Starter
Staying in touch

1 Match the communication devices in the photos with the speakers.

1 I'd feel lost without it. It's a pity they're so expensive to use. I'm always running out of credit.

2 It definitely makes staying in more fun. We can get over 100 channels, although I'm not keen on all the adverts.

3 I share one with my brother and we're always fighting over using it. He spends ages uploading all his photos.

4 We had one installed about a month ago and it's changed how we learn. Next week we're going to connect to a class in the USA.

4 Complete the sentences with the adjectives from the box.

> simultaneous   virtual   time-consuming
> face-to-face   unreliable

1 I prefer a _____ conversation because you can learn a lot from people's expressions.

2 Social networking sites offer people the chance to make friends although it's in a _____ world.

3 I never send letters now. The postal service can be _____; letters often don't arrive on time.

4 Megan was having _____ chats online with various friends.

5 I prefer checking my spelling on the computer. Using a dictionary is too _____.

Reading

I love sending text messages and getting them is even better.
How do you keep in touch with your friends?
Do you prefer talking on the phone or texting? Why?

Alinka

More soon ... watch this space!

1 Read the blogs and match them with the pictures.

2 For questions 1–12, choose from the people A–D. Some of the people may be chosen more than once. When more than one answer is required, these may be given in any order.

> **Reading Tip:** multiple matching
>
> Read the texts quickly to locate the information you are looking for.

Who

can't help listening to other peoples' conversations?	1 ☐
thought it was a good idea to obtain something?	2 ☐
agreed to let a friend borrow a device?	3 ☐
uses the Internet to learn new words and phrases?	4 ☐ 5 ☐
thinks actually talking to people face-to-face has disadvantages?	6 ☐ 7 ☐
has received a threatening message?	8 ☐
likes to know what's happening around the world?	9 ☐
thinks traditional methods of communication are slow?	10 ☐
was initially told that they couldn't use certain websites?	11 ☐
thinks advertising ruins the pleasure of reading about current events?	12 ☐

http://www.everyonesblogging.com/

Thanks to mobile phones, email and the Internet, maintaining contact with friends and events around the world is easier than ever. We asked four teenagers what they do to stay in touch.

A

16 April   9.05AM

Aleksander
Ukraine
I wasn't really interested in the news until a friend recommended that I got an iPod Touch. Now I've literally got the news at my fingertips. Simply by touching the screen, I can tune in to the weather forecast, the international news headlines or even the sports results. I get a real buzz on school trips when I can check out the news from home without using my laptop. Once I downloaded a podcast of an interview with my favourite pop group. My iPod Touch guarantees that I stay in touch with friends and events. Looking at a small screen in my hand has a lot more appeal than flicking through a newspaper or browsing through magazines full of publicity. My online translator also means that I can use it for German homework. When a friend wanted to know how I was getting such fantastic results in the vocabulary test I told him it was due to my iPod. I promised to lend it to him next time!

3 Find words in the text that mean the following.

1 a feeling of excitement (paragraph A)
2 advertising (paragraph A)
3 something you are crazy about and can't stop doing (paragraph B)
4 a feeling of being uncomfortable (paragraph B)
5 feel very embarrassed by something (paragraph B)
6 didn't agree to (paragraph C)
7 something that is suitable or useful (paragraph D)
8 by mistake (paragraph D)

Keep in touch!

16 April   11.33AM

Monika
Poland

My mobile phone is my lifeline and if I'm honest I think texting has become a bit of an obsession with me. I never miss a chance to glance at my Inbox for messages. It's a reassurance to know that your friends have been in touch, but a disappointment when they haven't! Sometimes eavesdropping is unavoidable, especially when people talk loudly into their phones in a public place. The other day I overheard a girl telling her boyfriend that she had been feeling ill that morning and that she had decided to stay at home. She was obviously lying because she was on the bus! A mobile phone connects you to friends without the awkwardness that you might feel face-to-face. On the other hand, you can't make out when somebody is blushing or avoiding eye contact. I was asked the other day if I wanted a phone that displays the image of the caller. I told them I would cringe if anybody saw me first thing in the morning!

16 April   1.17PM

Theo
Greece

How you keep in touch is a matter of personal preference but I tend to use social networking sites. What I love is how I can track down friends I haven't seen for ages. You can interact with your mates online without feeling obliged to actually get together or make arrangements. At first my dad refused to let me go on them; he said that the sites made you think you had friends when some of the contacts were little more than strangers. I told him to try one of the sites. He insisted he wasn't going to like it, but now he logs on every day! Having simultaneous chats online with instant messaging or MSN is a means of socialising even if it is in a virtual world. Our French teacher asked us if we would like to brush up on our French by chatting online to some students in France. Now I use MSN to pick up new expressions! Our class also writes a daily blog in French and we invite our French friends to comment on it. One student told me my French had been awful at first, but reassured me that it was improving. It's a better alternative to dull text books.

16 April   8.22PM

Natalia
Russia

Well, I admit I'm terrible at writing letters. They take too long and I'm useless at spelling. Nobody my age writes letters any more because the process of writing and then posting them is too slow and unreliable. They don't call it snail mail for nothing, do they? I prefer email because it's less time-consuming and you usually get a faster reply. Needless to say, being able to spell check your email is an added convenience for people like me! Mind you, there are disadvantages. Sometimes you can accidentally send an email to the wrong person. Once I sent an angry email to a friend telling her she had upset me the day before. The trouble is I sent it to the wrong person who then told everybody I had been nasty to her. Another problem is that my email is regularly bombarded with spam that takes me ages to get rid of. Once I received a chain email. It said that I had to email ten friends or something terrible would happen to me! I warned my friends to ignore it and then deleted it. I think we take email for granted now but it encourages people to stay in touch.

CHATROOM

Monika and Natalia talk about texting and emailing. How might these methods affect our written language?

WebSearch

www.channelone.com
wn.com.TeenNews

Vocabulary

Word formation: words from the text

1 Complete the sentences with the correct form of the words in capitals. Be careful, two words do not change form. All the words are from the reading texts on pages 78 and 79.

Body language and facial ¹_____ (EXPRESS) can often betray what a person is really thinking, which is why meeting ²_____ (STRANGE) and even friends can sometimes be difficult or embarrassing. Some people find it hard to deal with this ³_____ (AWKWARD) and prefer the ⁴_____ (CONVENIENT) of messaging or texting rather than a face-to-face conversation. People's ⁵_____ (PREFER) for sending messages electronically is understandable. You can catch up with friends and make ⁶_____ (ARRANGE) without actually having to speak to anybody! However, there are disadvantages to instant communication. For some, the ⁷_____ (APPEAL) of staying in touch can become an ⁸_____ (OBSESS). Those who frequently text friends get a strong feeling of ⁹_____ (DISAPPOINT) if those friends don't respond instantly. After all, texting and emailing, just like any form of communication, is a two-way ¹⁰_____ (PROCESS).

Communication and language

2 Match the phrases with the definitions

1 avoid eye contact
2 speak/talk face-to-face
3 mind your own business
4 keep/stay in touch with
5 lose touch with
6 master a language
7 speak one's mind
8 have contacts

A stop communicating
B learn a language very well
C not look into somebody's eyes
D talk to someone directly
E say exactly what you think
F communicate regularly
G know people who can help you
H not interfere in a situation that doesn't involve you

3 Complete the sentences with phrases from Exercise 2.

1 Emily keeps asking me if I'm going to get married. I wish she would _____ .
2 'You haven't spoken to Paul for ages,' 'I know, I've _____ him.'
3 People who are shy often _____ because it makes them feel awkward.
4 I don't want to phone or text James. I'd rather we _____ .
5 Sandra will give you an honest opinion. She always _____ .
6 The best way to _____ is to live in the country for at least a year.
7 I _____ who could help you with the computer problem.
8 When she went to live in Greece, she _____ her friends by email.

The news

4 Match the information with the links on a website.

1 the temperature in Moscow
2 gossip and news about celebrities
3 the website's opinion on the news
4 advertisements for jobs or items for sale
5 articles by people who regularly write for the site
6 an article about a book or film
7 the latest headlines
8 a report about someone who has died

Breaking News ☐
Weather Forecast ☐
Columns ☐
Show Business ☐
Editorial ☐
Classifieds ☐
Reviews ☐
Obituaries ☐

Idioms

5 Match the idioms with the definitions.

1 Your homework is to **learn** this list of verbs **by heart**.
2 Will you answer me, or say something – anything? Honestly, it's **like talking to a brick wall**!
3 I told Mark to meet me at the cinema but he went to the café instead. We must have **got our wires crossed**.
4 **Keep me posted** on the situation with Candy. If she phones, let me know.
5 When the president said he had lost the money he **was being economical with the truth**.
6 Jack promises that he's going to work harder, but **actions speak louder than words**.

A wasn't giving all the necessary information
B remember something without needing to read it
C what people do is more important that what they say
D misunderstood each other
E having a conversation with someone who refuses to answer
F give me up-to-date information

Phrasal verbs

6 Match the phrasal verbs with the definitions.

1 track down
2 tune in to
3 pick up
4 make out
5 check out
6 flick through
7 brush up on
8 get together

A look through a book or magazine quickly
B be able to hear, see or understand something
C practise sth you already have knowledge of
D watch or listen to a programme
E meet up with a friend
F learn something by listening to someone
G find someone after a difficult or long search
H get more information about something

7 Choose the correct answer.

1 A great way to **track down / pick up** new vocabulary is to listen to song lyrics.
2 I've **flicked through / tracked down** the TV guide, but I can't find anything I want to watch.
3 Julia never reads a newspaper, but she often **tunes in to / makes out** the radio for the headlines.
4 While I was staying with a family in Spain, I was able to **check out / brush up on** my Spanish.
5 I'm hoping to **check out / get together** with some old school friends during the summer break.
6 I can't **make out / pick up** what it says on that sign. Can you read it?
7 I think we should buy the newspaper to **flick through / check out** what's on this weekend.
8 After a long search the police finally **brushed up on / tracked down** the bank robber.

Back up your vocabulary

8 Read the text and choose the best answer (A, B, C or D) for each gap.

1 A total
  B snail
  C instant
  D technical

2 A modern
  B breaking
  C column
  D editorial

3 A keep
  B lose
  C have
  D connect

4 A columns
  B classifieds
  C obituaries
  D editorial

5 A rain
  B climate
  C chain
  D weather

6 A flick
  B touch
  C turn
  D move

7 A look
  B check
  C catch
  D see

8 A master
  B interact
  C eavesdrop
  D overhear

Newspapers no more

In a world of modern communication and ¹_____ messaging, newspaper sales are suffering. Gone are the days when people eagerly awaited the newspaper to find out about that day's ²_____ news. Thanks to the Internet those who like to ³_____ in touch with world events can log on to a free news website. Many sites offer the same features as a quality newspaper - from the website's own views on events in the ⁴_____, to features written by the site's regular columnists. One click will take you swiftly to the ⁵_____ forecast without the need to ⁶_____ through endless pages of advertisements. Most online news sites also offer regular video links so that you can ⁷_____ out the latest news. Readers are also invited to ⁸_____ with other readers by using the newspaper's forums where they can leave comments and express their opinions.

CHATROOM

- Do you ever read a newspaper?
- Do you think it is important to keep up with the news? Why/ Why not?

Grammar
Reported speech

> **reported statements**
> *He said that the sites **made** you think …*
> *When a friend wanted to know how I **was getting** such …*
> *I overheard a girl saying she **had been feeling** ill and that she **had decided** to stay at home …*
> *One student told me my French **had been** awful at first.*
> **reporting verbs**
> *I **promised** to lend it to him.*
> *He **insisted** he wasn't going to like it.*
> *… a friend **recommended** that I got an iPod Touch.*
> *I **warned** my friends to ignore it.*
> **reported commands and requests**
> *I told him **to try** one of the sites.*
> *I was asked the other day **if I wanted** a phone that displays …*
> **other changes**
> *Once **I** sent an angry email to a friend telling **her** she had upset me **the day before**.*

See **Grammar File**, pages 168 and 169

"My teacher isn't qualified to teach spelling!
She spells U 'y-o-u'. She spells BRB 'r-e-t-u-r-n'.
She spells BFN 'g-o-o-d-b-y-e'..."

1 Choose the correct answer.

1 'I'm going to read the newspaper.'
  Paul said that he **was going to read / was reading** the newspaper.
2 'Did you see the lottery winner on the news?'
  They asked if I **saw / had seen** the lottery winner on the news.
3 'Do you like the book you're reading?'
  He asked if I **did like / liked** the book I **was reading / read**.
4 'I may call you later.'
  She told him she **might / would** call him later.
5 'He's sent a lot of emails today.'
  He said he **sent / had sent** a lot of emails that day.
6 'What will you be doing in the summer?'
  She asked what I **would do / would be doing** in the summer.
7 'I didn't check my emails last night.'
  Thomas said that he **didn't check / hadn't checked** his emails **last night / the night before**.

2 Complete the conversation with reported speech.

Lucy: Hi Alice. Did you see Kate last night?
Alice: Yes, I did. She said ('I've had an email from Max.')
1 _____

Lucy: Lucky Kate! What did he say?
Alice: He said ('It was great to meet you and your friends at the beach.')
2 _____

Lucy: Is that all?
Alice: No. He told Kate ('I'm planning a party for my friends next week.')
3 _____

Lucy: Do you think that includes us?
Alice: Well, he said ('I'll email the details tomorrow.')
4 _____

Lucy: That's great! I hope we get an invitation.
Alice: Oh, we will. At the end of his email he said (I can't find your friends' email addresses.')
5 _____

Lucy: And …
Alice: And he asked her ('Do you think your friends can come?')
6 _____

Lucy: Great! That must mean us. I hope Kate told him ('They will definitely be here.')
7 _____

3 Complete the reported requests and commands.

1 'Will you text me this afternoon?'
  Amy asked him _____.
2 'Can you buy me a newspaper?'
  He asked them _____.
3 'Open the door for me, please.'
  He asked them _____.
4 'Don't call me after 9 pm.'
  She told him _____.
5 'Get off my computer!'
  He told her _____.
6 'Email us with all the gossip!'
  They told him _____.

After all our online chats, it's great to finally meet you in person.

Same here.

4 Rewrite the sentences with reported speech using the correct form of the verbs from the box.

> complain   persuade   deny
> recommend   boast   accuse

1 'I speak excellent English.'
Max _____ excellent English.
2 'It's unbelievable. This letter has taken a month to arrive.'
She _____ a month to arrive.
3 'You've been reading my letters!'
He _____ his letters.
4 'I think it would be better to send an email because it's quicker.'
The boss _____ an email.
5 'We're glad you finally agreed to come out, Sandra.'
Sandra's friends finally _____ go out.
6 'We didn't send him the message!'
They _____ the message.

5 Complete the diary with the pronouns from the box.

> her   us   we   she   their   it   his   them

Tuesday

Just got back from Dan's party. He said
¹_____ was going to be fantastic and he
was right. Last week his parents told
²_____ that we could all stay for the night.
They suggested that ³_____ took sleeping
bags and camped in ⁴_____ garden. I know
that Dan isn't keen on camping, but he told us
that ⁵_____ parents were worried about
the noise. You see, Dan had asked our friend
Julia to bring ⁶_____ guitar. She's in a
rock group and sings really well. He said they
didn't want us to disturb ⁷_____ with the
music. They needn't have worried because in the
end Julia decided not to come. She said that
⁸_____ hated camping!

6 Complete the sentences with the correct time phrases.

1 He said he had arrived (three days ago)
_____ .
2 Amy told them the party would be (next Saturday)
_____ .
3 They said they weren't free (tonight)
_____ .
4 We asked if they could come (tomorrow)
_____ .
5 I told them I had seen Mark (last week)
_____ .

7 Complete the second sentence so that it has a similar meaning to the first. Use the word in capitals.

1 'Don't lie, Charles!' Jenny said.
NOT
Jenny _____ lie.
2 'Was there a good film on TV last night?'
ASKED
Jim _____
a good film on TV the night before.
3 'Let's look on Facebook,' she said.
SUGGESTED
She _____ on Facebook.
4 'I saw him last week,' he said.
PREVIOUS
He said he _____ week.
5 'Don't open chain emails!' the teacher told them.
WARNED
The teacher _____ chain emails.
6 'I'm sorry I lied to you.'
APOLOGISED
She _____ to him.

Back up your grammar

8 Read the text and think of the word which best fits each space. Use only one word in each space.

When the head teacher of a primary school in England told parents ¹_____ the school ²_____ going to teach a new language, there was a mixed reaction. Ardwell School is a multi-racial school where more than twenty languages are already spoken. 'She told us ³_____ to worry as the plan would help the children communicate better', said one parent. 'She told ⁴_____ that the children ⁵_____ be learning Makaton, a special sign language that had ⁶_____ tried in other schools.' 'Basically she persuaded us ⁷_____ give it a go,' admits another parent. The results have been undeniably successful. One teacher who learnt Makaton with his class claimed that another language in the classroom had ⁸_____ been a problem. He said that the kids seemed to like it and believed it had given ⁹_____ more confidence with ¹⁰_____ communication skills.

CHATROOM

- What has your teacher told you about learning English? Was it useful?
- Have you ever complained about something in a shop? What did you say?

Listening

Listening 1

1 Look at the photos from the news. What do you think the stories are about?

2 Listen to a recording of the news. Which photos are related to the news items mentioned?

3 Listen again and complete the notes.

The News

1 Type of company with problems:
_____

2 Staff not happy with:
_____

3 Average number of emails in a day:
_____

4 Amount of junk mail:
_____

5 Office communication discussion (when?):
_____

6 Interactive whiteboards to be supplied to:
_____

7 Robert Pattinson's new role as:
_____

8 Film tickets phone number:
_____

Listening 2

4 You will hear six short conversations. Choose the best answer, A, B or C.

> **Listening Tip: multiple choice**
> ○ Read the questions and decide what information you are looking for.
> ○ As you listen, cross out any options which you are sure are wrong.

1 Listen to the phone conversation. What is it about?
  A a business meal
  B an office party
  C a formal lunch

2 Listen to the speakers. Who are they?
  A a photographer and a newspaper editor
  B a journalist and a restaurant owner
  C a newspaper editor and a writer

3 Listen to the phone message. What does the speaker ask for?
  A news about a friend's trip
  B a friend's phone number
  C a letter

4 Listen to the speakers. What has happened?
  A They've missed the film.
  B They've misunderstood each other.
  C They didn't do their homework.

5 Listen to the announcement. What is it about?
  A the weather
  B the traffic
  C holidays

6 Listen to the speakers. What are they talking about?
  A how people use their computers
  B what people do in their free time
  C how people read the news

Logged in

AlinkaJ

Sometimes you can't help eavesdropping on conversations. *What about you? Do you ever eavesdrop on conversations in cafés or restaurants?*

More soon ... watch this space!

Speaking
Solving a problem

1 Look at the pictures. What do you think is the matter with the girl?

2 Find out who the girl is and what the problem and possible solutions are by asking these questions.

- Who is the girl in the photo?
- What is the problem?
- What are the possible solutions?
- What are the disadvantages of each solution?

See page 125 for Teacher/Student B information.

3 What do you think Magda should do? Offer some advice to help solve the problem. You can choose one of the solutions in the pictures, or create your own solution to the problem. Use the phrases from the Language Upload box to help you.

Speaking Tip: solving a problem

- Make sure you understand what the problem is.
- After you have understood the information, be clear about your opinion and remember to refer back to the information to explain your final choice.

4 Listen to Joe offering his advice.

- Is his opinion the same as yours?
- What reasons does he mention?
- Tick the phrases in the Language Upload box that he uses.

5 Now answer the questions. Use the ideas below to help you.

1 Would you like to spend a month in London? Why/Why not?
2 If you were going to London for a month how would you keep in touch with your friends at home?
3 How would you try and meet new people on a language course?
4 Do you think that a language course in England is the best way to master the language? What else could you do?

meet people from other countries

see the sights

miss friends

pick up everyday phrases

chat online

instant messaging

text

invite them for a drink/a meal

suggest going for a walk/swim

Language Upload

Giving your opinion

I think that …
I don't think it would be a good idea to …
Furthermore, …
Besides …
As well as that, I think …

Making suggestions/Giving advice

I would advise her to …
I suggest -ing …
I think she should …

Explaining your reasons

If she went to … , she could …
If she did … , she'd have to …
The advantage of doing that would be …
The disadvantage of doing that would be …

Writing: An Article

Before you write

1   Answer the questions.

1   In your opinion, which of the two photographs shows the best way to learn a language?
2   How will learning English help you in the future?
3   How can your computer help you with learning a language?
4   Is everybody capable of learning a second language?

2   Read the advert and highlight the phrases which tell you what you must do.

Win a language course in New York!

'We should have every child speaking more than one language.'
Barack Obama

Write an article commenting on the quotation from US President Barack Obama. Explain why learning other languages is important and what you think Barack Obama meant by it. The winning article will be published in next month's magazine.

3   Read one student's competition entry. Choose the best title.

A   Successful communication.
B   More languages, more jobs!

How do you feel about learning other languages? For many of us, it's great fun, but it can be a time-consuming process. What's sure, though, is that it's an essential part of everyone's education.

First of all, if you know how to speak other languages, you can interact with people from other countries. This means that you can apply for better jobs; international companies need people who can email, phone or speak face-to-face with foreign customers.

Apart from that, a second language helps you to learn about other cultures. If you master another language, you can share ideas. I'm sure people get on better when they can understand each other. It's when people get their wires crossed that they get frustrated.

All in all, I believe that knowing other languages helps us to keep in touch with the rest of the world. When he said that every child should speak more than one language, I think that Barack Obama wanted to make us realise that communication between different countries and cultures is extremely important.

4   Read the article again and underline the topic sentences in paragraphs 2, 3 and 4.

5   Look at the main ideas from the article. Number them in the order they appear.

Learning how other people live   ☐
International communication   ☐
The language learning process   ☐
Languages at work   ☐

6   What six expressions or phrases from this unit has the writer used to describe language and communication?

1   … you can interact with other people from other countries.
2   _____
3   _____
4   _____
5   _____
6   _____

7   Answer the questions.

1   How does the writer attract the reader's attention? Give an example.
2   What expressions does the writer use to give an opinion?
3   How does the writer
   ●   introduce an idea (para 2)?
   ●   give more information (para 3)?
   ●   conclude the article (para 4)?

8   Complete the sentences with your own ideas.

1   Learning a language can be fun when …
2   What I find difficult about learning another language is …
3   You can brush up on a language by …
4   After studying in the classroom you should …
5   You can only master a language if …

Time to write

9 Read the task and tick (✓) the ideas that are important for you.

An online language magazine wants students around the world to write an article on the best way to keep in touch with friends. Write between 120 and 180 words.

talking face-to-face ☐
email ☐
MSN ☐
mobile phone ☐
writing a blog ☐
texting ☐
sending letters ☐
social networking sites ☐

10 Write notes for each of the ideas you have ticked above. Organise your notes into four clear paragraphs.

Para 1
_____
_____
_____

Para 2
_____
_____
_____

Para 3
_____
_____
_____

Para 4
_____
_____
_____

11 Think of a short title for your article.

12 Now write your article. Use the Writing Checklist and Memory Flash to help you.

Writing Checklist: An Article

Have you
1 got a good title?
2 begun your article with an interesting sentence or question to attract your reader?
3 used the ideas from your notes?
4 organised your ideas in paragraphs?
5 covered all the points in the task?
6 talked about your opinions and your experience?
7 used expressions and vocabulary from this unit?
8 used expressions that connect ideas and conclude the article?

Memory Flash

Beginning the article
How do you feel about …?
Have you ever …?
You may have noticed that …
Is it a good idea to …?

Giving an opinion
I (really) think/believe …
What's sure is …
I'm sure …
In my opinion …

Connecting ideas
First of all …
In the first place …
To begin with …
As well as that …
Apart from that …
In addition to …

Concluding
All in all …
On the whole …
To conclude …

Vocabulary

1 Complete the text with the words and phrases from the box.

comment   keep you posted   blog   stay in touch
tuned in to   contacts   master the language
overheard   pick up

http://www.travelsinrussia.com

travelsinrussia.com

Hi Everybody,

Today is the first day of my journey around Russia and as some of you have asked me to ¹_____, I've decided to write a daily ²_____. I'm going to add some photos which I know you'll want to ³_____ on! I arrived in Moscow last night and it was freezing. I ⁴_____ a man in the hotel say it was going to get a lot colder. I haven't managed to ⁵_____ much Russian yet, but I've got a whole year to spend here. When I ⁶_____ the TV last night, I couldn't understand a word! A cousin of mine has some ⁷_____ at the university, so I hope to meet up with them soon. It will be really good to interact with some Russians of my age and hopefully I'll ⁸_____ before I leave! Well, a very tiring first day. Keep reading and I'll ⁹_____!

2 Choose the word or phrase that best completes the sentence.

1 Read the _____ in the newspaper to find out which famous people have died.
   A headlines   C obituaries
   B classified   D reviews

2 Jack didn't like it when his teacher _____ on his poor handwriting.
   A glanced   C commented
   B eavesdropped   D displayed

3 Writing a blog was too _____ and he gave it up once he found a job.
   A simultaneous   C convenient
   B virtual   D time-consuming

4 Can you tell me what the message says? I can't _____ without my glasses.
   A pick it up   C flick through it
   B make it out   D brush up on it

Grammar

3 Complete the second sentence so that it has a similar meaning to the first. Use the word in capitals.

1 'I didn't speak to Jake after the match,' said Tom.
   DENIED
   Tom _____ to Jake after the match.

2 'Perhaps it would be better to phone him with the news,' said Sandra.
   RECOMMENDED
   Sandra _____ him with the news

3 'Are they talking about me?' he asked.
   WERE
   He asked _____ about him.

4 'Don't forget to write soon,' she said to her boyfriend.
   REMINDED
   She _____ soon.

5 'I won't listen to you any more,' she said to him.
   TOLD
   She _____ listen to him any more.

6 'Can I call you tonight?' Charles asked her.
   IF
   Charles asked _____ that night.

7 'Where did you find your phone?' Sam asked him.
   FOUND
   Sam asked Mark _____ phone.

4 Choose the word or phrase that best completes the sentence.

1 He asked me _____ his message.
   A if I get   C did I get
   B if I had got   D had I got

2 Max said he would see the film _____.
   A the following day   C following day
   B the day before   D the previous day

3 I promised Anna that I _____ her some photos that night.
   A send   C have sent
   B will send   D would send

4 The teacher recommended that _____ the Internet to learn vocabulary.
   A we had used   C we did use
   B we were using   D we used

5 In the end, she told him _____ to be alone.
   A that she did want   C that she wanted
   B if she wants   D what she wanted

6 In her text she said she _____ at the Internet café by 9 p.m.
   A is   C is be
   B would be   D will have been

My parents are really pessimistic about the future. They worry about global warming, war, hunger ... lots of things. I'm the opposite – I'm an optimist. I think we can make the world a better place if we try. How about you? Are you optimistic or pessimistic about the future? Why?

8 Future Fears

Vocabulary Starter
Natural disasters

1 Use the pictures to complete the crossword.

2 Complete the sentences with the words from the box.

> erupted   heatwave   drought   rural   seeds
> tidal wave   tremor   urban   waste

1 This is a terrible _____. It hasn't rained for two years.
2 Water the _____ to help them grow.
3 We produce so much unwanted _____ every day, that there is nowhere left to put it.
4 We're in the middle of a _____ with temperatures of over 40°C every day.
5 This is a _____ society in which most people live in villages and work on the land.
6 Some of the problems faced by people living in _____ environments include overcrowding and traffic pollution.
7 When the Icelandic volcano _____, it caused chaos throughout Europe.
8 A few days after the earthquake, there was another strong _____ which shook the houses again.
9 The beach house was destroyed by a five-metre high _____.

3 Replace the underlined words and phrases with a word from the box in the correct form.

> collide   dump   garbage   leak   starve   toxic   wipe out

1 Don't put those newspapers in the <u>rubbish</u> bin. They can be recycled.
2 The fish have all died because of <u>poisonous</u> chemicals.
3 We didn't have any water because there was a <u>hole</u> in the pipe outside.
4 The captain was arrested for <u>throwing</u> rubbish in the ocean.
5 The money from our song will go to people who are <u>dying of hunger</u>.
6 A dangerous disease could <u>kill</u> millions of people.
7 Two cars <u>hit each other</u> outside our school but, luckily, no-one was hurt.

CHATROOM
- What environmental problems exist in your area? Which are the worst?
- What is your biggest worry about the future? What can we do to prevent problems in the future?

Crossword:
1 Across: V (VOLCANO)
4 Down: LAVA
2 Down: E
3 Down: M
5 Across: T
6 Down: ASH

Reading

1 Read the texts and match the headings with the paragraphs. There is one heading you do not need.

- [ ] Dirty habits
- [ ] Weather worries
- [ ] Moving misery
- [ ] Falling objects
- [ ] Uncontrollable technology
- [ ] Travel troubles

2 Read the texts again and decide whether the statements are true (T), false (F) or not mentioned (N).

1 No-one was killed in the 2010 snowstorm in the USA.
2 Jackie knows that the summer will be hot this year.
3 Lisa couldn't fly to Canada because the plane's engines stopped working.
4 The last meteor to hit Earth was in Tunguska, Russia, in 1908.
5 Tunguska is not a built up area.
6 It wasn't always illegal to pollute Lake Onondaga.
7 Genetically modified crops have disadvantages as well as advantages.
8 Earthquakes occur more often in urban areas than in rural ones.

Reading Tip: true / false / not mentioned

Answers are 'not mentioned' if the statement talks about an idea that isn't in the text at all, even if you know it to be true or false yourself.

THE END OF THE WORLD?

What are the dangers facing us today?

A Global warming is a misleading term. Climate change is the phrase which is used by scientists and meteorologists. We are experiencing more extremes, not just of heat, but of cold, high winds and heavy snow and rainfall. Everyone remembers Hurricane Katrina which hit New Orleans in 2005, but the USA suffered another storm in February 2010. Blizzards paralysed the capital city, Washington DC, leaving 350,000 people without power. The snow in my hometown of Baltimore was an amazing 96 centimetres deep! I think the world will suffer more similar freak conditions in the future. Maybe, this summer, we'll have a heatwave. I think I'll have some solar panels put into the roof just in case!

Jackie, *Baltimore, USA.*

B Natural disasters worry me. The tsunami in 2004, which caused deadly tidal waves in the Pacific and earthquakes in places like China and Chile, always seemed so far away but, in April 2010, my family and I were due to fly from Scotland to Canada. Our flight was cancelled because of a volcano in Iceland. It had erupted under a glacier and it was too dangerous for planes to fly through the cloud of ash caused by the erupting volcano. In fact, the cloud of volcanic ash hung over Europe for weeks and people were forced to wait for days at airports or return home by train or coach. The lava is more spectacular and dangerous locally, but it is the ash which is the real killer. A mega volcano is believed to have erupted about 77,000 years ago, which caused a seven-year winter and nearly wiped out the entire human race.

Lisa, *Glasgow, Scotland.*

C It's amazing what threats to the planet you can find out about on the Internet. In March 2009, a meteorite with a width of 30 metres only just missed colliding with the Earth. And what's even more shocking is that it had only been spotted two days earlier! I read on the Internet that a similarly sized meteor hit Tunguska in Russia in 1908. A total of 80 million trees were destroyed over an area of 2000 square kilometres. If it had landed in a built-up area, the loss of life would have been immense. Improvements have been made in finding such objects and we're learning how to push them out of our orbit so that they will fly harmlessly by. We should be able to do this in the next ten years, so keep your fingers crossed until then!

Ben, *Swindon, UK.*

D The local lake here, Onondaga Lake, is the most polluted lake in the USA. There are leaks from old pipes and, even though laws have been passed, some local industries are claimed to still be deliberately dumping waste into the lake. It's made me read more about the problem of toxic and hazardous materials being dumped worldwide. Did you know that a scientist called Charles Moore has discovered what he calls the 'Great Pacific Garbage Patch'. It's made up of about 100 million tons of rubbish stretching from California to Japan. It is almost like a plastic soup. It is twice the size of the United States. Fish will die out and the oceans may end up like Onandaga Lake – just because people won't change their way of life.

Janine, *Syracuse, NY.*

E Overpopulation is a real problem. I know genetically modified crops increase the amount of food we can grow, even if there is a drought, but in some ways they are worse for farmers than traditional crops. Farmers can't grow new plants from last year's seeds. New seeds have to be bought every year. Farmers can't afford them and may starve. In order to survive, people have to leave rural areas for urban ones. Conditions there are often worse for them. Many of them don't have access to clean water and they live in overcrowded buildings. These are often unsafe, especially in areas which are prone to earthquakes. Even a small tremor could cause a massive disaster. We should be trying to help people live better lives in their traditional homelands, not forcing them to leave home to survive.

Dominique, *Quebec, Canada.*

3 Find these words in the text and choose the correct meanings.

1 extremes (paragraph A)
   A typical conditions
   B new conditions
   C unusually bad conditions

2 paralysed (paragraph A)
   A destroyed
   B froze
   C brought to a stop

3 suffer (paragraph A)
   A experience something bad
   B cause problems
   C worry about problems

4 freak (paragraph A)
   A unknown   B unusual   C unsafe

5 threats (paragraph C)
   A dangers   B invasions   C illnesses

6 spotted (paragraph C)
   A seen   B stopped   C photographed

7 immense (paragraph C)
   A very small   B very possible   C very great

8 have access to (paragraph E)
   A have money   B own   C be able to use

CHATROOM

- Do you think any of the things in the text will happen in the future?
- What worries you most about the future?

WebSearch

http://www.recyclenow.com
http://www.greenpeace.org/international
http://www.nationalgeographic.com

Vocabulary

Word formation: words from the text

1 Complete the headlines with the correct form of the words in capitals. All the words are from the reading texts on pages 90 and 91.

1 Relief as cloud of _____ (VOLCANO) ash flies _____ (HARM) by after lucky change in wind direction

2 Government accused of publishing _____ (MISLEAD) information about our _____ (CROWD) cities. The problem is much worse than we thought.

3 _____ (LOSE) of life caused by new form of _____ (DEAD) flu tops 100,000.

4 _____ (IMPROVE) in secret spy-camera technology could stop ships dumping _____ (HAZARD) waste at sea.

The weather

2 Replace the underlined words in the sentences.

1 There was <u>heavy snow and high winds</u> along the east coast of the USA last night.
  A a blizzard   B a tsunami
2 <u>The air was full of heat and moisture</u> all day.
  A It was humid   B It was stormy
3 It was too warm for real snow, so we got <u>a mixture of snow and rain</u>.
  A sleet   B hail
4 The air was heavy with <u>a mixture of smoke and fog</u>.
  A frost   B smog
5 Don't go outside. It's <u>raining very hard</u>.
  A falling down   B pouring down
6 It was <u>a cloudy day</u>.
  A overcast   B foggy

Adjective-noun collocations

3 Match the adjectives with the nouns to make collocations.

1 acid	A weather
2 genetic	B fuels
3 extreme	C energy
4 finite	D rain
5 fossil	E issues
6 solar	F resources
7 green	G modification / engineering

4 Complete the sentences with collocations from Exercise 3.

1 There is no _____ here – no hurricanes, no tornadoes, not even much snow.
2 The world only has _____. Oil and gas won't last forever.
3 All houses should be built with panels in their roofs, so they can use _____ for light and heat.
4 Pollution rises into the atmosphere then falls as _____ , killing trees and poisoning lakes.
5 The _____ of crops has unknown effects on the environment.
6 _____ such as oil, gas and coal, are a major cause of pollution.
7 I'm very interested in _____ such as recycling, saving endangered animals and renewable energy.
8 Scientists want to help us, but I'm still worried about the possible harmful effects of _____.

Phrasal verbs

5 Choose the correct answer.

1 What will we do when the world runs _____ oil?
  A out of   B down on   C into
2 Could you do _____ electricity? Imagine no lights, no TV and no Internet.
  A through   B under   C without
3 We should recycle the things we throw _____.
  A over   B away   C off
4 Important species are dying _____ because of man's actions.
  A over   B up   C out
5 People in the third world have to live _____ far less than those in the developed world.
  A out   B on   C up
6 We need to find alternative energy sources before we use _____ all the fossil fuels.
  A up   B out   C off
7 You could cut _____ your use of electricity by switching off your computer at night.
  A out of   B down on   C into

Idioms

6 Complete the phrases with the words from the box.

> chickens   fingers   leg   oyster   sorry   touch

1 Keep your _____ crossed.
2 _____ wood.
3 Don't count your _____ before they hatch.
4 Break a _____!
5 Better safe than _____.
6 The world's your _____.

7 Complete the dialogues with the phrases from Exercise 6.

1 A: Why have you got raincoats and sleeping bags? You're only going on a day trip.
   B: Well, _____.

2 A: This is it. I'm going on stage in two minutes.
   B: _____!

3 A: I've heard that our flight might be cancelled. I hope it isn't.
   B: _____.

4 A: I don't know what to do with my life.
   B: You're only seventeen. _____. If you work hard you can do anything you want.

5: A: I'm going to pass my exams in June, I'll get a job and by August, I'll have enough money for a good holiday.
   B: _____.

6 A: How far is it?
   B: We should be there in half an hour; _____.

Dependent prepositions

8 Choose the correct answer.

1 Are you worried about the threat **of** / **about** / **in** an alien invasion **for** / **from** / **of** outer space?

2 The *Titanic* collided **with** / **in** / **on** an iceberg.

3 Do you have access **to** / **with** / **from** the Internet?

4 It's your first driving lesson. Try not to crash **in** / **into** / **to** any other cars.

5 Take an umbrella. The rain is absolutely pouring **down** / **out** / **off**.

6 Recycle glass. It can be turned **in** / **through** / **into** new bottles.

Word formation: measurement

9 Complete the text with the correct form of the words in capitals.

Astronauts get first look at their future home

'It's a disaster!'

The [1]_____ (STRONG) of Ben's feelings was obvious as he spoke to us. The bedrooms are ridiculously small. The [2]_____ (LONG) of each room is only two metres and the [3]_____ (WIDE) is just one metre. They need to [4]_____ (LONG) them to at least three metres and [5]_____ (WIDE) them to two metres.

Stephanie Philips was also upset. 'The [6]_____ (HIGH) of the roof is just one and a half metres. Ben and I won't be able to stand up straight. They have to [7]_____ (STRONG) it too,' she added.

One luxury for the astronauts is a swimming pool, but Ben still wasn't happy. 'The pool is only half a metre deep. We can't swim in water of that [8]_____ (DEEP). They need to [9]_____ (DEEP) it to at least two metres or, better still, not have a pool and use the money for other improvements.'

The reaction of government officials will only [10]_____ (HIGH) the astronauts' anger as they refused to accept the complaints and said that they should be grateful for this chance to live on a different planet for six months.

Back up your vocabulary

10 Read the text and choose the best answer (A, B, C or D) for each gap.

Join our Internet DVD rental club and get ONE FREE legal download today.

The Day After Tomorrow
A film about the effects of global warming. The melting of the ice caps causes a new ice age which results in extreme [1]_____ conditions all over the USA. A group of people escape into the public library as the winds strengthen and temperatures fall. They are forced to live [2]_____ snacks from a food machine as a huge ice storm approaches. Will they survive?

Armageddon
Scientists have discovered a huge [3]_____ which will [4]_____ with the Earth in just eighteen days. A group of astronauts are sent into space to destroy the giant rock with a nuclear bomb, but time is running [5]_____. Will their plan work or will the human race be wiped [6]_____?

Apollo 13
The true story of the moon landing that never was. The astronauts blast off and leave the Earth with no problems, but then things start to go wrong. They cancel the moon landing and have to [7]_____ without heat to save power. It's now a race to get home before they use [8]_____ all their oxygen. Will they make it in time? It's down to luck now – they just have to keep their fingers crossed and hope for the best.

1 A weather	B waste	C storm	D rain
2 A from	B over	C out	D on
3 A volcano	B meteorite	C tsunami	D tremor
4 A hit	B throw	C smash	D collide
5 A off	B out	C over	D along
6 A off	B out	C through	D down
7 A make	B do	C cut	D run
8 A up	B down	C off	D out

CHATROOM

What is the weather like in your country at different times of the year? Have you ever experienced extreme weather conditions?

More practice on pages 138–139

Grammar
Passive voice

> passive voice
> Hundreds of homes **are destroyed** by extreme weather events every year.
> The East Coast **was hit** by blizzards.
> At ten o'clock last night, we **were being driven** to the airport.
> Improvements **have been made** in finding such objects.
> It **had only been spotted** two days earlier.
> Scientists are sure that we**'ll be contacted** by aliens in the future.
> Our class is going **to be given** a talk on green issues.
> The oceans **can be cleaned** up if we increase the penalty for illegal dumping.
> New seeds **have to be bought** every year.
> Are you worried about the Earth **being hit** by a meteorite?
> impersonal structures
> **It is known** that fossil fuels will run out this century.
> **It has been claimed** that genetically modified crops would solve the problem of famine.
> A mega volcano **is believed to have erupted** about 77,000 years ago.

See **Grammar File**, page 170

1 Complete the text with the correct passive form of the verbs.

Saving the environment

In Germany, the town of Vauban was the first town to ban cars from the town centre. The idea is sure ¹_____ (copy) by other towns in the near future. In the city of Freiburg, cars can only ²_____ (park) in public car parks, not on private land. That means that car parking charges have to ³_____ (pay) by any resident who owns a car.

Recently, normal light bulbs ⁴_____ (ban) by the EU. This was not a popular decision in some places. Many British people hate ⁵_____ (tell) what they can and can't do. When the decision ⁶_____ (make), newspapers were full of angry comments about freedom and democracy.

Waste needs ⁷_____ (reduce) and different countries have different methods of doing this. In England, people can ⁸_____ (fine) if their bins are overfull. However, despite such policies, less waste ⁹_____ (recycle) in Britain than in many other countries. Many people believe that policies which ¹⁰_____ (introduce) at the moment are not very effective.

2 Rewrite the sentences in the passive, starting with the words in bold.

1 Many cities charge **people** to drive into the centre.
_____

2 Someone must teach **Jimmy** about saving energy.
_____

3 You shouldn't plant **genetically modified crops** too close to normal crops.
_____

4 We're going to reduce **carbon emissions** by 10 percent over the next ten years.
_____

5 Governments are passing **new environmental laws** all the time.
_____

6 They should make **school dinners** more healthy.
_____

3 Rewrite the sentences using the passive or impersonal passive structures.

1 We know that American cars travel a total of four billion miles every day.
A American cars *are known* to travel a total of four billion miles every day.
B It *is known* that American cars travel a total of four billion miles every day.

2 Some people have said that wind power is 100 percent 'clean'.
A Wind power _____ to be 100 percent 'clean'.
B It _____ that wind power is 100 percent 'clean'.

3 People say that Mount Rumpke is made entirely of garbage.
A Mount Rumpke _____ entirely of garbage.
B _____ Mount Rumpke is made entirely of garbage.

4 People expect scientists to find an alternative to petrol in the next twenty years.
A Scientists _____ an alternative to petrol in the next twenty years.
B It is expected that an alternative to petrol _____ in the next twenty years.

5 People thought that Pluto was a planet until 2006.
A Pluto _____ a planet until 2006.
B _____ that Pluto was a planet until 2006.

4 Complete the second sentence so that it has a similar meaning to the first. Use an impersonal passive structure.

1 People claim that one ton of recycled paper saves 1200 litres of oil.
It_____.

2 People in the Middle Ages believed that the moon was completely smooth.
The moon_____.

3 Some people have said that a super volcano in Lake Toba killed 90 percent of the world's population about 75,000 years ago.
It_____.

4 Environmentalists think that extreme weather events are getting worse due to global warming.
Extreme_____.

Causative *have*

I'll have some solar panels put on the roof.
Have you had an earthquake shelter built in your garden?

See **Grammar File**, page 171 ⟫

5 Write sentences with the causative *have*.

1 I / just / my computer / repair
I've just had my computer repaired.

2 My mum / her hair / cut / at the moment
_____

3 The school / will / the electricity / check / next week
_____

4 My dad / going to / his tyres / change / soon
_____

5 We / need / our satellite dish / fix
_____

6 Complete the sentences using the causative *have* so that they are true for you.

1 I've never had …
2 I always have …
3 Next week, I'm going to have …
4 I should have had …
5 I need to have …

7 Read the text and think of the word which best fits each space. Use only one word in each space.

The First International Conference of Young Scientists

It ¹_____ held in 1994 in Visegrad, Hungary. It ²_____ been planned the year before by representatives of universities in Minsk and Budapest. The conference gives 14–18 year old school students a chance to learn about methods of scientific research. The students create projects and ³_____ them assessed by experts and feedback ⁴_____ given to the students at the conference.

It ⁵_____ hoped that participants in such conferences will ⁶_____ encouraged to go on to study science at university. Science subjects ⁷_____ known to be less popular than in the past, so anything which boosts student numbers has ⁸_____ be welcomed.

2010 is a special year for the ICYS as, for the first time ever, the conference has moved outside Europe, to Indonesia. As we write, the conference is ⁹_____ organised on the magical island of Bali. Eager students all over the world are, at this moment, ¹⁰_____ their hair cut, their suits cleaned and their microscopes checked in readiness for the big occasion.

CHATROOM

Which of these jobs could you do yourself? Which would you have to have done by somebody else?

• Your hair needs cutting.
• Your room needs painting.
• A button has come off your shirt.
• You need to put a satellite dish up for your TV.
• You want to put a new DVD drive in your computer.
• Your bike tyre needs changing.

Listening

Listening 1

1 Look at the photo. What does it show? What do you know about this idea?

 **2** You will hear six people talking. Choose the best answer, A, B or C.

Listening Tip: multiple-choice questions

The speaker will probably mention all three options in some way. Don't make up your mind until the recording has finished.

1 The person isn't worried about flu now because
  A she understands the problem well enough.
  B her children are grown up.
  C there are other things to think about.

2 The woman is upset because
  A her children didn't take the problem seriously.
  B of someone else's irresponsible behaviour.
  C her children were so frightened.

3 The speaker is upset about
  A the effects of global warming.
  B her teacher's lessons about global warming.
  C her friends' attitude towards the lessons.

4 The speaker believes
  A he could make money from domestic robots.
  B that a lot of people would lose their jobs because of domestic robots.
  C domestic robots should be used in factories.

5 The speaker thinks the invention of e-books would
  A make it easier to become famous.
  B make him better off financially.
  C reduce his chances of becoming a writer.

6 The speaker thinks that DNA research will
  A prevent some illnesses.
  B cut crime.
  C benefit employees.

Listening 2

3 You will hear five people talking about problems caused by the weather. For each speaker choose the correct statement (A–F). There is one extra statement which you don't need to use.

Listening Tip: multiple matching

Think of synonyms for the words in each statement. Even if these aren't used in the listening, it will help you to focus on what you are likely to hear.

Speaker 1 ☐
Speaker 2 ☐
Speaker 3 ☐
Speaker 4 ☐
Speaker 5 ☐

He/She ...
A had to buy an important piece of equipment.
B was too brave.
C listened to the wrong advice.
D had heard an incorrect weather forecast.
E made the most of their situation.
F spent a lot of money because of the weather.

Logged in

SantiagoX15

The most frightening weather I've ever been in was when I was camping in France. There was a storm right overhead. I was really scared.
What's the most frightening experience you've ever had because of the weather?

More soon ... watch this space!

Speaking
Comparing two pictures

1 Look at the two pictures of life in the future and answer the questions.

Which picture shows an optimistic view of the future? Which picture best represents your own idea of life in the future?

2 You will hear someone talking about the pictures. How did she answer the questions in Exercise 1?

3 Listen again. What synonyms does the speaker use for words which are unknown to her?

skyscrapers	*tall buildings*
domes	_____
greenhouse	_____
pollution	_____
depressing	_____

Speaking Tip: comparing two pictures

Don't panic if you don't know or can't remember a word for something in the photo. Think of it as a good opportunity to demonstrate your ability to paraphrase and give definitions.

4 How could you describe these things if you didn't know the words or forgot them in the exam?

laptop	_____
whiteboard	_____
in rows	_____
modern	_____
webcam	_____
flat screen	_____

5 Match some of these adjectives with the pictures below. Add any other words you can think of.

> comfortable relaxing fun serious
> practical unlikely expensive noisy

6 Now work with a partner to carry out this task. Use the Language Upload box to help you.

> Compare two photographs of possible classrooms of the future and say which you prefer and why.

Language Upload

Describe something you don't know the word for

It's a kind/type/sort of …

Comparing something to another object

It looks like …
It's similar to …
It's shaped like …
(It's) like they have/use in …

Describing similarities and differences

Both pictures show … / The two pictures both show …
Although both pictures show … , the first is … , but the second is …
The second picture isn't so …
The two photos have a lot (of things) in common.

Giving an opinion

My view is that …
What I think is …

Writing: An Opinion Essay
Before you write

1 Imagine you have a billion euros to spend to make the world a better place. Which of these projects would be the most useful and why? Put the other projects in order of usefulness.

- Research into and creation of clean energy sources
- Research into genetic engineering to improve the production of crops for food
- A space exploration programme sending astronauts into space and, if possible, to the moon
- Building of sea defences to protect coastal towns from possible future rising sea levels
- Free broadband Internet connection for everyone

2 What possible uses could space exploration have for life on Earth?

3 Read the task. Tick (✓) the points you would mention in your answer.

> Our government should spend more money on space exploration. Do you agree or disagree? Write between 120 and 180 words, giving reasons for your answer.

- Possible benefits of space exploration ☐
- Actual benefits from past exploration ☐
- History of space exploration ☐
- Other projects to spend money on ☐
- Your personal opinion ☐
- Best science fiction films you have seen ☐

4 Read one student's essay. Did he/she include the same points as you ticked in Exercise 3?

5 In which order did the writer place these paragraphs?

A Paragraph (for or against the statement in the task) outlining *opposite* point of view to the writer's.

B Paragraph summing up the writer's opinion.

C Paragraph (for or against the statement in the task) outlining the writer's point of view.

D Introductory sentence, rhetorical question and a short answer to the question.

1 B-A-D-C	2 A-C-D-B
3 D-C-A-B	4 D-A-C-B

6 Find words and phrases in the text which are similar in meaning to these words from the task.

should	_____
spend money	_____
space exploration	_____

The government has to provide many important services, but has a limited budget. Is it right to spend enormous amounts of money on space exploration? In my opinion, it is not.

There are several arguments against spending money on exploring space. To start with, money ought to be used for improving the lives of ordinary people, in particular the poor and the sick, before we waste money on anything else. Hospitals and schools need to be built and improved. Apart from this, it is essential to invest money in protecting the environment.

There are people who have the opposite point of view. They claim that new technology such as mobile phones has been developed because of the space programme. It has also been argued that the US space programme costs just fifteen cents per person per day, although it seems to me that there are better ways for this money to be spent.

All things considered, I believe that governments should concentrate on making improvements in their people's day-to-day lives, not on more space exploration.

7 Read the essay again and decide which of these statements is true.

When writing an essay you
- should try not to use the same words that are in the task.
- can use the words in the task once or twice, but should also try to rephrase them for variety.
- must always copy the words from the task exactly as they are written.

8 Look at the Writing Checklist. Find and underline examples of these points in the essay. They may appear in more than one paragraph.

Time to write

9 Read the task. Which person makes these statements. Write A or B.

'Green issues should be taught as a separate subject from other sciences in schools.' Do you agree or disagree? Write between 120 and 180 words giving reasons for your answer.

I agree …   A

I disagree …   B

1 It is important that students understand the issues clearly.
2 There isn't enough room in the timetable.
3 Teachers don't have the knowledge.
4 There are less important subjects that could be removed from the timetable.
5 We need to do everything we can to help the planet.
6 It is too subjective to be a school subject.
7 Important issues will come up in Biology, Geography or other subjects.
8 If students study the subject at school, they may go on to study it at university and then work in the field in the future.

10 Decide whether you agree with the statement in the task and why. There won't be room to include all the points from Exercise 9. Choose two which support your argument and one or two that oppose your argument.

11 Write your essay, using the Writing Checklist and Memory Flash to help you. Remember to make a plan first like the one in Exercise 5.

Our head teacher is very interested in the environment. Even our uniform is green.

Writing Checklist: An Opinion Essay

Does your essay include

1 a clear reference to the topic of the essay in the opening paragraph?
2 an eye-catching statement or question in the opening paragraph to attract the reader's attention?
3 impersonal passive structures: *It is said that, It has been argued that*?
4 clear linking of ideas in a logical sequence?
5 your own opinion stated clearly? This is always given in the conclusion, but can also be stated in the introduction as long as it is phrased differently each time.
6 a number of items showing a good range of vocabulary for this level?
7 justifications for the arguments?

Memory Flash

Expressing opinion

I believe …,
In my view, …
It seems to me …

Listing points

There are several arguments …
In the first place,
To start with,
To begin with,
Apart from this,
Another reason is …

Introducing contrasting viewpoints

There are people who have the opposite point of view.
They claim that …
It has been argued that …

Introducing examples

for instance
such as
in particular
especially

Concluding

Taking everything into account,
All things considered …

Revision 8

Vocabulary

1 Complete the dialogues with the words from the box. There is one extra word.

> ash   drought   fossil   leak   sleet   urban

1 A: It says here that oil is running out.
   B: Not just oil. All _____ fuels will be gone in fifty years.
2 A: It's amazing how lifestyles have changed over the years.
   B: I know. 75% of people now live in _____ areas. A hundred years ago it was 25%.
3 A: Hooray! Winter is nearly over.
   B: Oh great! The snow is turning to _____ and, next week, it'll be pouring with rain!
4 A: People here are starving.
   B: Yes, and if the _____ continues, the situation will get even worse.
5 A: Here's the newspaper. There's nothing in it.
   B: Nothing in it? Didn't you read about the cloud of _____ from the volcano in Iceland?

2 Choose the word or phrase that best completes the sentence.

1 There's a protest about the government transporting _____ materials by train through built-up areas.
   A immense   C remote
   B hazardous   D overcast
2 You can't just _____ your old monitor here. You have to take it to a special recycling area.
   A dump   C waste
   B leak   D erupt
3 We've been seeing more and more examples of _____ weather in the world recently.
   A paralysed   C finite
   B extreme   D acid
4 There's a danger that a meteorite will collide _____ an important satellite.
   A to   C on
   B with   D in
5 We'll have to _____ the amount of fuel we use if the price keeps on going up.
   A live on   C do without
   B use up   D cut down on
6 Let's plant these _____ and hope that it rains soon so that they will grow.
   A seeds   C threats
   B leaks   D tremors

Grammar

3 Complete the second sentence so that it has a similar meaning to the first. Use the word in capitals.

1 Scientists are watching the progress of Hurricane Kate.
   WATCHED
   The progress of Hurricane Kate _____ scientists.
2 We need to strengthen our sea defences in the next five years.
   TO
   Our sea defences _____ in the next five years.
3 Some people think that there may be life on Mars.
   IS
   It _____ that there may be life on Mars.
4 A lot of people believe that hurricanes and storms are getting stronger.
   TO
   Hurricanes and storms _____ getting stronger.

4 Complete the dialogue with the correct passive form of the verbs.

John S: Mr Galileo? Hello. BBC News. Can I ask you a few questions?
Galileo: Of course.
John S: How did you get your idea for your theory that the Earth moves round the Sun?
Galileo: Well, it was from research that ¹_____ (carry out) several years ago in Poland by Copernicus. Before Copernicus, the Earth ²_____ (believe) to be in the centre of everything with the Sun and planets rotating around us. Now, it ³_____ (know) that, in fact, our planet travels round the Sun.
John S: Your findings are said by some people ⁴_____ (be) wrong and it ⁵_____ (think) that you ⁶_____ (arrest) soon. Are you worried at all?
Galileo: Not at all.

Most of my friends are into fashion, even the boys! We don't wear uniform to school, so it can be difficult deciding what to wear every day. What about you? Do you wear the same style clothes as your friends? Is fashion important to you?

9 Looking Good!

1 _____ trousers

2 _____ shoes

3 _____ running top

4 _____ jeans

5 _____ T-shirt

6 _____ coat

7 _____ sweatshirt

Vocabulary Starter
Fashion

1 Label the pictures with words from the box.

> high-heeled patterned hooded
> baggy tight-fitting flared sleeveless

2 Use one word from each group to complete the phrases.

> round middle fair clean medium well

> built height shouldered
> haired shaven aged

1 He's neither too tall, nor too short. He's of *medium height*.
2 She doesn't walk with a straight back. She's _____ .
3 He hasn't got a beard or moustache. He's _____ .
4 Her hair is blonde. She's _____ .
5 He's big and strong. He's _____ .
6 She's aged between 45 and 55 years. She's _____ .

3 Match the words with the definitions.

1 retail
2 charity
3 bargain
4 volunteer
5 ethical
6 outfit
7 showcase
8 catwalk

A something you buy cheaply or less than its usual price
B morally good and right
C the stage that models walk on in a fashion show
D a set of clothes that you wear together
E an organisation that helps people who are poor, ill, etc.
F offer to do something without being paid
G a show or display of someone's best qualities
H the business of selling things in shops

CHATROOM
- How would you describe your best friend/your teacher?
- What do you like most about your own appearance?

Reading

1 Look at the photos taken at the Urban Youth Clothes Show. What do you think you can do at this event?

2 Read the brochure. What is there to do or see at the show that you *didn't* think of in Exercise 1?

The Urban Youth Clothes Show

About Us

Created five years ago as a showcase for youth talent, the Urban Youth Clothes Show has since become a unique event for 14 to 24 year olds. Whether you aim to be a high flyer in fashion design or just have a passion for fashion, make it a day to remember. This year's show will be held in the new Highfield Exhibition Centre in London and has the backing of some major investors in the fashion trade.

The Competition

**Young designer of the year award.
'Something old, something new'**
Each year young designers are invited to submit a design based on a theme. This year it's 'Ethical Fashion' and wannabe designers have the challenging task of turning a tired, second-hand garment into a must-have fashion item. As well as awarding a cash prize, the show's organisers will assist the winner in creating a front cover look for a leading fashion magazine. So, if you'd rather be in the competition than watch it, it's time to let your imagination run wild! Visitors to the show can bid for the winning creation in an auction to raise money for charity.

The Catwalk

All of the innovative designs will feature in an end-of-show catwalk. Many of the show's visitors look forward to this final performance and claim it's the highlight of the show.

The Shopping

Shop till you drop with affordable retail therapy!
Bargain hunters can enjoy strolling around the stands where high street retailers will be offering unbeatable deals.

If it's jeans you're after, snap up a bargain at Mean Jeans. Whether you prefer wearing baggy or tight-fitting, faded or flared, Mean Jeans has something in stock to suit you.

Planning to dress up for the end-of-year party, but haven't got a clue what to wear? Check out Posh Frocks for chic dresses and tailor-made suits. Whatever your shape or size they can make it fit! Matching accessories are also on offer.

Pick out your summer footwear at Coast Shoes. It's got a new range of funky sandals from high-heeled glamour to comfortable flip-flops.

The past is back! Retrospective is using the Urban Youth Clothes Show to launch its new summer range of retro clothing. Come and pick out the latest striped swimwear or try on one of their lightweight jackets. But you'd better get there fast as Retrospective says demand is fast outgrowing supply.

The Pleasure

Do you hate having bushy eyebrows or being too spotty? Or perhaps you just wish you were fair-haired or dark-skinned like your friend? Let our volunteer make-up artists and hairdressers help you make the best of yourself. After shopping, indulge yourself with a relaxing makeover and let the experts advise you on how to achieve the right image. Places are limited so you'd better book now to avoid missing out on the event of the year!

The Exhibition

Fashion through the ages
On loan from one of London's outstanding exhibitions, the Urban Youth Clothes Show has obtained some amazing costumes. Take a step back in time and marvel at the vintage costumes made for Russian aristocrats at the Tsar's famous ball of 1913. There will also be a demonstration of ballroom dancing. Perhaps you remember admiring the glamorous outfits of old Hollywood films? A rare selection will be available for public viewing at the Urban Youth Clothes Show. Admission is free to all ticket holders.

Tickets

Tickets can be bought on the day and cost £26. The price includes:
→ A goody bag filled with treats
→ A free health drink at the *Zest* juice bar
→ A guaranteed seat at the catwalk performance

All competitors are allowed to bring one guest only. Admission is half price for family members.

Do you prefer to avoid the queues? Then, book online. A booking fee of £2 is payable. Please note, this fee cannot be refunded.

3 Read the brochure again and choose the best answer (A, B, C or D).

1 The Urban Youth Clothes Show was started
  A because investors thought it a good idea.
  B to demonstrate the abilities of young people.
  C because there weren't enough young people in the fashion trade.
  D to get young people interested in fashion.

2 This year competitors have to
  A create something that will sell well.
  B transform an old item of clothing.
  C make something that can be used in a magazine.
  D use their imagination.

3 What will happen to the winning design?
  A It will be sold.
  B One of the visitors will have it as a prize.
  C It will be given to a charity.
  D It will be photographed for a fashion magazine.

4 Where will you be able to buy something that has been made just for you?
  A Mean Jeans   C Retrospective
  B Coast Shoes   D Posh Frocks

5 Retrospective is urging customers to get there quickly
  A because their jackets are perfect for summer.
  B because they've lots of retro clothes in stock.
  C because they are running out of clothes.
  D because now is a good time to buy swimwear.

6 What can the volunteer make-up artists teach you?
  A how to relax
  B how to get bushy eyebrows
  C how to pick the right style for you
  D how to deal with spots

7 The costumes on display from Russia were
  A worn by wealthy people at the Tsar's parties.
  B made to show the Tsar's elaborate taste.
  C made for the Tsar.
  D worn by Hollywood stars.

8 If you pay £2 more
  A friends and family can join you.
  B you won't have to wait to get in.
  C you can collect your ticket early.
  D you can guarantee a seat at the catwalk.

4 Find words or phrases in the brochure that mean the following. The relevant sections are given in brackets.

1 someone who is very good at their job (About Us)
2 organisations or people who put money into something to make it succeed (About Us)
3 offer the highest price (The Competition)
4 include something as a special or important part (The Catwalk)
5 attractive things that you add to what you are wearing (The Shopping)
6 let yourself do something that you enjoy (The Pleasure)
7 when you change the way you look completely (The Pleasure)
8 special things that you give to someone else or yourself (Tickets)

CHATROOM

- Why do you think the Urban Youth Clothes Show is so popular?
- Do you think a clothes show for young people would be a good idea in your town? Why/Why not?

 WebSearch

http://www.fashion-era.com
http://www.teenvogue.com

Vocabulary

Word formation: words from the text

1 Complete the text with the correct form of the words in capitals. All the words are from the reading text on page 102.

Every year at my school we have a fashion show to raise money for our school trip. It has the ¹_____ (BACK) of a local fashion ²_____ (RETAIL) that lends us outfits and ³_____ (ACCESSORISE). The most unusual ⁴_____ (CREATE) are made by the design students at school. As well as the catwalk, young hairdressers will be giving ⁵_____ (DEMONSTRATE) on how to deal with problem hair or how to look ⁶_____ (GLAMOUR). After the show ⁷_____ (VISIT) will be able to look around the stands that sell clothes and beauty products.

Clothes

2 Match the adjectives with the definitions.

1	chic	A	modern, different and interesting
2	lightweight	B	old, but good quality
3	faded	C	not heavy, for warmer weather
4	retro	D	suitable for a serious occasion
5	scruffy	E	fashionable and stylish
6	formal	F	based on a style from the past
7	vintage	G	untidy
8	funky	H	less bright than it used to be

3 Complete the sentences with adjectives from Exercise 2.

1 I left my T-shirt out in the sun and now it's _____.

2 It's a warm day for a picnic. I think I'll just take a _____ jacket.

3 I found an old pair of shoes that were worn in the 1920s. Collecting _____ clothing is my hobby.

4 I don't think those trousers are _____ enough for an interview. You'd better wear a suit and tie.

5 I like to be fashionable, but I don't wear the same things as my friends. I choose clothes that are _____ and a bit unusual.

6 Jake is relaxing at home in his old, _____ jeans but he'll change to go out.

7 Anna's bought a _____ dress that is an exact copy of one worn in the 1950s.

8 You always wear the latest fashions and know how to dress well. I wish I could be as _____ as you!

Verbs

4 Complete the text message with the correct form of the verbs from the box.

> match   suit   fit

Amy
Just found the perfect dress for your party. Couldn't believe they had my size and it ¹_____ me perfectly. It's very retro so it ²_____ the 1980s theme of your party. Unfortunately it doesn't ³_____ my shoes, so I'll have to get some new ones! C U L8R

Describing appearance

5 Complete the table.

> thick hair   spotty   tanned   rosy cheeks
> wrinkles   an oval face   balding
> bushy eyebrows   a brunette   fair-haired

He/She has got …	He/She is …

6 Complete the dialogue with the words from the box.

> muscly   dark-skinned   braces   pale
> overweight   toned   freckly   skinny

Anna: Honestly, look at my arms. I only sat in the sun for a few minutes yesterday and they're already ¹_____.

James: It's because you're ²_____. You should be careful in the sun.

Anna: I know. I'd love to be ³_____ like you and have black hair and brown eyes.

James: Everybody wants to change how they look. I'd like to be more ⁴_____, but I hate doing sport.

Anna: Me too. I get embarrassed wearing shorts because my legs are too ⁵_____.

James: What are you talking about? You've got fantastic legs. At least you don't have ⁶_____ that everybody sees when you smile!

Anna: You look fine. But, we should do more sport anyway. I don't want to be ⁷_____ when I'm older.

James: Right. Let's start tonight. We'll go weight-training at the gym.

Anna: Fine, but I don't want to end up too ⁸_____ like one of those professional body-builders!

Consumerism

7 Match the <u>underlined</u> phrases with the definitions.

1 We're going on a <u>shopping spree</u> to London. I want something new for Clare's party.
2 During the sales most shops offer <u>unbeatable deals</u> because they want to tempt customers to buy more.
3 If you show the <u>voucher</u> when you pay, you will get a ten percent discount.
4 I'm sorry but the only size we have <u>in stock</u> is 37.
5 Every time they <u>launch</u> a range of clothing they invite a celebrity to the shop.
6 We were so fed up with our exams that we decided to go shopping for some <u>retail therapy</u>.
7 The jeans were so popular that <u>demand outstripped supply</u> and they had to order more pairs.
8 All customers have the right to <u>a refund</u> if they take the product back to the shop within 30 days.

A fewer were available than were needed
B a trip to the shops when you buy lots of things
C money returned to you if you are unhappy with something you bought
D shopping for pleasure
E a kind of ticket that can be used to pay for things instead of money
F things that are sold cheaper than anywhere else
G make a new product available to be sold
H available in the shop

Phrasal verbs

8 Match the phrasal verbs with their definitions.

1 miss out on (sth)
2 sell out (of sth)
3 dress up
4 snap (sth) up
5 show (sth) off
6 pick (sth) out

A wear special clothes
B buy something quickly
C choose from a selection of things
D let others see something you're proud of
E sell everything so there is nothing left
F not have the chance to do something you want

9 Complete the sentences with the correct form of the phrasal verbs from Exercise 8.

1 My parents said I have to _____ for my cousin's wedding, but I'm not very keen on wearing smart clothes.
2 The trainers are such a good price. You'd better get there fast before they _____.
3 I didn't have a lot of time to shop, but I managed to _____ a bargain in a local boutique.
4 Sandra was very pleased with the dress she had made at school and couldn't wait to _____ it _____ to the rest of the class.
5 Charlie _____ the funkiest jacket from the new range and was very pleased with his choice.
6 I love the end-of-year party – there's no way I would _____ the best event of the year!

Back up your vocabulary

10 Choose the correct answer.

1 I prefer _____ jeans to straight ones because I can wear them over my boots.
  A flared   B faded   C vintage   D striped
2 That jacket doesn't _____ you properly. It's too tight across your back.
  A match   B suit   C fit   D wear
3 Amy's gym classes have done her good. She looks very fit and _____ these days.
  A overweight   C toned
  B skinny   D tanned
4 You can't go out in those _____ clothes. People will think you don't look after yourself.
  A neat   B smart   C scruffy   D chic
5 The fresh air has done you good. I haven't seen you with such _____ for a long time.
  A bushy eyebrows   C a brunette
  B thick hair   D rosy cheeks
6 Let's go to London for some _____. You know we'll feel better for it.
  A vouchers   C retail therapy
  B shopping spree   D high street retailers
7 In the past families often used to _____ up in smart clothes for dinner.
  A pick   B snap   C dress   D take

┌─ CHATROOM ─────────────────────┐
• When was the last time you dressed up? How did you look?
• Do you look for a bargain when you're buying clothes? Why/Why not?
└────────────────────────────────┘

Grammar
Gerunds and infinitives

gerunds

*Bargain hunters can enjoy **strolling** around the stands.*
***Shopping** at the Urban Youth Clothes Show is something all visitors enjoy.*
*…the task of **turning** something old into a fashion item.*

infinitives

*Whether you aim **to be** a high-flyer in fashion or …*
*Are you planning **to dress up** for the party?*

infinitive and / or gerund

*Do you prefer **to avoid** the queues?*
*Whether you prefer **wearing** baggy or tight-fitting …*
*Remember **to book** your tickets today!*
*Perhaps you remember **admiring** the glamorous outfits of old Hollywood films?*

be allowed, make, let

*Visitors will **be allowed to buy** the winning garment.*
*We can't **make** you **visit** us.*
***Let** your imagination **run** wild!*

would rather, prefer to, had better

*… if you**'d rather be** in the competition **than watch** it …*
*Do you **prefer to avoid** the queues?*
*Friends and family **had better buy** their own tickets …*

See **Grammar File**, pages 172 and 173

1 **Choose the correct answer.**

 New    Reply

Subject: Fantastic day at the Urban Youth
         Clothes Show

Hi Nina,

After ¹*missing / miss* the bus this morning, we finally got to the Urban Youth Clothes Show. We had booked our tickets online but Julia had forgotten ²*bringing / to bring* them with her! Luckily one of the organisers let us in and it was amazing. We especially enjoyed ³*watching / to watch* the show on the catwalk. We spent ages ⁴*looking / to look* at the stands. I was thinking of ⁵*buying / to buy* something funky, but in the end I decided ⁶*getting / to get* some baggy jeans from Mean Jeans. It wasn't possible ⁷*trying / to try* them on because there were too many people, but fortunately they look OK. Before we left, we managed ⁸*visiting / to visit* the exhibition. We were really tired but it was worth ⁹*seeing / to see* the designs. All in all it was an amazing day. Perhaps you'd like ¹⁰*coming / to come* next year?

Write soon,

Emma

2 **Complete the conversation with the correct form of the verbs.**

Lucy: What are you planning ¹_____ (wear) for this year's fancy dress party, Nick?

Nick: I'm not sure yet. I usually try ²_____ (avoid) dressing up. Last time I spent ages ³_____ (get ready) for it and I ended up ⁴_____ (feel) really embarrassed.

Lucy: That's a shame. ⁵_____ (wear) different costumes should be fun. I don't mind ⁶_____ (help) you if you want.

Nick: That would be great. I was planning ⁷_____ (go) into town on Saturday. Do you want ⁸_____ (come) with me?

Lucy: Great. I'm really good at ⁹_____ (choose) fancy dress costumes. Perhaps you could be a Hollywood gangster.

Nick: OK. But what if you don't manage ¹⁰_____ (find) me something cool? I might look stupid.

Lucy: I'll do my best, Nick.

3 **Tick (✓) the pairs of sentences that have the same meaning.**

1 I stopped shopping in the sales.
  I stopped to shop in the sales. ☐

2 We hate missing out on a good party.
  We hate to miss out on a good party. ☐

3 Jake prefers buying second-hand clothes.
  Jake prefers to buy second-hand clothes. ☐

4 Can you remember to use the voucher?
  Can you remember using the voucher? ☐

4 **Complete the second sentence so that it has a similar meaning to the first. Use the word in capitals.**

1 I prefer to wear tight-fitting clothes.
  RATHER
  I _____ tight-fitting clothes.

2 Emily's parents didn't give her permission to go to the party.
  ALLOWED
  Emily _____ to the party.

3 My school forbids us to wear jeans.
  LET
  My school _____ jeans.

4 Alex should buy some new school shoes.
  BETTER
  Alex _____ some new school shoes.

5 Nobody forced him to get his hair cut.
  MADE
  Nobody _____ his hair cut.

6 They'd rather look for a bargain in the sale.
  PREFER
  They _____ for a bargain in the sale.

Articles and determiners

> **articles**
>
> … **an** auction to raise money for charity.
>
> This is **the** show for you.
>
> Admission is free to all ticket holders. (no article)
>
> **determiners**
>
> **a few** bargains
>
> **Each** year, young designers …
>
> **All of** the innovative designs …
>
> **Many of** the show's visitors …
>
> **Some of** the best high street retailers …
>
> **None of** the items are available yet.

See **Grammar File**, page 173

5 Correct the sentences.

1 It's such exciting event!
2 That's my jacket! Yours is striped one.
3 Fashion is a major industry in twenty-first century.
4 She has an very individual style.
5 Coco Chanel was one of world's most famous fashion designers.
6 Paul's got a curly hair.
7 Those boots were bargain! Only twenty euros!
8 It's an European fashion show.

6 Choose the correct answer.

1 The summer sale only attracted **a few / a little** customers.
2 **All of / None of** the visitors have arrived yet.
3 The drop in price made **little / few** difference to the number of sales.
4 The clothes show attracted **much / many** publicity.
5 I need **some / a few** help with the decorations.
6 We've got **plenty of / much** time to get ready.

"I **am** dressed for success! Of course, my idea of success may not be exactly the same as yours."

7 Choose the word or phrase that best completes the sentence.

1 We've got _____ ideas for the next fashion show.
   A much   C a little
   B none of   D a few
2 I didn't like the dresses in that shop. _____ of them were the right colour.
   A Not any   C Nothing
   B None   D No one
3 Look at all those shopping bags! She must have bought _____ things.
   A lot of   C a lot of
   B little   D few
4 _____ the designers are already working in the fashion industry.
   A Much of   C Most
   B Many of   D Less of
5 You don't need to hurry. We've got _____ of time.
   A a number   C few
   B much   D plenty

Back up your grammar

8 Read the article and think of the word which best fits each space. Use only one word in each space.

In the past few years, the demand for cheap clothing in [1]_____ west has produced a highly competitive labour market where children as young as five [2]_____ allowed to work in difficult conditions. Many [3]_____ the factory workers are women and young children who work for a wage that would be unacceptable elsewhere. International pressure has finally begun to [4]_____ some clothing companies realise that they have to [5]_____ these children have time for an education. There's no doubt they would [6]_____ be [7]_____ books in school than be made [8]_____ work at a sewing machine all day. But, unless more is done to support these children few [9]_____ them will manage [10]_____ escape poverty.

CHATROOM

• Do you have more or fewer clothes than your friends?
• Which items do you have most of? Jeans, T-shirts or accessories? Explain your answer.

Listening

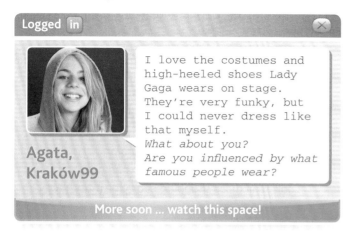

Logged in

Agata, Kraków99

I love the costumes and high-heeled shoes Lady Gaga wears on stage. They're very funky, but I could never dress like that myself.
What about you?
Are you influenced by what famous people wear?

More soon ... watch this space!

Listening 1

1 Listen to Tom's talk on the radio and decide whether the statements below are true (T), false (F) or if there is no information (NI).

> **Listening Tip: true, false, no information**
> Read the questions and think of synonyms for the key words and phrases.

1 Tom and his friends didn't use to like shopping.
2 Most people prefer cotton clothes because they're a natural product.
3 Cotton is grown in countries with little water.
4 The factories get rid of the chemicals by washing the cotton.
5 Many people have died because of the polluted water from the cotton industry.
6 Watching the programme made Tom realise he didn't have enough cotton clothes.
7 Tom hadn't worn all the shirts in his wardrobe.
8 Shopping had become a routine for Tom and his friends.
9 Last year Tom didn't go to the shops at all.
10 The experience has made Tom more creative.

Listening 2

2 You are going to listen to a radio interview with a fashion designer, Sylvia. Before you listen, tick (✓) what you think Sylvia will talk about.

- International fashion shows ☐
- Why fashion is important for teenagers ☐
- How travelling influences her work ☐
- The changes in the world of fashion ☐
- The importance of advertising ☐
- How much money she makes ☐
- The role of footballers ☐

3 For questions 1–7, choose the best answer, A, B or C.

1 When did Sylvia discover what career she wanted?
   A after she finished art college
   B when she got her first job
   C when she was working with a designer
2 What's the main consideration for Sylvia when she chooses a design?
   A that teenagers will buy the designs
   B that teenagers will like the designs
   C that the designs are right for teenagers
3 What does she do after seeing clothes at the catwalk shows?
   A She tries to copy them.
   B She makes them suitable for teenagers.
   C She shows the outfits to teenagers.
4 What's the advantage of making clothes in India?
   A They can be sold more cheaply.
   B The clothes are better quality.
   C Poor people get trained.
5 What does Sylvia's company think of child labour?
   A It agrees with it.
   B It needs it.
   C It disagrees with it.
6 How can a famous person help sell an item of clothing?
   A by wearing it in public
   B by buying it
   C by having a photo taken in it
7 How have boys' attitudes changed to how they dress and look?
   A They don't like sports clothes any more.
   B They realise they've got more choice.
   C They now feel it's OK to be interested in fashion.

CHATROOM

- What's the fashion at the moment for your age group?
- What do you think has been a 'bad' fashion item? Why?

Speaking
Reaching a decision

1 Why do people change their appearance?

2 Listen to Mark talking to a friend about his appearance. Tick (✓) what he has changed.

Hair ☐   Nose ☐
Skin ☐   Eyes ☐
Body ☐   Clothes ☐

3 Match the words and phrases from the box with the pictures.

> get braces   do weight-training
> wear make-up   get a haircut
> use hair gel   shop for new clothes

4 Work with a partner. Choose two of the photos and talk about changing your appearance in these ways. Use these phrases to help you.

1 I think that … is a bad/good idea because …
2 I would never try to … because …
3 I'm sure … is the best/quickest way …
4 It's better to …
5 I like … because …

5 Listen to two people discussing two of the pictures. Tick (✓) the expressions from the Language Upload box that they use.

6 Now complete this task with your partner. Use phrases from the Language Upload box. You should speak for about three minutes.

> How successful would these methods be in changing the way you look?
>
> Which two methods would you suggest trying?

Speaking Tip: reaching a decision

Listen to your partner and make sure you answer his/her questions and ask for his/her ideas.

Language Upload

Getting started

Let's start with this picture.
Shall we look at the pictures one by one?
Why don't I/you begin with the first picture?

Structuring the conversation

Shall we move on to the second picture?
Let's see. We haven't talked about/mentioned …
I think we've looked at all the pictures.

Asking for and responding to ideas

Do you think that's important?
What do you feel about … ?
Yes, I hadn't thought about that.
I'm not sure about that.
I suppose you're right.
I agree/I don't agree with you.

Reaching a decision

Let's make our suggestions.
I think I would choose/recommend/suggest …
I suggest, first … and second … because …

Writing: A Review
Before you write

1 Read the advert and tick (✓) the sentences that are true.

1 Teenagers will probably read the review. ☐
2 The review will give information on several shops. ☐
3 The review will include your opinion. ☐

Do you like shopping?

Do you have a favourite shop? What's good or not so good about it? If you recommend it, tell us why. The best review will be in the first edition of our new teen magazine *Rebel* and the winner will receive vouchers up to the value of €200 to spend in the shop of their choice!

2 Read the review. What does the writer like about Tara?

Great retail therapy at Tara

My favourite shop is Tara. It's one of the main high street retailers and most large towns have a branch. My local shop is huge and it sells brilliant clothes for men and women of all ages. The shop has several sales during the year with lots of unbeatable deals.

I like shopping at Tara because it offers a wide selection of clothes at prices most of us can afford. It sells smart clothes, but there's also a funky range for teenagers. Some of the high-heeled sandals and baggy T-shirts for this summer are fantastic.

The only bad thing about Tara is that sometimes it's crowded and I hate waiting to try clothes on. It's also advisable to check clothes carefully as sometimes the quality isn't as good as in other shops.

If you like fashion, then I would recommend you include Tara on your next shopping spree. The company has an informative website where you can find out when the sales are on, so don't miss out on all the amazing bargains!

3 In which paragraphs do these points appear in the review?

… the bad points about the shop
… the name of the shop
… a final recommendation to the reader
… what the shop sells
… the good points about the shop

4 Underline words or phrases in the review which the writer uses to describe

1 the shop
2 the style of the products in the shop
3 the prices
4 the disadvantages of the shop

5 Find words or phrases in the review that mean the following.

1 principal (paragraph 1)
2 very big (paragraph 1)
3 big choice (paragraph 2)
4 it's a good idea (paragraph 3)
5 which includes lots of information (paragraph 4)

6 Tick (✓) the determiners that are used in the review.

a lot of	☐	all	☐
lots of	☐	several	☐
each	☐	other	☐
every	☐	most	☐
some	☐	many	☐
any	☐	both	☐

Time to write

7 Look at the consumer website and complete the table with two advantages and two disadvantages for each method of shopping.

http://www.teenthing.com

calling all teenagers!

Do you look for unusual items in your local market, snap up bargains in the nearest shopping centre or do you get your retail therapy online? Write a review telling us about your favourite way of shopping and why you recommend it. The winner will receive £200 worth of clothes.

Outdoor market	Shopping centre	Online
+	+	+
+	+	+
−	−	−
−	−	−

8 Complete the sentences with your own ideas about shopping using the gerund or infinitive.

1 I spend a lot of time *looking for* bargains online.
2 I prefer _____ to _____ .
3 I refuse _____ .
4 I usually regret _____ .
5 I recommend _____ .
6 _____ online is _____ .

9 Choose a title for your review or use your own idea.
- Online is best!
- Shopping spree at a shopping centre!
- Market bargains!

10 Now write your review. Write between 120 and 180 words. Use the Writing Checklist and Memory Flash to help you.

Writing Checklist: A Review

Does your review include

1 four paragraphs, each with a clear purpose?
2 background information?
3 good and bad points?
4 your opinion?
5 a clear recommendation at the end?
6 interesting adjectives?
7 vocabulary from this unit?
8 correct use of gerunds, infinitives, articles and determiners?
9 present tenses?

Memory Flash

Beginning the review

My favourite ...
It's ... (short description)
It sells ...

The good points

It's friendly/huge/personal ...
The clothes are ... (funky, retro, vintage, etc.)
The choice is ...

The bad points

However, there are disadvantages, ...
Sometimes the ... is disappointing.
It's not as ... as ...

Giving your opinion

I prefer ... because ...
I like ...
I think that ...

Recommending

I would recommend ...
I strongly recommend ... because ...

Vocabulary

1 Complete the description with the words from the box.

> scruffy medium toned vintage braces
> fair-haired rosy cheeks

My best friend

What I like about my best friend, Sam, is that she's got ¹_____, which means she always looks fit and healthy, as though she's just been out in the fresh air. I'm quite envious that she's ²_____ because in the summer her hair gets even lighter and it looks very attractive. She's of ³_____ height. She's definitely not as short as I am, but she's not too tall either. She hates having to wear ⁴_____, but it's only for a few months more — then she'll have a great smile! We don't really dress the same. She's not as ⁵_____ as I am, because I never wear anything but jeans and comfortable T-shirts. I think she knows more about good style because she likes buying ⁶_____ clothes that are old but that look really good quality. Sam's mad about sports and has a very ⁷_____ body.

2 Choose the correct answer.

1 I had no idea we were going to **run out of** / **miss out on** the T-shirts so quickly. I'll have to order some more.
2 We could use the window display to **dress up** / **show off** the new summer range.
3 Jack took ages choosing his jeans. In the end he **picked out** / **snapped up** some faded ones.
4 As soon as the shop doors opened, people rushed in to **snap up** / **run out of** the bargains.
5 Everybody is **showing off** / **dressing up** for the end-of-year party, but I haven't got anything to wear.
6 It's a pity you didn't come shopping with us. You **picked out** / **missed out on** some great deals.

Grammar

3 Choose the word or phrase that best completes the sentence.

1 Alex said he didn't mind _____ while Anna tried on the dress.
   A to wait   B waiting   C wait   D waited
2 They hope _____ their own shop one day.
   A to open   B open   C opening   D to opening
3 We strolled along the street and enjoyed _____ in the shop windows.
   A to looking B look   C to look   D looking
4 Jo is the new shop assistant. She's only been here _____ weeks.
   A few   B a little   C a few   D little
5 For one day only, _____ customer will receive a 10 percent discount.
   A every   B many   C all   D all of
6 Tim buys lots of clothes online, but he _____ go shopping in town.
   A prefer to   B 'd rather C 'd better D prefers

4 Complete the second sentence so that it has a similar meaning to the first. Use the word in capitals.

1 Julia advised her friend to go back to the shop.
   HAD
   'You _____ back to the shop,' said Julia.
2 She won't meet many friends at the show.
   FEW
   She _____ friends at the show.
3 I don't want to go to the shopping centre today.
   RATHER
   I _____ the shopping centre today.
4 'Don't forget to take some money'.
   REMINDED
   Her mum _____ some money.
5 I hate it when I have to wait in a queue in a shop.
   STAND
   I _____ in a queue in a shop.
6 Will your boss give you permission to leave early today?
   LET
   Will your boss _____ early today?
7 George's parents didn't let him wear scruffy clothes to the wedding.
   ALLOWED
   George _____ scruffy clothes to the wedding.
8 There isn't much choice in this shop.
   LITTLE
   There _____ in this shop.

I'd love to travel but, being from New Zealand, that's not easy. When I leave school, I'm going to spend six months travelling round Europe and working. There are so many places I'd like to see. What about you? How easy is it to travel to different countries from where you live? Where would you like to go?

10 A Small World

Vocabulary Starter
Landscape and travel

1 Match the words with the pictures.

> bay cliffs lagoon
> mainland pebbles

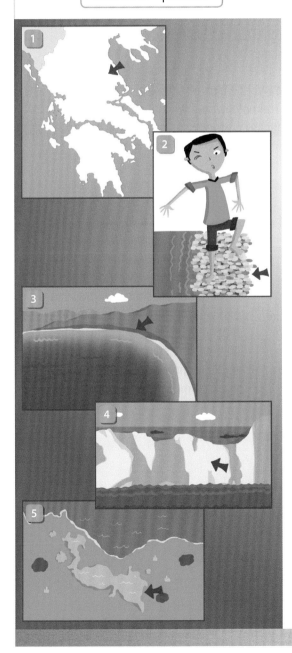

2 Match the words (1–8) with their underlined synonyms.

1 besides
2 breeze
3 whizzing
4 infuriates
5 plunge
6 hike
7 emerged
8 towered

A Pop up advertising <u>really angers</u> me.
B The buildings <u>rose</u> high above my head.
C My friends and I have a lot in common <u>in addition to</u> going to the same school.
D We went on a ten kilometre <u>walk</u>.
E There was a <u>gentle wind</u> blowing.
F A strange figure <u>appeared</u> from the fog.
G The toy plane was <u>moving very quickly</u> round the room and we couldn't catch it.
H I never believed that James would <u>jump suddenly and quickly</u> into the icy water.

3 Number the clues to the crossword.

```
                          ²
        ¹ C H E C K I N   N
              ⁴           A
    ³ B U D G E T  ⁵ F    V
            E      E      I
  ⁶ S U R C H A R G E     G
            M             A
          ⁷ P R I O R I T Y
            N             E
        ⁸ B A S E
            L
```

extra money you have to pay on top of the normal price ☐
a building at an airport where passengers arrive and depart ☐
very low in price ☐
the amount you have to pay for something ☐
the place where you leave your luggage at the airport ☐
find which way you need to go using a map or directions ☐
a central place you stay from where you travel to other places ☐
allowing you to do something before other people ☐

CHATROOM
What are the advantages and disadvantages of travelling by plane?

Reading

Logged in ⊗

I write a travel blog with photos and information from my holidays. It's like a souvenir for me – and it's cheaper than buying souvenirs in tourist shops. *Do you upload holiday photos to the Internet on a webpage, social networking site or blog?*

WellingtonSoutherncross1

1 Read the text and tick (✓) the subjects the writer talks about.

- The outward journey ☐
- The accommodation ☐
- The return journey ☐
- The nightlife ☐
- Booking the tickets ☐
- Places they visited ☐

12 Twelve places to see …

The Scilly Isles

Eguisheim

Nessebar

Siwa Oasis

Odessa

Telc

Lefkada

Vilnius

Brasov

Sopron

Kransjka Gora

Gdańsk

LEFKADA

We travelled here last summer and had a great time. It's an island, but it's connected to the mainland by a movable bridge. It moves to let the boats pass. We didn't see this happening …
We travelled on one of the budget airlines (I won't say which one!). Of course, once we'd paid the online check-in fee and the credit card surcharge and priority boarding fee the fares were probably higher than a normal airfare. My dad won't listen to reason, though. ☐1☐ Being a technophobe, he can't actually use the airline's website, so I have to print off the e-tickets for him and write down the booking reference number so he won't lose it. ☐2☐ He keeps all the print-outs carefully, but he's convinced that they won't be acceptable to the check-in staff at the airport. Watching him anxiously checking and rechecking the tickets always makes me giggle, which infuriates him. I just can't help it, though!

Having successfully passed through check-in, we headed for the plane. The in-flight entertainment consisted of three noisy children behind us and a middle-aged man snoring loudly in the window seat next to me. Priority boarding doesn't really work when everyone uses it, so Mum and I sat apart from Dad and chatted about our plans. ☐3☐ He likes his peace and quiet!

So, to Lefkada …

We stayed in the town of Nydri, which was a lively resort and a good base to explore from. The hotel where we stayed (or 'at which we stayed' as my English teacher prefers!) was quiet and friendly. We rented a car and did a lot of sightseeing. On the first day we headed north. After looking round Lefkada town, we went to the nearby lagoon. If you like birdwatching, it's a great place to spend the day. ☐4☐

My favourite day was when we went to Porto Katsiki, which is a stunning beach at the foot of some towering white cliffs. The best thing about the day was that we didn't travel by car. Dad had read that the road was very narrow and the route difficult to navigate. And navigation isn't his strongest skill! Mum had read that the walk down to the beach from the car park (and back

up again) was very steep. [5] Nydri is a major port and, besides the ferries to other islands, there are also cruises to beaches on Lefkada. Approaching the beach from the sea presented a great photo opportunity.

The weather was gorgeous, of course, and, on the one windy day when we didn't fancy being on a beach, we had a pleasant hike through the olive trees to the Nydri waterfalls.

One more place I must mention is Vassiliki. It's in a bay and they get an afternoon breeze there, which is known locally as Eric (don't ask me why!). It's a great place for windsurfers. [6] Pretty soon, the whole bay is full of brightly coloured sails whizzing to and fro. The only slight drawback is that the beach doesn't have much sand – it's mainly pebbles. Still, my trusty plastic beach shoes kept me protected.

On the journey back, the plane was held up for five hours. No reason was given. Still, you don't expect reasons from budget airlines, do you? [7] Taking off at 5 a.m., we saw the sun rising in the east and the view of the islands was incredible. Luckily, drowsiness had slowed the other passengers down and I was able to get a window seat this time. I got some amazing shots of the island, the Croatian coast, Venice and the Alps. After that, we plunged into thick cloud. The next thing I saw was the terminal building at Heathrow Airport. I shook Mum awake. 'We're home,' I said. 'Are we?' she replied, sleepily, 'How sad.'

2 Read the text again and match the sentences with the gaps in the text. There is one sentence you do not need.

Reading Tip: missing sentences

When you have completed the task, read through the text to make sure it makes sense in terms of both grammar and meaning.

A I don't think he was too upset by that!
B As a result, we went by boat.
C That wasn't what he'd expected at all.
D He's obsessed with documents.
E Actually, apart from an uncomfortable night at the airport, it was a real bonus.
F He sees the adverts for £10 tickets and falls for them every time.
G If your parents like it, but you don't, it isn't!
H Some of them are locals and some are tourists.

3 Find words or phrases in the text that mean the following.

1 getting on a plane (line 6)
2 certain that something is true (line 11)
3 laugh quickly (line 13)
4 breathing noisily while asleep (line 17)
5 amazingly beautiful (line 30)
6 wonderful (line 43)
7 backwards and forwards (lines 51 and 52)
8 disadvantage (line 52)

CHATROOM

Imagine you were going to make a website called 'Three places that I've seen and you must see'. Work in groups and tell each other which places you would write about and why.

 WebSearch

http://www.1000beforeyoudie.com
http://www.lefkas.net
http://www.ionian-islands.com

Vocabulary

Word formation: words from the text

1 Complete the blog with the correct form of the words in capitals. All the words are from the reading text on pages 114 and 115.

Dad's new toy!

Last month, my dad got a new GPS ¹_____ (NAVIGATE) system for his car. I don't know why. He's a real ²_____ (TECHNOLOGY) and hasn't even learned to use the CD player, yet!

The first time he used it, we were going to a hotel for Easter. He spent so much time ³_____ (ANXIOUS) checking and ⁴_____ (CHECK) the directions that I was scared we were going to have an accident. In the end, he got lost and out came the ⁵_____ (TRUST) old maps, which he gave to me. It was late by this time and I looked at them ⁶_____ (SLEEP). In the end, ⁷_____ (DROWSY) forced Dad to stop at a hotel for the night and we arrived a day late. I don't think he'll be so ⁸_____ (OBSESSION) with techno-gadgets from now on!

Travel arrangements

2 Complete the mini dialogues with words from the box.

> aisle confirm e-tickets fares
> insurance reservation

1 A: Why don't you sit next to the window?
   B: No, I'd rather be next to the _____ , so that I can stretch my legs.

2 A: What are all those bits of paper?
   B: They're our _____ . I booked on the Internet.

3 A: How do you know that the booking has worked?
   B: They'll send us an email to _____ that the money has gone through.

4 A: What's this extra £30 for?
   B: _____ , just in case we have an accident.

5 A: The flight to Paris is £20 or the train costs £80.
   B: I can't understand why train _____ are so expensive.

6 A: We should be able to find a hotel easily when we arrive.
   B: I'm not so sure. I think we should make a _____ before we leave.

Landscape

3 Match the words with the descriptions.

1	lagoon	A	an area of fruit trees
2	bay	B	a deep narrow valley with steep sides
3	orchard	C	a narrow passage of water between two areas of land
4	headland		
5	gorge	D	the top of a mountain
6	moor	E	a steep rock at the edge of the sea
7	summit	F	a lake of sea water separated from the sea by a small strip of land
8	strait		
9	cliff	G	land sticking out into the sea
10	tide	H	the regular rising and falling of the level of the sea
		I	a wild area of high land, covered with rough grass
		J	an area of the sea, partially enclosed by a curve in the land

Collocations

4 Choose the correct answer.

A: We can pay extra for ¹priority / previous / preview **boarding** and get on the plane before the other people.
B: How much is it?
A: It's expensive. Twenty euros per person.
B: Never mind. Pay it.

A: Do you want a window seat?
B: No, I'd prefer ²a middle / a corridor / an aisle **seat**. I might need to get up and go to the toilet.

A: Is this Palermo?
B: No, it's Rome.
A: But we're going to Palermo. Is there something wrong?
B: No. There are no ³open / direct / one-way **flights** to Palermo so we have to get off here and get a ⁴further / destination / connecting **flight**.

A: What a lovely holiday. It's a shame we have to go home. Why didn't you get ⁵a free / an open / a clear **return**?
B: I was worried there wouldn't be any free places.

A: The couple in the next room have changed the date of their flight home free of charge.
B: Maybe they paid a ⁶flexible / changeable / moveable **fare**.
A: What's that?
B: It's a slightly more expensive ticket but you can change the dates if you want.

Phrasal verbs

5 Complete the sentences with one word from each box.

> fill   get   held   print   pull   take   turn

> away   back   in   off   out   up x2

1 The plane was _____ by a thunderstorm and we missed our connecting flight.
2 Can you _____ the e-tickets for me, please?
3 Good afternoon. Please could you _____ this form and then I'll show you to your room.
4 We need to _____ from home for a few days.
5 Don't park. Just _____ by the entrance and I'll jump out.
6 Ladies and gentlemen, we have a problem and we will have to _____ .
7 Have a rest, _____ some time _____ work and relax.

Word formation

6 Complete the table.

Verb	Noun	Adjective
accompany		(un)
announce		-
-		available
refund		(non-)
afford	-	
-	expense	
-		(in) convenient
reserve		-

7 Complete the text with the correct form of the words in capitals.

CostCut Airlines

For safety reasons, we cannot allow ¹_____ children under the age of twelve on our flights. Flight times do sometimes change at the last minute. Passengers must listen carefully to all ²_____ at the airport.   ACCOMPANY

ANNOUNCE
AVAILABLE

The ³_____ of budget tickets is limited. Unfortunately, these tickets are ⁴_____ . However, our flexible tickets are very ⁵_____ compared to our more ⁶_____ competitors.   REFUND
AFFORD
EXPENSE

Our information desk is ⁷_____ located inside the entrance to the airport and is open every day.   CONVENIENT

To make a ⁸_____, visit our website.   RESERVE

Prepositional phrases

8 Choose the correct answer.

1 What **in** / **on** / **at** -flight entertainment is there?
2 Welcome **on** / **in** / **at** board.
3 Most of the cabins are **below** / **under** / **down** deck.
4 Let's go **on** / **out** / **in** deck for a bit of fresh air.
5 You must pay for the ticket **on** / **in** / **for** advance.
6 Shall we stop somewhere **en** / **in** / **over** route?
7 Travelling by train is much cheaper if you buy an **out** / **over** / **off** -peak ticket.

Back up your vocabulary

9 Choose the word that best completes the sentence.

1 There was a rocky _____ at each end of the bay.
   A headland B moor   C lagoon   D strait
2 I always book my tickets a long time in _____ to get the best prices.
   A front   B ahead   C forward   D advance
3 A(n) _____ return is useful if you don't know when you want to come back.
   A open   B flight   C direct   D preview
4 The walk through the _____ was stunning although I was worried about falling rocks.
   A strait   B moor   C gorge   D lagoon
5 The _____ is coming in and soon all this will be under water.
   A strait   B breeze   C tide   D bay
6 I need to _____ away from work for a few weeks.
   A turn   B pull   C take   D get

CHATROOM

Which of the landscape features from Exercise 3 can you see in your country? Where are they? What do you know about them?

I told you we should have paid for priority boarding!

Grammar
Clauses

relative clauses
*I love the model gondola **that** I bought in Venice last year.*
*There was a pool, **where** we spent most of our time.*
*I keep thinking about last July, **when** I saw the Mediterranean for the first time.*
*We stayed with a friendly couple **who** had three children.*
*I keep in touch with a couple of people from the camp **whose** email addresses I wrote down.*
*The people to **whom** I was sending the email own a holiday home.*

participle clauses
***Having** successfully **passed** through check-in, we headed for the plane.*
***After looking** at the town, we went to the nearby lagoon.*
***Before leaving**, I bought several souvenirs.*
***Taking off** at 5 am, we saw the sun rising in the east.*

See **Grammar File**, page 174

1 Combine the sentences with a relative pronoun.

1 We went to a small café on the seafront. We ate fresh fish there. (WHERE)

_____

2 We were stuck in a traffic jam at 6 o'clock. Our plane took off. (WHEN)

_____

3 The police stopped a man from boarding the plane. He had been acting suspiciously. (WHO)

_____

4 The bay is in the south. This is the most popular part of the island. (WHICH)

_____

5 I met Matthew Teller. His guide books are really excellent. (WHOSE)

_____

2 Rewrite these sentences using preposition + relative pronoun to make them more formal.

1 The bed we slept in was amazing.
The bed in which we slept was amazing.

2 The hotel we stayed at looked like a palace.

_____

3 The shop we bought our souvenirs from was tiny.

_____

4 The people we talked to advised us to visit the lagoon.

_____

5 The friend I got this model Eiffel Tower from loved Paris.

_____

6 The family we went on holiday with complained about everything.

_____

3 Complete the second sentence so that it has a similar meaning to the first.

1 We walked along the cliffs and saw dolphins swimming in the sea.
Walking _____ .

2 The breeze blew gently, which cooled the hot sunbathers down.
Blowing _____ .

3 My dad searched the airline website, where he discovered a lot of hidden charges.
Searching _____ .

4 The group arrived at the crowded resort and wished they had booked a room in advance.
Arriving _____ .

5 I printed out the e-tickets and noticed that Dad had booked the wrong dates.
Printing _____ .

4 Look at the diary entries and write sentences using the words given.

Day 1: a.m. visited the national museum
        p.m. went shopping   (after)
Day 2: a.m. swam in the lagoon
        p.m. had a wakeboarding lesson (before)
Day 3: a.m. got up late
        p.m. sunbathed   (after)
Day 4: a.m. walked through the gorge
        p.m. took a boat to the next island (after)
Day 5: a.m. said goodbye to my friends,
        flew home   (before)

5 Report Pia's messages using the form 'Having done …'

Having set off on holiday with her parents, Pia kept in touch with her friends by Twitter.

1 We've just climbed the Eiffel Tower. Now we're going for lunch.

2 I've just waved goodbye to Bari. Now I'm going to look round the boat.

3 We've arrived in Rhodes. Now we've got to find our hotel.

4 Dad and I have built a sandcastle. Now we're waiting for the tide to come in and destroy it!

5 I've spent all my money! I can't buy any more souvenirs.

Question tags and echo questions

question tags
You **don't expect** reasons from budget airlines, **do you?**
There**'s** a beach here, **isn't there?**
echo questions
'We're home,' I said. '**Are we?**' she replied.
'I swam here last year.' '**Did you?** Was the water warm?'

See **Grammar File**, page 175

6 Complete the sentences with question tags.

1 These are olive trees, _____?

2 You've never walked through this gorge before, _____?

3 That's not the right beach, _____?

4 The in-flight entertainment was awful, _____?

5 Your dad brought the e-tickets with him, _____?

6 Everyone knows how to book tickets online, _____?

7 Let's pay for priority boarding, _____?

8 I'm going to have the window seat, _____?

CHATROOM

Use question tags to ask your partner four questions about his/her holidays.

7 Put the responses in the correct places and then complete them with the correct echo question.

Ann: Did you know much about Portugal before you went?

Ben: No. I never read guide books before a holiday.

Ann: ¹*Don't you? But it's good to know something about the place you're going to.*

Ben: I like it to be a surprise. Actually, I wasn't looking forward to this holiday at all.

Ann: ² _____

Ben: Oh yes. Portugal's beautiful but I didn't want to go with my parents.

Ann: ³ _____

Ben: No, they annoy me on holiday. Anyway, in the end I was glad I went.

Ann: ⁴ _____

Ben: I met some really cool people and spent most of my time with them.

Ann: ⁵ _____

Ben: No, I think they were pleased to have some time on their own.

A _____? Don't you get on with them?

B _____? Didn't your parents mind?

C _____? What happened to make you change your mind?

D _____? But it's good to know something about the place you're going to. ✓

E _____? I'd love to go to Portugal.

Back up your grammar

8 Read the email and think of the word which best fits each space. Use only one word in each space.

New   Reply

Peter and Jill,
We're having a great time here in Russia.
Day 1: ¹_____ arrived in Moscow, we were taken to our hotel ²_____ we had time to unpack and rest.
Day 2: ³_____ eating a big breakfast, we visited Red Square and St Basil's cathedral. Our guide, ⁴_____ English was perfect, told us everything we needed to know. Having ⁵_____ a few (!) photos, we had lunch.
Days 3-10: We joined the M/S *Glushkov*, a beautiful boat ⁶_____ which we spent seven nights cruising to St Petersburg. The best day was the second, ⁷_____ we stopped at Kostroma. The boat also took us to Kizhi which was another highlight thanks to Andriy, without ⁸_____ we would have missed a lot of the attractions.
Love, Cathy and Greg

More practice on pages 144–145

Listening

Listening 1

🔊 **1** Listen to an interview at an airport. After each section of the interview, you will hear two questions. Choose A, B or C.

Listening Tip: multiple-choice questions heard but not written

You won't know what the questions are before you hear them, so it is important to look at the choices given and make notes about what they refer to while you are listening.

Part 1: Interviewing a tour guide

1 A twelve
  B sixteen
  C twenty-five
2 A three o'clock
  B one o'clock
  C half past twelve

Part 2: Interviewing a member of the tour party

3 A three months ago
  B last Christmas
  C a year ago
4 A the parties
  B the price
  C the range of activities

Part 3: Problems at the airport

5 A Lois
  B Mark
  C Chris
6 A It left Corfu.
  B It arrived in London.
  C It was due to leave London.

Part 4: About to leave

7 A He drives a minibus.
  B He works at a hotel.
  C He works at the airport.
8 A They are still missing.
  B They are boarding the plane.
  C They are waiting for Carey.

WebSearch

http://whc.unesco.org/en
http://www.spain.info
http://www.agni.gr

Listening 2

🔊 **2** You will hear someone talking about holidays in Spain. Complete the sentences with a word or short phrase.

Listening Tip: sentence completion

○ Look at the sentences and predict the kind of word you are listening for.
○ Write numbers as figures not words to save time.
○ Make sure the complete sentence with your answer in it makes sense.

Monfrague National Park

Notes for website article

Speaker: Javier Alonso (Google him later)

1 Nine of Spain's national parks are on _____.
2 Monfrague National Park is near the _____.
3 The Portuguese spelling of the River Tagus is _____.
4 There are a total of _____ pairs of black vultures in the park.
5 To walk to Monfrague Castle from the car park takes about _____.
6 Cave paintings show us that people have lived in the area for more than _____.
7 The architecture in Caceres is a mixture of Gothic, Renaissance, Roman and _____.
8 Every May, in the Plaza in Trujillo, there is a _____.
9 The best airport to arrive at for Caceres is _____.
10 The cost of a train ticket from Lisbon is about _____ that of a train ticket from Madrid.

Logged in ⓘ ⊗

There are fourteen national parks in New Zealand. I think I can name four of them! Egmont Park has got a volcano in it. It's the wettest part of New Zealand and there is a rainforest there, too.

How many national parks do you know in your country?

Describe the landscape in them.

WellingtonSoutherncross1

More soon ... watch this space!

Speaking
Discussing pros and cons

1 Look at the discussion topic and try to think of four arguments for and four arguments against the statement.

> Although air travel is a major cause of air pollution, more and more people travel by plane nowadays. Air fares should be made much more expensive in order to protect the environment.

Arguments for	Arguments against
• People would avoid unnecessary journeys.	• Planes don't pollute as much as other forms of transport
•	•
•	•
•	•

4 With a partner look at a second discussion topic.

Student A: Think of four arguments for the statement.

Student B: Think of four arguments against the statement.

Don't show each other your arguments.

> Mass tourism has harmed many areas of the world and should be strictly controlled.

5 Discuss the topic with your partner, using the arguments you noted in Exercise 4. Use the phrases from the Language Upload box to help you.

Speaking Tip: asking for clarification

Don't be afraid to ask the examiner or your partner to repeat or clarify their comments if you don't understand them at first.

Language Upload

Giving opinions

As far as I'm concerned, …   To my mind, …
In my opinion, …   I think …
It seems to me, …   I'm sure that …

Accepting and rejecting other arguments politely

Of course … , but …
You are absolutely right, … but …
However, …
Yes, but don't forget that …
That's all very well, but …
I see what you mean, but …
Well, yes, you're right.
Well, that's possible, but …
Remember though that …

Giving examples

For example, …
If … , will/would …

2 Listen to two people discussing this topic. Who is for and who is against? What arguments do they use for and against the statement?

3 Listen again and tick the words and phrases in the Language Upload box that you hear.

Writing: Instructions

Before you write

1 **Look at the writing task and answer the questions.**

A friend of yours is arriving in your country from Britain. Write a letter telling your friend how to get to your town from the nearest airport. Warn him/her about any problems he/she may have and how they can overcome them. Write between 150 and 200 words.

1 What's the best way of getting from the airport to the city centre?
2 What problems might someone have at the airport / finding the transport / on the transport?
3 If there is no airport in your town, how would somebody get from the city where the airport is to where you live?
4 How could your friend contact you on the way?

2 **Read the letter. What are the writer's answers to the questions in Exercise 1?**

Dear Sharine,

I'm so excited that you're coming! When you arrive, first take a bus from the airport. The bus stop is right outside the terminal building. Buy a ticket from the driver and then validate it in one of the machines on the bus. Be careful! If you don't, you could be fined.

Stay on the bus until it comes to the end of the route. That's the train station so you can't get lost. There are three different types of trains. Local trains are very cheap, but very slow and uncomfortable. Intercity trains are expensive and you have to pay for a seat reservation. The best trains are the normal 'fast' trains. They're fairly quick and much cheaper than the intercity ones.

You'll be travelling late in the evening, so don't travel in first class. The train won't be too crowded and first class may be very empty and not so safe. Travel in second class. Make sure you get on the right train! In fact, ask someone on the platform.

Remember to send me an SMS as soon as you know which train you'll be on and I'll meet you at the station here.

See you soon,
Tamas

3 **Cover the letter in Exercise 2. Look at the pictures and give instructions. Use the verbs in the box to help you.**

| ask buy send take travel validate |

4 **Complete the sentences with words from the box.**

| as soon as be careful don't make sure remember until |

1 _____ to change some money before you try to buy your bus ticket.
2 _____ get off the bus before the end of the route.
3 _____ at the train station.
4 _____ you don't get on the wrong train.
5 Let me know _____ you arrive.
6 Don't get on a train _____ you're sure it's the right one.

5 **Look at the Writing Checklist. Find and underline examples of these things in the letter. They may appear in more than one paragraph.**

6 Read the advert and the task and answer the questions below.

Holiday home exchange – free holidays ... all over the world

How does it work?
Send details of where you want to go and where you live and we will try to find someone who wants to stay in your home. Everything is free! No fees, no membership, nothing!

Top tips
Be honest – people will be upset if you promise a four-bedroom home and only have two bedrooms. There are forums on the website where you might get talked about!

Be flexible – there may not be anyone on a small Greek island who wants to swap homes with you, but there may be several people in the Mediterranean area.

Your family are having a home-exchange holiday with an English-speaking family. A fifteen-year-old girl will be using your bedroom while you are away. Leave a note for her warning her of any possible problems and giving instructions on how to overcome them.

---

1 What problems might someone face if they had to use your bedroom for a week while you were away?
2 What instructions would you give them to help them overcome these things?

7 Complete the table with the notes.

- lamp
- difficult to open
- don't move it or it will go out and you'll be in the dark
- It isn't very strong
- Push the frame – not the glass!
- sometimes crashes
- save your work regularly
- the bed

Equipment	Problems	Instructions
computer		
	loose cable	
window		
		Don't jump on it.

8 Which of the sentences is most appropriate for the task? Why?

1 A I'm so excited that you're going to stay in my bedroom!
  B A warm welcome to my bedroom.
2 A If you encounter any problems in the course of your journey, you can text me on 0048 601311347.
  B Remember to send me an SMS as soon as you arrive.
3 A With kind regards.
  B See you soon.

9 Make a plan and write your letter. Use the Writing Checklist and Memory Flash to help you. Write between 150 and 200 words.

Writing Checklist: Instructions

Does your letter include
1 a reason for writing the instructions?
2 sequencing words such as *first, then, as soon as,* etc.?
3 imperative forms?
4 expressions to emphasise instructions?
6 expressions to give warnings?
7 reasons for the instructions and personal preferences?
8 appropriate style of language depending on who the instructions are for?

Memory Flash

Sequencers

First …	Then …	As soon as …
Second …	After that …	until …

Emphasising

Remember …	Make sure that …
Be careful …	Let me know if …

Imperatives

do / don't

First conditional

If … , … will …	Provided that …
Unless …	As long as …

Personal recommendations

If I were you, I wouldn't …
It's not a good idea to …

Vocabulary

1 Complete the advert with the correct form of the words from the box. There is one extra word.

> accompany afford announce
> insure refund reserve

FLY WITH SMALL-WORLD AIRLINES

You can get a great deal if you book online NOW!

Our offer:

◇ ¹_____ prices even for flexible fares.

◇ Special child minders for ²_____ children aged between eight and thirteen.

◇ Regular ³_____ about flying times, delays and other important information sent to your mobile.

◇ 24 hour 'thinking time' during which you can cancel or change your ⁴_____ without charge.

◇ Free travel ⁵_____ of up to $10,000 per person.

2 Complete the sentences with the correct word.

> bay cliffs gorge headland
> lagoon orchard summit

1 We walked through a lovely _____ full of apple and pear trees.

2 You must be careful when climbing down the _____ because if it rains heavily it can flood very quickly.

3 You can't swim in the _____ because the water isn't very clean, but it's a great place to watch the birds which come there to feed.

4 We were all exhausted when we reached the _____ of the mountain, but the fantastic view was worth the climb.

5 We sailed around the _____ into a glorious _____ .

6 Danger! Don't walk too close to the edge of the _____ .

Grammar

3 One of the four underlined words is incorrect. Decide which one it is and cross it out.

1 The boat <u>in</u> <u>which</u> <u>we</u> reached the island <u>it</u> was small.

2 <u>Having</u> <u>arrived</u> at the lagoon, <u>where</u> we decided <u>to</u> have a picnic.

3 <u>While</u> <u>I</u> <u>checking</u> my e-ticket, I realised that I <u>had</u> spelt my name wrongly.

4 <u>Is</u> the name of this bay <u>is</u> 'The Bay of Naples', <u>isn't it</u>?

5 <u>From</u> <u>whom</u> <u>did</u> you receive the guidebooks <u>from</u>?

6 The family <u>whose</u> house <u>we</u> were staying <u>in</u> <u>they</u> left a really helpful note.

4 Read the text and choose the best answer (A, B or C) for each gap.

Welcome to Sochi!

Come to Sochi, ¹_____ you can swim in the beautiful Black Sea.

²_____ relaxing in the sea, take a trip to the mountains for a glorious view. ³_____ seen the view, visit Europe's most northerly tea plantations. You didn't know that there were tea plantations here, ⁴_____? In fact, the city is Russia's only sub-tropical resort.

Come to Sochi, ⁵_____ is the longest city in Europe and ⁶_____ tennis club saw the young Maria Sharapova and Yevgeny Kafelnikov take their first steps onto the tennis court.

Come to Sochi in June, ⁷_____ millions attend Russia's biggest annual film festival.

'⁸_____?' you ask. Yes, they do, but don't take my word for it. Come and see for yourself in Sochi, Russia's most fashionable resort.

1	A when	B which	C where
2	A Having	B After	C When
3	A After	B Having	C When
4	A knew you	B didn't you	C did you
5	A what	B which	C where
6	A which	B who	C whose
7	A when	B where	C at which
8	A Does it	B Do they	C Is it

Speaking Activities

Unit 3

Page 37, Exercise 3, Student B Course Information

Young Drivers' Course	
Course content	Practice: driving skills – how to control a car; individual practice with instructor in special dual control cars Theory: how a car works – and how to look after it; safety on the road, what to do in an emergency
Target students	Teenagers who are too young to get a driving licence but want to learn driving skills now
Requirements	None, except minimum age 14
Dates	1 week in July
Fees	£100

Page 37, Exercise 6, Student A Course Information

Music Course	
Course content	Mornings: students learn to play new instrument or improve skills and techniques on instrument they already play Afternoons: students practise together in a mixed instrument band Group puts on musical performance at the end of the course
Target students	Teenagers and young adults with an enthusiasm for music
Requirements	No formal qualifications needed but enthusiasm essential; students should be available some evenings for extra practice
Dates	Two weeks in August
Fees	£200

Sports Week	
Course content	Students spend 1 week doing intensive training in one or (maximum) two sports. Choose from: tennis, football, cricket, hockey, basketball, swimming, golf, climbing, ice-skating
Target students	Teenagers aged 14–17 who are fit and energetic
Requirements	Students must be fit and be good at teamwork; they must be able to attend morning and afternoon sessions. No beginners
Dates	1 week in July
Fees	£100

Unit 5

Page 61, Exercise 8, Role play

Student B

You are a shop assistant. Find out what the problem is. Offer to replace the item. If the customer refuses, offer a refund. Begin the role play by saying.
'Hello Sir/Madam. Can I help you?'

Student A

The situation

You are in a computer shop. You were given a new laptop for your birthday but when you took it out of the box there was a problem with the screen. You don't feel happy with the make. Your partner is the shop assistant.
Your goal
Explain the problem. Ask if you can exchange it for another make.

Unit 7

Page 85, Exercise 2, Teacher/Student B Information

Who the person is	Magda, my cousin	
Problem	Got bad marks in English and needs to make progress fast. Her parents want her to study through the holidays, but Magda doesn't want to stay at home studying on her own.	
Solutions	Do English course in London and speak English all day, meet English people and learn about their culture.	Do summer course in home town; English lessons every morning and free time in the afternoon to go out with friends.
Disadvantages	She might miss her friends. It might be expensive.	She might not make very fast progress. She might get bored.

1 **Read the text and choose the best answer (A, B, C or D) for each gap.**

Robert Lindsay

Robert Lindsay is one of Britain's best loved actors. He originally planned to become a drama teacher but a friend persuaded him to go to London for a(n) [1]_____ at the Royal Academy of Dramatic Arts. He was accepted and has been working ever since.

He appeared in several sit-coms in the 1970s which led [2]_____ offers of theatre work. He has appeared [3]_____ stage many times, including in the musical *Me and My Girl* which was a huge success [4]_____ the box office. He also [5]_____ a song for Derby County Football Club, his local team, which is played before every match.

He is now best known for starring in the sit-com *My Family* in which he plays the [6]_____ of bad-tempered dentist, Ben Harper. The programme, which is shown [7]_____ BBC 1, has been running for over ten years. There have been ten [8]_____ with a total of over one hundred [9]_____ . There have been eight main [10]_____ members over the years, although not all of them are still in the show. The show has over seven million [11]_____ fans who watch it every week. It is also popular on [12]_____ such as BBC America, ABC Australia and Nickelodeon in Germany.

1	A audition	B appearance	C practice	D performance
2	A for	B on	C through	D to
3	A in	B off	C on	D up
4	A on	B at	C in	D with
5	A rehearsed	B recorded	C restored	D rewarded
6	A series	B rash	C role	D cast
7	A in	B from	C with	D on
8	A series	B channels	C exhibitions	D performances
9	A casts	B episodes	C programmes	D locations
10	A role	B staff	C cast	D union
11	A anxious	B cautious	C sensitive	D loyal
12	A programmes	B channels	C series	D episodes

2 **Use the same word to complete both sentences.**

1 A I blacked out and didn't _____ to for several hours.

   B I'd love to _____ across something old and valuable in our attic.

2 A After the match, the players ended _____ at a Chinese restaurant.

   B Cheer _____; you'll meet someone else soon.

3 A I don't know how we _____ through that terrible journey.

   B Cheryl wanted the lead role but only _____ a minor part in the play.

4 A This song brings _____ happy memories.

   B When you look _____ on your childhood, how do you feel?

5 A The film was made _____ location in Mexico.

   B The excitement started _____ page one and continued right to the end of the book.

3 Choose the word or phrase that best completes the sentence.

1 Seeing your name _____ print gives you a great feeling.
  A in   B on   C for   D at

2 I ended up with a lot of bruises and a _____ eye.
  A rash   B blue   C bumped   D black

3 Paula has a really _____ idea for a new film.
  A exciting   B excited   C excitement   D excite

4 Dad has been really _____ lately; he always seems angry and fed up.
  A grateful   B grumpy   C honest   D creative

5 I _____ to send you some designs for the album cover, but I forgot.
  A was going   B am going   C used to   D would

6 How many _____ are there on this album?
  A charts   B tracks   C releases   D lyrics

7 I missed the train so I was late for the _____ ; the conductor was really annoyed with me.
  A portrait   B rehearsal   C album   D series

8 I need some advice, but I don't know who to _____ to.
  A lead   B stick   C turn   D come

4 Complete the text with the correct form of the words in capitals.

New dating agency survey

When somebody joins a dating agency, what exactly are they looking for? 75 percent of women said they wanted someone who was ¹_____ . **AFFECTION**
Another factor that women looked for was ²_____ . For men, more **HONEST**
so than women, ³_____ is very important. **APPEAR**

    What happens when these people meet? Unfortunately, the experience
is often ⁴_____ . The biggest problems are not with looks, but with **DISAPPOINT**
⁵_____ . Men seem to cause more problems than women. They are **BEHAVE**
often accused of being ⁶_____ and, in a surprisingly large number **MATURE**
of cases, of being too ⁷_____ . It seems that they want to prove that **COMPETE**
they are somehow 'better' than the woman, even when this is obviously
not the case.

    This, of course, causes a lot of ⁸_____ , especially for people **FRUSTRATE**
who have been on a number of dates and still not found anyone suitable.
However, men in the survey accused some women of being ⁹_____ **DECIDE**
and unable to decide whether to continue the relationship or not. This
might sound ¹⁰_____ , but people using dating agencies tend to be **LOGIC**
more critical of prospective partners than those who haven't.

5 Complete the dialogues with the words from the box. There is one extra word.

> audition   proof   anxious   lyrics   rash   swollen

1 A: What's wrong with you?
   B: I'm _____ to find out how I did in my exam.

2 A: Are you sure it was Debbie who broke your watch?
   B: Yes, but I don't have any _____ .

3 A: Are you feeling all right?
   B: No, not really. I got stung by a bee and my arm is all _____ .

4 A: Do you like this song?
   B: It's OK, but I don't understand the _____ .

5 A: Have you got a part in the play?
   B: Not yet. I've got to go to the theatre for a(n) _____ first.

6 Choose the correct words to complete the conversation.

What ¹_____ to at the moment?

A are you listening   C do you listen
B you listening   D did you listen

It's the new song by The Hopping Turtles.
It ²_____ in the charts for ages.

A used to   C has been
B had been   D would be

Who are they? ³_____ of them!

A I'd never heard   C I'm never hearing
B I never hear   D I've never heard

They're an American band. I ⁴_____ a track
from their album on an online radio station.

A hearing   C heard
B was hearing   D have heard

You ⁵_____ strange music ever
since I've known you!

A have liked   C had liked
B used to like   D would like

I ⁶_____ listening to music which is
unusual and creative.

A am loving   C loved
B would love   D love

It's ⁷_____ you formed a band.
I'm sure you'd be good.

A hour   C rather
B should   D time

I ⁸_____ be in a band. I played the guitar.

A used to   C would
B could   D have

Really? How often did you practise?

We ⁹_____ meet every Monday after school.

A used   C would
B had   D has

Did you ever play live?

No, we split up after we ¹⁰_____ two rehearsals.
We realised that we weren't very good.

A have had   C would have
B had had   D were having

But that's exactly the sort of band that
you like. One that isn't very good!

7 Choose the word or phrase that best completes the sentence.

1 While you _____ your homework, I found a great game on the Internet.
   A were finished   B had finished   C have finished   D were finishing

2 Royce wrote me a long email telling me everything he _____ since we last met.
   A has done   B did   C was doing   D had done

3 I realised that someone _____ my letters before I got them.
   A was reading   B has read   C has been reading   D is reading

4 On average, one house _____ in our street every month.
   A is selling   B has sold   C was selling   D is sold

5 Yahoo used to be the biggest search engine, but by 2000, it _____ in popularity by Google.
   A has overtaken   B had overtaken   C has been overtaken   D had been overtaken

6 I _____ to be lonely, but now I have lots of friends.
   A would   B was   C used   D had

7 Sean _____ to have a party, but his parents wouldn't let him.
   A had gone   B was going   C would   D has been

8 I _____ Brad Pitt on Twitter since he was in the film *Ocean's Thirteen*.
   A have been following   B was following   C had been following   D have been followed

8 Complete the second sentence so that it has a similar meaning to the first.
Use the word in capitals.

1 Someone has invited me to join a social networking site.
INVITED
I _____ to join a social networking site.

2 My parents often went cycling before I was born.
WOULD
My parents _____ before I was born.

3 When I looked down, I realised that someone had taken my bag.
BEEN
When I looked down, I realised that _____ .

4 I started this book in December and I still haven't finished it.
READING
I have _____ December and I still haven't finished it.

5 I stopped liking meat after we visited a sausage-making factory.
OFF
I _____ after we visited a sausage-making factory.

6 Our old Maths teacher would get very angry if we made silly mistakes.
USED
Our old Maths teacher _____ very angry if we made silly mistakes.

7 I don't really want you to borrow my new jacket.
RATHER
I _____ borrow my new jacket.

8 My plan was to finish my homework before the film started on TV.
GOING
I _____ my homework before the film started on TV.

9 Read the article about Mark and think of the word which best fits each space. Use only one word in each space.

Mark Stevens turns his back on Hollywood

Mark Stevens has been performing on stage for many years now, but he
[1]_____ never appeared in a film before. He probably won't appear in
one again. Although he often [2]_____ to say that he would never leave
the theatre for the bright lights of Hollywood, he [3]_____ tempted by
a very large amount of money and the promise of an interesting role.
When he first read the part, he was [4]_____ to turn it down, but for
some reason he changed his mind. It was a bad mistake. When he left
England, he was cheerful and [5]_____ good health. Three months
later, he returned, exhausted. [6]_____ he was watching the film on its
opening night, he collapsed and had to be rushed to hospital. The film did
very badly [7]_____ the box office and his illness didn't save him from
hurtful reviews. Speaking from his hospital bed, last August, Mark told
reporters that he [8]_____ learned an important lesson and that, from
now on, he was going to stick [9]_____ the stage where he felt much
happier. Since then, he has [10]_____ offered the lead role in a new play
in London. He [11]_____ feeling well again and has almost forgotten
the events of last year. Last week, I interviewed Mark in his car while
he was [12]_____ driven from his home in the country to the theatre in
London for rehearsals. This is what he told me ...

1 Read the text and choose the best answer (A, B, C or D) for each gap.

Training to be a football manager

If you've got a passion for football and think you know how to ¹_____ out a first class team, then being a football manager might be a ²_____ option for you. First, you should continue your education. Look for universities that offer a ³_____ in Physical Education or sports science. While this ⁴_____ will be essential, you should also spend time with a local football club and offer to help them. It's vital that you study the game and the players carefully and ⁵_____ up with ideas on how they can improve.

If you have ⁶_____ from university this will be an advantage when you ⁷_____ for your first job. You need to demonstrate that you have academic ability, but that you also have ⁸_____ experience to do the job.

Those who make it as professional, ⁹_____ football managers can often earn a very competitive ¹⁰_____ doing something that they love!

1	A	call	B	take	C	turn	D	work
2	A	profession	B	salary	C	title	D	career
3	A	degree	B	training	C	interview	D	experience
4	A	label	B	qualification	C	graduate	D	form
5	A	keep	B	come	C	speed	D	catch
6	A	revised	B	graduated	C	passed	D	trained
7	A	apply	B	attend	C	send	D	ask
8	A	so	B	too	C	such	D	enough
9	A	overtime	B	excessive	C	full-time	D	underpaid
10	A	salary	B	membership	C	bonus	D	payment

2 Complete the sentences with the prepositions from the box.

> down   with   out   up with   on   over   through to   off   up (x2)

1 I feel like trying something completely different. Perhaps I'll take _____ singing or acting.
2 Slow _____ , will you? You're driving much too fast on this narrow road.
3 Let's work _____ how much money we'll need to take on holiday.
4 Why don't you call Sam? You can always count _____ him to give you an honest opinion.
5 The goalkeeper was sent _____ the pitch after he got aggressive with another player.
6 After twisting his ankle Max couldn't keep _____ the other runners.
7 Guess what! We've got _____ the finals on Saturday!
8 If this company is taken _____ , a lot of people will lose their jobs.
9 The factory has to speed _____ production if it's going to satisfy its customers.
10 It's not easy to deal _____ angry customers.

3 Choose the word that best completes the sentence.

1 Because I work in this shoe shop, I get a good _____ here – 25% off.
   A account   B discount   C count

2 After you _____ from university, you'll have to look for a good job.
   A graduate   B graduation   C post-graduate

3 She was _____ because of her bad behaviour during the match.
   A qualified   B disqualified   C qualification

4 My mum gets a lot of _____ from her work.
   A satisfaction   B satisfied   C satisfying

5 After your _____ , you should be able to find work in an international company.
   A train   B trainer   C training

6 If you'd like to take up _____ , you can do a course in the Alps.
   A snowboarder   B snowboarding   C snowboard

7 Emma works as a sales _____ , but she's looking for another job.
   A assistance   B assist   C assistant

8 He is _____ and usually makes friends very easily.
   A confide   B confident   C confidential

4 Complete the text with the correct form of the words in capitals.

According to a report from a leading recruitment [1]_____ , there has been an increase in the number of vacancies for fitness [2]_____ and personal trainers. The jobs require a specialist [3]_____ of health and fitness, as well as an ability to deal with a wide range of people. The more [4]_____ applicants are usually advised to pursue a period of [5]_____ at a sports college before looking for employment. Salaries in this profession are often [6]_____ and will depend on age and experience. The job can be very [7]_____ and includes the possibility of [8]_____ travel, especially for those willing to work in hotels abroad.

AGENT

INSTRUCT
KNOW
EXPERIENCE
TRAIN

NEGOTIATE
ENJOY
NATIONAL

5 Choose the word or phrase that best completes the sentence.

1 We're playing cricket this afternoon. Can I borrow your _____ please?
   A bat   B club   C board   D stick

2 Charlie never _____ jogging. He'd rather ride his bike.
   A play   B goes   C does   D practises

3 The workers were told that their _____ would be reduced from five to four weeks.
   A annual bonus   B overtime   C flexible hours   D paid holiday

4 I've left my car at the _____ to be repaired.
   A garage   B warehouse   C clinic   D company

5 Adam's nose was broken because he wasn't wearing a _____ .
   A helmet   B wetsuit   C face guard   D net

6 He's not keen on team sports, but he enjoys doing _____ at his local karate club.
   A basketball   B martial arts   C cards   D golf

7 Amanda works in the clothing _____ of a large shop in town.
   A company   B department   C office   D factory

8 'Why aren't you playing hockey today?' 'The match has been _____ due to bad weather.'
   A taken over   B turned out   C sent off   D called off

9 I know why you hate _____! It's impossible to do it when your clothes and books are all over the floor!
   A vacuuming   B collecting   C ironing   D painting

10 The new clothes shop is _____ more staff. I'd love to work there.
   A counting on   B taking on   C working out   D taking up

6 Complete the second sentence so that it has a similar meaning to the first. Use the word in capitals.

1 They didn't try snowboarding because it looked so dangerous.
TOO
Snowboarding looked _____ try.

2 The player's behaviour was so bad he was sent off.
SUCH
It _____ that the player was sent off.

3 We'll have dinner when you get home.
UNTIL
We _____ you get home.

4 I've never seen such a scary film.
THE
That is _____ I've ever seen.

5 Windsurfing was easier than I had expected.
AS
Windsurfing _____ I had expected.

6 James had bought more cakes than he needed for the party.
MANY
James had bought _____ for the party.

7 It was such a stressful job that he left.
SO
The job _____ he left.

8 I'll finish these emails before I leave the office.
TIME
By the _____ , I'll have finished these emails.

9 These trousers are too short to wear with these shoes.
ENOUGH
These trousers _____ to wear with these shoes.

7 Read the article about careers and think of the word which best fits each space. Use only one word in each space.

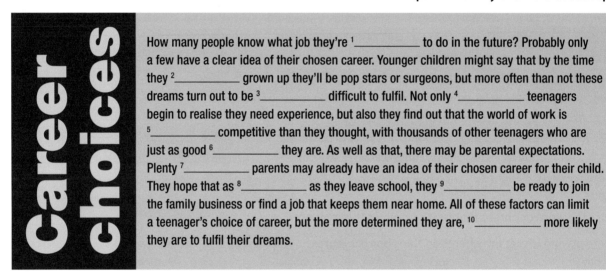

Career choices

How many people know what job they're [1]_____ to do in the future? Probably only a few have a clear idea of their chosen career. Younger children might say that by the time they [2]_____ grown up they'll be pop stars or surgeons, but more often than not these dreams turn out to be [3]_____ difficult to fulfil. Not only [4]_____ teenagers begin to realise they need experience, but also they find out that the world of work is [5]_____ competitive than they thought, with thousands of other teenagers who are just as good [6]_____ they are. As well as that, there may be parental expectations. Plenty [7]_____ parents may already have an idea of their chosen career for their child. They hope that as [8]_____ as they leave school, they [9]_____ be ready to join the family business or find a job that keeps them near home. All of these factors can limit a teenager's choice of career, but the more determined they are, [10]_____ more likely they are to fulfil their dreams.

8 Choose the word or phrase that best completes the sentence.

1 This time next week we _____ in Paris.
A 'll sightsee   B 'll be sightseeing   C sightsee   D 're sightseeing

2 We haven't seen Peter for ages, so I think I _____ him later.
A 'll call   B going to call   C would call   D am calling

3 She's very talented. Not only _____ beautifully, but she also speaks four languages.
A does sing   B she sings   C does she sing   D sings she

4 _____ you hear about the job, give me a call.
A Until   B By the time   C As soon as   D While

5 'How was the snowkiting?' 'Fantastic! It's ages since I've had so _____ fun!'
A few   B many   C little   D much

6 We're only five minutes late for the match. We _____ much.
A won't have missed   B not miss   C will be missing   D aren't missing

7 'I've never been keen on boxing.' '_____'
A Neither do I.   B Neither I.   C So have I.   D Neither have I.

9 Choose the sentence, A, B, C or D, which is closest in meaning to the sentence given.

1 I will apply for the job if you help me with the application form.
   A I will not apply for the job if you don't help me with the application form.
   B I won't apply for the job even if you help me.
   C If you help me, I won't apply for the job.
   D You will help me if I apply for the job.

2 Martial arts can be as dangerous as boxing.
   A Martial arts are less dangerous than boxing.
   B Martial arts and boxing are equally dangerous.
   C Neither martial arts or boxing are dangerous.
   D Boxing is not as dangerous as martial arts.

3 He's such a good runner that I think he'll be a professional one day.
   A He runs so fast that he's almost a professional.
   B Only professionals can run better than he can.
   C He doesn't run well enough to become a professional.
   D Since he runs so well, it's possible he'll be a professional in the future.

4 Not only do I play rugby, but I also do athletics in my spare time.
   A Neither rugby nor athletics are my hobbies.
   B Both rugby and athletics are my hobbies.
   C I play rugby, but I prefer doing athletics.
   D I'd like to play rugby and do athletics in my free time.

5 Max isn't old enough to apply for the job.
   A Max is too old to apply for the job.
   B Max won't apply for the job when he's older.
   C Max is too young to apply for the job.
   D Max is the right age for the job.

6 The warmer the weather became, the more Julia enjoyed windsurfing.
   A Julia liked windsurfing more as the weather got warmer.
   B Julia only likes windsurfing in warm weather.
   C Julia didn't like windsurfing while it was cold.
   D Julia was less enthusiastic about windsurfing in hot weather.

10 Complete the second sentence so that it has a similar meaning to the first.

1 That match was so exciting that I want to see it again.
It was _____ .

2 Your tennis racquet is better than mine.
My tennis racquet _____ .

3 She failed the Maths test and the Science test.
Not only _____ .

4 The opening of the new shop is on Tuesday.
The new shop _____ .

5 They'll give Kate her present at the weekend.
Kate _____.

6 The weather forecasters predict rain at the weekend.
The weather forecasters say _____.

7 You will never find a better job than this!
This is _____!

8 We'll tidy up before you get home.
By the time _____.

11 Complete the text with the words and phrases from the box.

| By the time | such | As soon as | is going to be | quicker than |
| the more nervous | too much | as good as | enough | so many |

Emily is about to start her first job. ¹_____ she gets up, she takes a long, warm shower and tries to remember the names of the people she ²_____ working with. There are ³_____ of them that she knows she'll forget their names. She's never been ⁴_____ her friends at remembering things. ⁵_____ she goes down to the kitchen, her mum has prepared a special breakfast but there's ⁶_____ of it and Emily can't face it. The longer she looks at the food ⁷_____ she feels. After a quick coffee she decides to head to the bus stop. She'd like to walk, but there isn't ⁸_____ time. The bus journey is much ⁹_____ she thought it would be. When she arrives early at the office she's greeted warmly. Her nerves vanish as she realises it isn't ¹⁰_____ a terrifying place after all.

1 Complete the dialogues with the words from the box. There is one extra word.

> click   delete   download   insert   restart   upload

1 A: Something's wrong. The computer screen has frozen.
   B: Switch it off and _____ it. It should be OK afterwards.
2 A: Hey look! Free films and games.
   B: Don't _____ anything from that site. It's not legal.
3 A: How do I go to the home page on this website?
   B: _____ on the link on the left of the screen.
4 A: I can't wait to see my friends and show them my photos.
   B: Why don't you _____ your photos to the web, then your friends can see them now.
5 A: I don't need this file anymore.
   B: You can _____ it then.

2 Choose the word or phrase that best completes the sentence.

1 The cat jumped on my laptop and _____ the screen; I was furious!
   A spilled   B scratched   C ripped   D crushed
2 If your printer isn't working, first check that the _____ is connected to the computer.
   A file   B software   C cable   D drive
3 The laptop isn't working because the _____ is dead.
   A wireless   B battery   C glitch   D cable
4 Click on the _____ at the top of the page to go to the site you want.
   A link   B join   C connect   D copy
5 This program should protect your computer against _____ .
   A injuries   B diseases   C viruses   D illnesses
6 Danny went down on his knees and, presenting Imelda with a diamond ring, he _____ to her.
   A arranged   B attracted   C proposed   D engaged
7 Some of my old school friends are organising a _____ next week.
   A generation B sibling   C reunion   D relationship
8 Natalie's parents are _____ and will probably get divorced soon.
   A separated B connected C opposite   D engaged
9 I've got three _____; two brothers and a sister.
   A spouses   B siblings   C fiancées   D widowers
10 My mum's _____ name was Fisher.
   A modem   B main   C married   D maiden

3 Complete the sentences with the correct form of the words from the box. There is one extra word.

> child   favourite   free   hand   neighbour   relation

1 When we first moved here, this used to be a quiet, pleasant _____ .
2 I don't believe that Nicole's _____ with Joe will last long.
3 You give your children too much _____ . They need more rules.
4 There are only a _____ of people that I can really call friends.
5 I had a difficult _____ and did badly at school.

4 Read the text and choose the best answer (A, B, C or D) for each gap.

A bad day

I went to see my friend Jack today. We get on really well – that's to say, we did! Jack was using his computer when I arrived so we surfed the ¹_____ for a while and then I told him I could make his computer run faster. I'd ²_____ a copy of some free software I'd found onto a CD, so I inserted the ³_____ into the drive. A message came up on the screen, 'Before you ⁴_____ this programme, you should first back ⁵_____ all important files'. Jack looked worried but I told him it wasn't necessary. The computer started making some very strange noises – there was obviously ⁶_____ wrong. Suddenly, the screen went ⁷_____ .

'Never mind,' I said. 'I'll fix it.' I tried to restart the computer, but nothing happened. I told Jack that the problem was probably overheating and not my disk at all, so I ⁸_____ the computer apart to have a look and clean out the dust. Jack wanted me to ⁹_____ it all back together but, just at that moment, I dropped it. Bits of cable came out and Jack started shouting. His mum came into the room and told him ¹⁰_____ for making so much noise. I couldn't help laughing so he threw me ¹¹_____ . Now I don't know what to do.

Jack, if you're reading this (unlikely I know with a broken computer) – I'm sorry and I wish I could ¹²_____ the clock back to this morning.

1 A net	B page	C file	D screen		7 A blank	B out	C crash	D empty
2 A done	B had	C made	D sent		8 A put	B got	C turned	D took
3 A file	B disk	C icon	D cable		9 A put	B take	C make	D get
4 A make	B turn	C run	D find		10 A up	B off	C out	D over
5 A out	B to	C off	D up		11 A off	B in	C up	D out
6 A the	B some	C a	D something		12 A make	B reach	C send	D turn

5 Complete the second sentence so that it has a similar meaning to the first. Use the word in capitals.

1 I hope you will stay in contact when you move.
TOUCH
I hope you _____ when you move.

2 You have to be brave and ask Emily to dance.
PLUCK
You have to _____ to ask Emily to dance.

3 Tia and William have gone out together.
DATE
Tia isn't here. She's gone _____ William.

4 I want to put my past behind me and start again.
FRESH
I'm going to _____ and put my past behind me.

5 Ellen is having a lot of problems.
THROUGH
Ellen is _____ a difficult time.

6 Do you have a good relationship with your older brother?
GET
Do you _____ your older brother?

7 With social networking sites, there's no reason to stop communicating with friends.
LOSE
You don't have to _____ friends nowadays because of social networking sites.

8 Don't sound too anxious – pretend you aren't interested.
HARD
Don't sound too anxious – _____ get!

6 Complete the responses with the correct phrases from the box. The function of each response is given.

> If only   had   I'll do   was able   must have   needn't have

1 A: Someone will have to phone Mia about the rehearsal.
   B: _____ that if you give me Mia's number.   OFFER

2 A: We're going to miss the train.
   B: _____ we'd got up earlier.   REGRET

3 A: There's no-one in the house.
   B: They _____ left a message somewhere.   DEDUCTION ABOUT THE PAST

4 A: We'll have to walk home; the last bus has gone.
   B: I wish we _____ a car.   PRESENT WISH

5 A: Did you break your leg while skiing?
   B: Yes. Luckily, I _____ to get to the hospital fast.   ABILITY

6 A: I checked your hard drive for viruses.
   B: You _____ done that. The computer is brand new.   LACK OF NECESSITY

7 One of the four underlined words is incorrect. Decide which one it is and write the correct form of the word.

1 There won't be a school trip to the mountains unless the rain stopped.
   _____

2 If only I didn't downloaded that game from the Internet last week, my computer would be OK now.
   _____

3 Something must had happened to Ula and Fran for them to be this late.
   _____

4 It was very kind of you but you needn't have spend so much time fixing my computer.
   _____

5 Provided the computer crashes while I am working, what will I do?
   _____

8 Choose the word or phrase that best completes the sentence.

1 I bought a game on eBay and I _____ get it to work on my computer.
   A don't   B can't   C mustn't   D wasn't able

2 You _____ out something about digital cameras before you bought one.
   A should have found   B should find   C would have found   D would find

3 Some old computer games _____ only be used on Windows 95 or 98.
   A can   B must   C need   D could

4 If I _____ about the new shop, I wouldn't have bought my laptop online.
   A know   B would know   C had known   D knew

5 You won't _____ find a good coat for under £50.
   A can   B can't   C manage   D be able to

6 You _____ able to use your phone in Croatia, so take it with you.
   A can't be   B can be   C may be   D must have been

7 You _____ to ask Peter about your problem. He knows a lot about relationships.
   A ought   B must   C would   D should

8 If you _____ on the icon on the left, you can see my photos.
   A click   B will click   C would click   D would have clicked

9 I wish I _____ more confident.
   A am   B was   C would be   D could

10 I wish I _____ everyone about my party.
   A didn't tell   B wouldn't tell   C hadn't told   D wouldn't have told

9 Complete the second sentence so that it has a similar meaning to the first. Use one of the phrases in the box in each sentence.

> was able to / wasn't able to   can / can't   have to / don't have to   might / might not   must / mustn't

1 It's not necessary for you to phone every five minutes.
(You / phone) _____ every five minutes.

2 I'm sure Toni has found her phone by now.
(Toni / found) _____ by now.

3 It's not possible that Erin failed her Maths exam.
(Erin / failed) _____ her Maths exam.

4 Do you think that Oliver managed to get a ticket for the match?
Do you think (Oliver / get) _____ a ticket for the match?

5 It's possible that these footprints were made by a wolf.
(A wolf / made) _____ these footprints.

10 Choose the sentence, A, B, C or D, which is closest in meaning to the sentence given.

1 If you back up your files, you won't lose your work.
  A You won't lose your files unless you back up your work.
  B As long as you back up your files, you will lose your work.
  C You might lose your work if you don't back up your files.
  D Provided that you back up your work, you will lose your files.

2 The only reason I know the answers is because I found a really useful website last night.
  A If I hadn't known the answers, I wouldn't have found the website.
  B I won't know the answers unless I find a good website.
  C I would have known the answers if I had found the website.
  D If I hadn't found the website, I wouldn't have known the answers.

3 I'm sure it's impossible that aliens visited the Earth in the past.
  A Aliens can't have visited the Earth.
  B It isn't necessary for aliens to visit the Earth.
  C Aliens didn't have to visit the Earth.
  D Aliens weren't able to visit the Earth.

4 Birgit didn't manage to upload her photos.
  A Birgit can't have uploaded her photos.
  B Birgit wasn't allowed to upload her photos.
  C Birgit wasn't able to upload her photos.
  D Birgit didn't have to upload her photos.

5 I'll copy this CD for you as long as you give me a blank CD.
  A I'll copy this CD for you unless you give me a blank CD.
  B If you had given me a blank CD, I would have copied the CD for you.
  C I'd copy this CD for you if I had a blank CD.
  D I won't copy this CD for you unless you give me a blank CD.

11 Read the article about regrets and think of the word which best fits each space. Use only one word in each space.

➡ TIME.............

TURNING BACK

People often ask themselves how their lives might have been different if they [1]_____ made different choices or done things differently. However, as [2]_____ as we don't make any really big mistakes, our decisions [3]_____ probably cause only minor changes.

For the rich and famous, each decision can make a huge difference to their lives. Take Molly Ringwald, for example. She was a big star in the 1980s with films like *Sixteen Candles* and *Pretty in Pink*. In 1990, she was offered the lead role in a new film called *Pretty Woman*. She turned it down. At the time, she was [4]_____ to choose exactly the parts she wanted. She didn't have [5]_____ take roles she didn't like. She was a star. But not for long ... If [6]_____ she could turn the clock back and change her mind.

In the end, an unknown actress called Julia Roberts got the part instead. The film was a huge success and the rest, as they say, is history. [7]_____ we could change history – what differences would we see? [8]_____ Molly Ringwald be as famous as Julia Roberts is today [9]_____ she had taken the part? Would Julia Roberts still [10]_____ unknown? Perhaps the film wouldn't have [11]_____ so successful. We will never know [12]_____ someone invents a time machine!

1 Choose the word or phrase that best completes the sentence.

1 The bathroom flooded when a pipe started _____ .
   A colliding   B starving   C leaking   D erupting

2 James was disappointed when he _____ his friends discussing his surprise party.
   A overheard   B eavesdropped   C glanced   D displayed

3 Removing the waste oil from the ocean will be a difficult and _____ process that could take months.
   A time-consuming   B virtual   C simultaneous   D rural

4 The football manager refused to _____ on the poor performance of the team.
   A display   B comment   C behave   D interact

5 If the workers decide to go on strike, it will _____ the factory's production output.
   A starve   B dump   C suffer   D paralyse

6 After years of _____ , farmers were unable to grow their own food and many people left in search of better land.
   A waste   B tremors   C heatwave   D drought

7 'Shall we go to that new restaurant in town?' 'I'm not sure. It hasn't had very good _____ in the local newspaper.'
   A classifieds   B editorials   C reviews   D columns

8 Don't throw away the receipt for your phone in case there's a problem with it. Yes, _____ .
   A better safe than sorry   B touch wood   C break a leg   D keep your fingers crossed

2 Complete the sentences with the correct form of the verbs from the box.

> collide   starve   spot   glance   browse   blush   suffer   erupt   dump   eavesdrop

1 Adam was jealous of his girlfriend and started _____ on her conversations.
2 We were having a coffee in that trendy new café when we _____ Daniel Craig from the James Bond film.
3 If it doesn't rain soon, people in the village _____ because they can't grow enough food.
4 When the volcano _____ , thousands of people will have to leave their homes.
5 The two racing cars _____ as they were going around the corner of the track.
6 'Would you like to try those dresses on?' 'No thanks, I'm just _____ !'
7 The children _____ in this heat; we should never have brought them to such a hot place.
8 We shouldn't _____ our waste in the sea. Pollution is killing the fish.
9 'What's happening in the news?' 'I'm not sure. I only had time to _____ at the newspaper this morning.'
10 Melissa felt embarrassed speaking to the whole class and found it difficult not to _____ .

3 Complete the sentences with the correct form of the words from the box. There is one extra word.

> tremor   seed   business   urban   preference   acid   editorial   issue   oyster

1 I don't care what you think. Sometimes I wish you would mind your own _____ .
2 James has always been interested in green _____ because he's a farmer and wants to produce food without harming the natural environment.
3 We were lying in bed when we felt the first _____ . It was as though the whole house was shaking.
4 Finding a way to reduce _____ rain is a national worry. We must recycle as much as we can.
5 Did you read the _____ in the local newspaper? I thought it was an interesting view of the economic crisis.
6 Although it seems incredible, foxes can survive in an _____ environment, living on rubbish from bins and walking the quiet streets at night.
7 Speaking three languages you could work anywhere you want. The world's your _____ .
8 If you're really interested in eating healthy food you should get some _____ and grow your own vegetables.

4 Read the text and choose the best answer (A, B, C or D) for each gap.

Vital means of communication

More advanced methods of communication have changed the way that we [1]_____ with each other and the world. In the developed world we are all aware of the advantages of [2]_____ in touch by texting, phoning, email and [3]_____ , which allows [4]_____ chats with multiple friends. Indeed, most of us would argue that we simply can't do [5]_____ our phone or laptop. But recent events of a catastrophic nature have shown that mobile phones and radios have become vital in developing countries. On 12 January, 2010, a massive earthquake occurred in Haiti at a [6]_____ of 8.1 miles. Approximately 200,000 people died and many roads and houses were destroyed. Only twelve days later, an emergency information service offered free text messages that would allow people to [7]_____ down missing relatives and seek advice on housing and food problems. Injured people were directed via text messages to the nearest hospital where they would have access [8]_____ medical care. Those without phones were advised to [9]_____ in to the local radio station for important news announcements. Survivors say that without such communication there would have been much greater [10]_____ of life.

1	A interact	B comment	C display	D overhear
2	A calling	B staying	C losing	D having
3	A advertising	B snail mail	C chain email	D instant messaging
4	A freak	B face-to-face	C immense	D simultaneous
5	A out of	B away	C without	D with
6	A depth	B length	C strength	D width
7	A track	B cut	C slow	D find
8	A in	B of	C to	D for
9	A move	B turn	C crash	D tune
10	A threat	B loss	C leak	D hazard

5 Complete the text with the correct form of the words in capitals.

New forecasting system could save lives

Weather forecasters are often criticised for their [1]_____ predictions that fail to prepare us for extreme weather. But, a team of specialists in [2]_____ have recently developed a system which it is hoped will be [3]_____ , but extremely efficient. They have designed sensors that can be positioned at a [4]_____ of seventy metres in ice. The sensors can record any change in temperature or movement of water over a period of time. If there is no movement for a certain [5]_____ of time, the sensors 'go to sleep' to save power. Once the [6]_____ of a reading increases, one of the sensors 'wakes' the other sensors up! Scientists are trying to convince environmental companies of the [7]_____ of these sensors for predicting floods and landslides and other events. They believe the [8]_____ that the sensors obtain could help us prepare for the destruction that is being caused by climate change.

RELY

ENGINEER
ECONOMY

DEEP

LONG
STRONG

CONVENIENT
MEASURE

6 Complete the second sentence so that it has a similar meaning to the first. Use the word in capitals.

1 The teacher won't let the students leave without finishing the exercise.
ALLOWED
The students _____ leave without finishing the exercise.

2 'Don't drop paper on the floor, Thomas!' said Mr Gilbert.
NOT
Mr Gilbert _____ drop paper on the floor.

3 'Why are you waiting here?' he asked me.
ME
He _____ waiting there.

4 'Will they be at the party?' John asked Laura.
IF
John asked Laura _____ at the party.

5 My mobile phone was stolen from my bag.
HAD
I _____ from my bag.

6 'What can we do to save the planet?' the students asked.
THEY
The students asked _____ to save the planet.

7 'When will they give you your results?' her parents asked.
GIVEN
Her parents asked when she _____ results.

8 They say the film was set in this town.
SAID
The film _____ set in this town.

9 The shop hasn't got any bread left.
RUN
The shop _____ bread.

10 'Why don't we go to the park this afternoon?' said Jane.
THEY
Jane suggested _____ to the park that afternoon.

7 Choose the word or phrase that best completes the sentence.

1 Patrick asked us _____ ready to go.
A that we were   B if we be   C if were we   D whether we were

2 The boy denied that _____ the laptop.
A he had taken   B he took   C he didn't take   D he was taken

3 Since the storm a lot of the old houses _____ .
A have repaired   B were being repaired   C have been repaired   D are repaired

4 Anna wanted to know _____ with her book.
A if I had finished   B if I finished   C did I finish   D if I had been finish

5 We _____ up by a strange noise on the balcony.
A were waking   B were woken   C had woken   D woke

6 The customers were so rude that the waitress _____ the restaurant.
A said that they leave   B told to leave   C said that they left   D told them to leave

7 James's hair grows very quickly. He has to _____ regularly.
A have it cut   B have cut   C be cut   D cut

8 The students will _____ by their good results in the test.
A encourage   B been encouraged   C be encouraged   D being encouraged

9 Different forms of solar energy _____ by humans since ancient times.
A had used   B has been used   C have been used   D were used

10 The government says that new methods for predicting climate change _____ next year.
A will be introduced   B will introduce   C are introduced   D introduce

8 Read the article about the 2004 tsunami and think of the word which best fits each space. Use only one word in each space.

Boxing Day Tsunami

On 26 December 2004, tourists and the inhabitants of Sumatra, Indonesia, [1]_____ taken completely by surprise when a thirty metre high wave crashed over the coast, wiping [2]_____ anything that was in its path. Scientists at the time said that it had [3]_____ one of the worst natural disasters in recorded history. A tsunami or giant tidal wave is caused [4]_____ moving tectonic plates that collide under the Earth's surface. More than 230,000 people from fourteen countries were killed and thousands [5]_____ their homes destroyed. Headlines around the world attracted a humanitarian response and more than seven billion dollars [6]_____ donated in aid. Most survivors said the day [7]_____ started just like any other day with no sign of what was to come, apart from one ten-year-old girl, who told reporters [8]_____ she had been having a ride on an elephant shortly before the tsunami struck. She said that after a short time, the elephant had begun to appear nervous and its owner [9]_____ her that she [10]_____ have to come back the next day. The owner was convinced that his elephant [11]_____ sense something and insisted they [12]_____ the beach straightaway.

9 Complete the second sentence so that it has a similar meaning to the first.

1 'Shall I do the exercise in this book?' she asked.
   She asked _____ .

2 'I won't speak to you again if you leave now!' Emma said to Adam.
   Emma threatened _____ .

3 My room is being painted today.
   I'm _____ .

4 'How much money did your parents give you, Maria?' asked Alex.
   Alex wanted to know _____ .

5 Careless driving caused this accident.
   This accident _____ .

6 'I promise I'll bring you your book tomorrow.'
   She promised _____ .

7 Nobody had seen her for three years.
   She hadn't _____ .

8 'You must email us while you're away.'
   They insisted _____ .

10 Choose the sentence, A, B, C or D, which is closest in meaning to the sentence given.

1 Julia reminded her friends that they had forgotten her birthday.
   A Julia's friends didn't have to be reminded it was her birthday.
   B Julia's friends remembered her birthday, but she forgot it.
   C Julia's friends wouldn't have remembered her birthday if she hadn't told them.
   D Julia's friends remembered that it was Julia's birthday.

2 The boys promised to bring some food if they were invited to the party.
   A If they were asked to the party, the boys said they would definitely bring food.
   B The boys said they would go to the party if there was food.
   C The boys wanted to invite people to bring food to the party.
   D The boys weren't sure if they should take food to the party.

3 Tyler spent ages having his hair coloured.
   A It didn't take long for Tyler to change the colour of his hair.
   B Another person coloured Tyler's hair and it took a long time.
   C Tyler coloured his hair very slowly.
   D Another person helped Tyler to colour his hair.

4 Lauren suggested her friends visited after she had eaten dinner.
   A Lauren didn't call her friends until she had eaten.
   B Lauren thought it was a good idea to eat before her friends visited.
   C Lauren suggested she ate after her friends visited.
   D Lauren wanted to eat with her friends.

5 Tom hated being made to wear smart clothes.
   A Tom didn't like having smart clothes made for him.
   B Tom hated not being allowed to wear smart clothes.
   C Tom had to wear smart clothes, which he hated.
   D Tom didn't like making smart clothes.

1 Complete the second sentence so that it has a similar meaning to the first. Use the word in capitals.

1 I'm afraid all our World Cup T-shirts have been sold.
OUT
I'm afraid we've _____ World Cup T-shirts.

2 There was no film when we flew from London to New York.
IN-FLIGHT
There wasn't _____ during our journey from London to New York.

3 We have to pay for the hotel before we arrive.
IN
We have to pay for the hotel _____ .

4 If there's any problem at all, we'll refund your money.
BE
You'll _____ there's any problem at all.

5 It's not necessary to wear smart clothes for the party – it's quite informal.
DRESS
You don't need _____ for the party – it's quite informal.

6 Just complete this form, please.
IN
Please can you _____ form?

7 We were too late to get any bargains in the shop.
OUT
We _____ all the bargains in the shop.

8 I'll see if we have any size 40 shoes.
STOCK
I'll see if there are any _____ .

9 Can we buy a ticket which allows us to choose when we come back?
OPEN
Can we buy _____ ticket?

10 Can we fly from London to Perth without changing planes?
FLIGHTS
Are there any _____ London to Perth?

2 Complete the text with the correct form of the words in capitals.

Celebrities turn out to see or to be seen?

A celebrity-packed audience turned out for an unusual fashion show last night. Instead of the usual [1]_____ female models wobbling along on the catwalk or [2]_____ males, we saw normal, healthy, even slightly [3]_____ models, who obviously enjoyed their food as much as their work. In place of [4]_____ clothes that normal people could never afford, we saw some [5]_____ bargains. Another difference from usual fashion designs was that the [6]_____ we saw today were not only the height of fashion, but also have almost unlimited [7]_____ as they are factory made rather than individually put together. So, what were all these celebrities doing looking at [8]_____ clothes, normally worn by men and girls-next-door with [9]_____ cheeks and natural smiles? Has show business gone [10]_____ at last?

SKIN
MUSCLE
WEIGHT

EXPENSE
BEAT
CREATE

AVAILABLE

AFFORD
ROSE
FUNK

3 Read the text and choose the best answer (A, B, C or D) for each gap.

Online clothes shopping

Is there any area of life that the Internet can't reach? While we search the Net for ¹_____ in CDs, computers and holidays, surely the joy of clothes shopping is to actually go to the shop and ²_____ the perfect dress, shirt, shoes or a complete ³_____; to feel it, try it on and make sure it ⁴_____. We can also ensure that the clothes we buy ⁵_____ us – that's what mirrors are for in changing rooms after all! If we're buying more than one item, we need to be sure that the pieces ⁶_____ each other and can be worn together. None of this is possible online, not even with the best virtual changing room software. ⁷_____ all this, clothes shopping is just fun!

However, all the high street ⁸_____ now have their own websites. Even ⁹_____ shops such as Oxfam or Cancer Research offer second-hand clothes online. All their clothes can be returned within twenty-one days and your money will be ¹⁰_____. But isn't it ¹¹_____ to wait for something in the post only to find that it's the wrong size? No more so than driving to a busy shopping centre, being ¹²_____ in traffic jams and searching for hours for a parking space.

1	A fares	B budgets	C reservations	D bargains
2	A pick out	B dress up	C show off	D pull up
3	A base	B match	C outfit	D showcase
4	A fits	B matches	C suits	D works
5	A like	B suit	C match	D dress
6	A match	B fit	C go	D look
7	A In addition	B Besides	C As well	D Apart
8	A terminals	B vouchers	C volunteers	D retailers
9	A volunteer	B retail	C charity	D vintage
10	A refunded	B insured	C reserved	D confirmed
11	A flexible	B infuriating	C towering	D convenient
12	A pulled up	B held up	C snapped up	D picked out

4 Complete the sentences with the correct form of the words from the box. There is one extra word.

> accompany   announce   bald   change   ethics   sleeve   spot   voluntary

1 My dad is definitely _____ , but he is very proud of the hair that he's still got!
2 The thief had bad skin – I mean he was quite _____ .
3 We need three _____ to help in our charity shop at weekends.
4 We only sell _____ products in our shop.
5 Did you hear the _____ ? The shop is about to close.
6 Only two _____ children are allowed in the shop at one time.
7 I prefer T-shirts to _____ shirts. I don't like my shoulders to be uncovered.

5 Complete the dialogues with the words from the box. There is one extra word.

> middle   oval   spree   hooded   vintage   voucher

1 A: Have you heard that the local shopping centre has banned teenagers from wearing _____ tops?
   B: Really? That's not fair.
2 A: What's your favourite kind of car?
   B: A _____ Rolls Royce Silver Shadow from 1934.
3 A: Malcolm's got a very round face.
   B: Yes, but his sister's is _____ .
4 A: My dad's forty-three but he won't admit that he's _____-aged.
   B: Well, he still looks young.
5 A: Why do you shop here?
   B: They give you a £10 _____ for every £100 you spend.

6 Complete the second sentence so that it has a similar meaning to the first. Use the word in capitals.

1 I'd rather not travel by plane.
PREFER
I'd _____ by plane.

2 Are you allowed to go out on dates?
LET
Do your parents _____ on dates?

3 What tasks do you have to do in your job at the boutique?
MADE
What tasks _____ do in your job at the boutique?

4 We should start to clean up now.
BETTER
We _____ clean up now.

5 There are only a few tickets left.
MANY
There _____ left.

6 The bargains I saw were on this website.
WHERE
This is the _____ the bargains.

7 Would you prefer to have pizza or pasta?
RATHER
What _____ , pizza or pasta?

8 Does your teacher let you talk during exams?
TO
Are you _____ during exams?

9 Is your dad forced to buy new clothes by your mum?
MAKE
_____ your dad buy new clothes?

10 If you want to lose weight, eat fewer sweets.
HAD
You _____ sweets if you want to lose weight.

7 Complete the conversation with the correct form of the verbs in brackets.

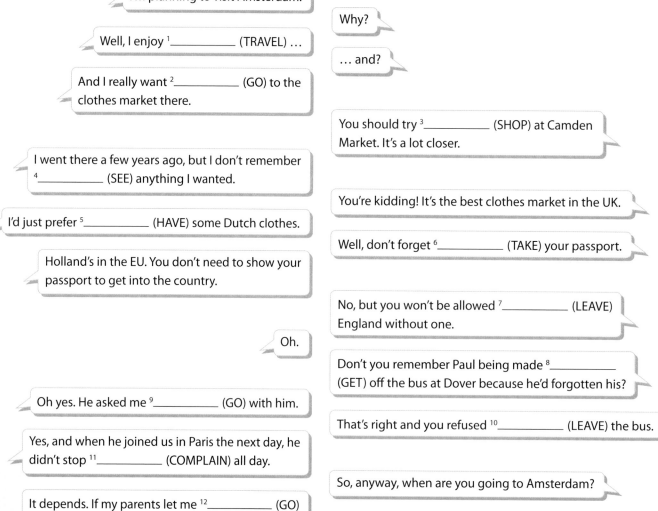

I'm planning to visit Amsterdam.

Why?

Well, I enjoy ¹_____ (TRAVEL) …

… and?

And I really want ²_____ (GO) to the clothes market there.

You should try ³_____ (SHOP) at Camden Market. It's a lot closer.

I went there a few years ago, but I don't remember ⁴_____ (SEE) anything I wanted.

You're kidding! It's the best clothes market in the UK.

I'd just prefer ⁵_____ (HAVE) some Dutch clothes.

Well, don't forget ⁶_____ (TAKE) your passport.

Holland's in the EU. You don't need to show your passport to get into the country.

No, but you won't be allowed ⁷_____ (LEAVE) England without one.

Oh.

Don't you remember Paul being made ⁸_____ (GET) off the bus at Dover because he'd forgotten his?

Oh yes. He asked me ⁹_____ (GO) with him.

That's right and you refused ¹⁰_____ (LEAVE) the bus.

Yes, and when he joined us in Paris the next day, he didn't stop ¹¹_____ (COMPLAIN) all day.

So, anyway, when are you going to Amsterdam?

It depends. If my parents let me ¹²_____ (GO) on my own, I'll go at half term. Hey, do you want to come too?

8 **Choose the word that best completes the sentence.**

1 There was no-one at the check-in desk when we arrived, _____ I thought was strange.
   A which   B what   C that   D who

2 From _____ did you hear about our website?
   A who   B whom   C which   D what

3 These are the shoes _____ I was telling you about.
   A what   B that   C who   D when

4 Is that the company _____ website is so infuriating?
   A whom   B which the   C whose   D who

5 I think we should stop here _____ at the map.
   A looking   B look   C to look   D looked

6 How late do your parents _____ you stay out?
   A allow   B make   C force   D let

7 Don't you think we _____ better take some sun cream?
   A should   B had   C would   D did

8 We're staying in _____ elegant hotel I was telling you about.
   A a   B an   C the   D –

9 It's only a small resort but there's _____ to do in the daytime and at night.
   A every   B lot   C many   D plenty

10 What would you _____ do this winter; go skiing or visit Egypt?
   A like   B prefer   C rather   D want

9 **Complete the sentences with the correct form of the verbs from the box. There is one extra verb.**

check in   confirm   lose   pay   take off   worry

1 At the airport, they made us _____ our shoes.
2 You'd better _____ weight if you want to wear that dress again.
3 Most airlines allow you _____ online now.
4 Would you like _____ in advance or when you arrive?
5 Stop _____ about your work and relax.

10 **Read the article about school rules and think of the word which best fits each space. Use only one word in each space.**

Why do schools hate fashion?

My dad told me that, at his school, the headmaster didn't ¹_____ them have long hair. A ²_____ years later, when punk was popular, they weren't allowed ³_____ have short, spiky hair.

School rules are always a bit confusing. At my school, the boys have to be clean-shaven and the teacher ⁴_____ them go home if they aren't. At my cousin's school, the older boys are ⁵_____ to look how they want and some of them have beards and moustaches.

At our school, we have a uniform until we are sixteen, after ⁶_____ we can wear whatever we like. Well, not exactly. Our head teacher, ⁷_____ clothes are always very elegant, hates scruffy jeans and old T-shirts. If your jeans are too faded or baggy, you ⁸_____ better be careful as you could be sent home to change.

I remember ⁹_____ sent home when I was fifteen because I was wearing make-up. The head sent my parents ¹⁰_____ letter telling them not to let me come to school like that again. All ¹¹_____ my friends have had notes like that too. It really infuriates us because we're not badly behaved children ¹²_____ cause problems, we're hard-working, polite students who like to express our personality through our appearance.

Word List

Unit 1

Personality and feelings

affectionate	grateful
anxious	grumpy
cautious	impatient
competitive	loyal
conduct	reward (v)
emotion	sceptical
enthusiastic	sensitive
excited	sociable
express	stressed

Words from the reading text

bark	insist
debated	issue
fed up	numerous

Word formation: words from the text

behave – behaviour
deep – depth
enthusiastic – enthusiasm
lonely – loneliness
prove – proof
research – researchers
sad – sadness
science – scientists

Word formation: nouns from adjectives

bored – boredom	honest – honesty
creative – creativity	impatient – impatience
excited – excitement	lonely – loneliness
frustrated – frustration	loyal – loyalty

Negative prefixes

disloyal	indecisive
illogical	unaware
immature	ungrateful
incapable	

Accidents and health

be in good health	have a bruise
be injured	have a bump (on your head)
be stung (by a bee)	have a rash
collapse	have a swollen (thumb)
have a black eye	trip over

Phrasal verbs

black out	get through
cheer up	go off
come to	turn to

Unit 2

Entertainment

album	programme
audition	record (v)
cast	release
channel	role
charts	series
episode	single
hit	track
lyrics	tune
on stage	

Words from the reading texts

anti-bullying campaign	debut
celebrity	heartthrob
columnist	superstar
convince	target
decade	

Word formation: words from the texts

comedy – comedian
criticise – criticism
fail – failure
famous – fame
influence – influential
make – remake
novel – novelist
success – successful

Art

exhibition	performance artist
gallery	portrait
landscape	sculptor
oils	watercolours

Adjectives ending in -ed and -ing

amazed – amazing	excited – exciting
disappointed – disappointing	exhausted – exhausting

Phrasal verbs

bring back	look back on
come across	settle for
come out	stick to
end up	turn down
lead to	

Prepositions + nouns

at the box office	on canvas
at the end	on location
in chapter (three)	on page (one)
in print	on stage
in the role of	(paint) in oils
on a TV channel	

Collocations

face an audience	get a part (in a play)
fail an audition	reach Number One in the charts
forget my lines	record an album
form a band	release an album

Word formation: nouns from verbs

appear – appearance	perform – performance
compete – competition	produce – producer
compose – composition	publish – publication
conduct – conductor	rehearse – rehearsal
entertain – entertainment	sculpt – sculpture
exhibit – exhibition	

Unit 3

Jobs and work

annual bonus	make-up artist
architect	negotiable
career	newsreader
discount	office
fitness instructor	overtime
flexible hours	paid holiday
form	paramedic
full-time	salary
interview	staff
label	working environment
lorry driver	

Words from the reading texts

catering	haulage
checkout	medical insurance
customer	nutrition
CV	proven
generous	qualified

Word formation: words from the texts

apply – application
fit – fitness
flexible – flexibility
free – freedom
play – player
qualify – qualifications
recruit – recruitment
responsible – responsibility
satisfy – satisfaction
succeed – successful

Work

comedian	plumber
journalist	surgeon

Compound nouns

estate agent	make-up artist
firefighter	sales assistant
fitness instructor	social worker
lorry driver	traffic warden

Workplaces

advertising agency	family business
clinic	fire station
company	garage
department store	head office
estate agency	warehouse
factory	

Education

degree	qualifications
experience	revise
graduate	training
passed	

Collocations

apply online	have mechanical knowledge
attend an interview	manage a team
be a team player	send your CV

Phrasal verbs

come up with	take on
count on	take over
deal with	turn out
keep up with	work out

Unit 4

Activities, equipment and dangers

bruise (v)	roll
bungee jumping	ski lift
face guard	ski run
goal	slope
helmet	snowboarding
hockey stick	snowkiting
ironing	spectator
kit	thrill-seeker
ledge	twist
off-piste	vacuuming

Words from the reading text

adrenaline junkie	require
excessive	somersault
housework	steep
participate	

Word formation: words from the text

active – activity
athlete – athletic
compete – competition
contest – contestant
excess – excessive
fashion – fashionable
participate – participants
tradition – traditional

Sports and equipment

athletics	martial arts
baseball	net
bat	pads
board	painting
boxing	racquet
cards	rugby
club	shuttlecock
cricket	snowboarding
golf	snowkiting
gymnastics	surfing
hockey	wakeboarding
ice-hockey	wetsuit
jogging	windsurfing

Verbs for sports

do – athletics, martial arts
go – jogging, snowboarding, snowkiting, surfing
play – cards, rugby

Phrasal verbs

call off	send off
catch up with	slow down
get through to	speed up
keep up with	take up

Word formation: adjective prefixes

confident – overconfident
experienced – inexperienced
legal – illegal
national – international
paid – overpaid / underpaid
qualified – disqualified / overqualified / underqualified
rational – irrational
standard – substandard

Unit 5

Computers

bug	glitch
cable	hardware
concerned	key in
connect	keyboard
convince	mouse
crash	post
damage	protect
database	query
delete	save
download	software
file	troubleshooter

Words from the reading texts

command	intervention
concern	media
cool off	reward
deposit	soak

Word formation: words from the texts

assign – assignment
fail – failure
imply – implication
print – printer
respond – response
solve – solution
technical – technicians
unfortunate – unfortunately

Computer equipment

battery	netbook
disk	screen
hard drive	wireless
modem	

Verbs related to computers

click on	put (sth) together
back up	restart
burn (a CD)	run (a program)
insert (in the disk drive)	surf
log off	take (sth) apart
log on	unplug
lose (files)	wipe off

Minor disasters

be destroyed by a virus	not work properly
crack	overheat
crash	rip
crush	scratch
drop	spill
go blank	there is something wrong
make a funny noise	with it

Friends, family and relationships

anniversary	play hard to get
blind date	pluck up (the) courage
divorced	propose
engaged	regret
generation gap	relationship
go on a date	reunion
go through (a difficult time)	separated
keep in touch (with)	tongue-tied
lose touch (with)	turn the clock back
make a fresh start	twins
opposites attract	

Words from the reading text

bombard	ignore
chatty	lacking in
come up	prevent
disastrous	tactics

Word formation: words from the text

believe – unbelievable
disaster – disastrous
engage – engagement
enjoy – enjoyable
fool – foolish
free – freedom
mature – immature
rude – rudeness
separate – inseparable
shy – shyness

Family and friends

bachelor	mother-in-law
close friend	online friend
ex-boyfriend	roommate
ex-girlfriend	sibling
father-in-law	spouse
fiancé	widow
fiancée	widower
in-laws	

Collocations

arranged marriage	generation gap
black sheep	maiden name
double date	opposite sex
fresh start	

Phrasal verbs

ask (sb) out	stay out
get on (well) with	stay up
move out	tell (sb) off
split up	throw (sb) out

Word formation: noun suffixes

bachelor – bachelorhood	hand – handful
bore – boredom	neighbour – neighbourhood
child – childhood	optimist – optimism
favourite – favouritism	relation – relationship
free – freedom	sex – sexism
friend – friendship	

Unit 7

Staying in touch

blush	mobile phone
browse	networking
chain email	overhear
comment	podcast
display	satellite TV
eavesdrop	simultaneous
face-to-face	snail mail
instant messaging	spam
interact	time-consuming
interactive whiteboard	unreliable
laptop	virtual

Words from the reading texts

accidentally	cringe
awkwardness	obsession
buzz (n)	publicity
convenience	refuse

Word formation: words from the text

appeal – appeal
arrange – arrangement
awkward – awkwardness
convenient – convenience
disappoint – disappointment
express – expression
obsess – obsession
prefer – preference
process – process
strange – strangers

Communication and language

avoid eye contact	master a language
have contacts	mind your own business
keep/stay in touch	speak/talk face-to-face
lose touch with	speak your mind

The news

breaking news	obituaries
classifieds	reviews
columns	show business
editorial	weather forecast

Idioms

actions speak louder than words
be economical with the truth
get your wires crossed
it's like talking to a brick wall
keep sb posted
learn (sth) by heart

Phrasal verbs

brush up on	get together	track down
check out	make out	tune in to
flick through	pick up	

Unit 8

Natural disasters

ash	rural
collide	seed
drought	starve
dump	tidal wave
earthquake	toxic
erupt	tremor
garbage	tsunami
heatwave	urban
lava	volcano
leak	waste
meteorite	wipe out

Words from the reading text

extremes	paralyse
freak	spot (v)
have access to	suffer
immense	threat

Word formation: words from the text

crowd – overcrowded
dead – deadly
harm – harmlessly
hazard – hazardous
improve – improvements
lose – loss
mislead – misleading
volcano – volcanic

The weather

blizzard	overcast
foggy	pour down
frost	sleet
hail	smog
humid	

Adjective-noun collocations

acid rain
extreme weather
finite resources
fossil fuels
genetic modification / engineering
green issues
solar energy

Phrasal verbs

cut down on	run out of
die out	throw away
do without	use up
live on	

Idioms

Better safe than sorry.
Break a leg!
Don't count your chickens before they hatch.
Keep your fingers crossed.
The world's your oyster.
Touch wood.

Dependent prepositions

access to	pour down
collide with	threat of
crash into	turn into
invasion from	

Word formation: measurement

deep – depth – deepen
high – height – heighten
long – length – lengthen
strong – strength – strengthen
wide – width – widen

Fashion

baggy	of medium-height
bargain	outfit
catwalk	patterned
charity	retail
clean-shaven	round-shouldered
ethical	showcase
fair-haired	sleeveless
flared	tight-fitting
high-heeled	volunteer
hooded	well-built
middle-aged	

Words from the reading text

accessories	indulge yourself
bid (v)	investor
feature	makeover
high flyer	treat

Word formation: words from the text

accessorise – accessories
back – backing
create – creations
demonstrate – demonstrations
glamour – glamorous
retail – retailer
visit – visitors

Clothes

chic	lightweight
faded	retro
formal	scruffy
funky	vintage

Verbs

fit
match
suit

Describing appearance

a brunette	overweight
an oval face	pale
balding	rosy cheeks
braces	skinny
bushy eyebrows	spotty
dark-skinned	tanned
fair-haired	thick hair
freckly	toned
muscly	wrinkles

Consumerism

a refund	retail therapy
demand outstripped supply	shopping spree
in stock	unbeatable deals
launch	voucher

Phrasal verbs

dress up	sell out (of sth)
miss out on (sth)	show (sth) off
pick (sth) out	snap (sth) up

Unit 10

Landscape and travel

base	lagoon
bay	mainland
besides	navigate
breeze	pebble
budget	plunge (v)
check-in	priority
cliffs	surcharge
emerge	terminal
fee	tower
hike	whizz
infuriate	

Words from the reading text

boarding	gorgeous
convinced	snore
drawback	stunning
giggle	to and fro

Word formation: words from the text

anxious – anxiously
check – recheck
drowsy – drowsiness
navigate – navigation
obsession – obsessed
sleep – sleepily
technology – technophobe
trust – trusty

Travel arrangements

aisle	fares
confirm	insurance
e-tickets	reservation

Landscape

bay	moor
cliff	orchard
gorge	strait
headland	summit
lagoon	tide

Collocations

aisle seat	flexible fare
connecting flight	open return
direct flight	priority boarding

Phrasal verbs

be held up	pull up
fill in	take (time) off
get away	turn back
print out	

Prepositional phrases

below deck	off-peak
en route	on board
in advance	on deck
in-flight	

Word formation

accompany – companion / (un)accompanied
afford – affordable
announce – announcement
available – availability
(in)convenient – convenience
expense – expensive
refund – refund / (non-) refundable
reserve – reservation

Grammar File

Unit 1
Present tenses

Form	Use	Example
Present simple I play He/She plays Do you play? Does he/she play? He/She doesn't play They don't play **Passive:** It is played	• permanent situations • general truths • regular actions • timetables (future) • in stories / reviews	*They **come** from London.* *Water **boils** at 100° Celsius.* *I **play** tennis on Fridays.* *The plane **leaves** at nine o'clock.* *The film **begins** in a forest …*
Present continuous I am singing He/She's singing We're singing Are you singing? Is he/she singing? I'm not singing He/She isn't singing They aren't singing **Passive:** It is being sung	• actions happening now • temporary situations • future arrangements • annoying habits	*The boys **are playing** football now.* *Dad **is travelling** abroad a lot this year.* ***Are** you **having** a party on Saturday?* *They**'re always arguing** about his homework!*
Present perfect simple I have seen He/She has seen Have you seen? Has he/she seen? He/She hasn't seen They haven't seen **Passive:** They have been seen	• actions completed at an unspecified time in the past • recently completed actions with a result in the present • situations that started in the past and have continued until now	*I**'ve travelled** by boat but I**'ve** never **travelled** by plane.* *I**'ve** just **had** a dance lesson and I feel exhausted!* *I**'ve been** friends with her since last year.*
Present perfect continuous I have been walking He/She has been walking Have you been walking? Has he/she been walking? He/She hasn't been walking We haven't been walking	• actions started in the past and continuing until now • actions started in the past that have ended recently but are still relevant in the present	*It**'s been snowing** heavily since last night.* *We**'ve been working** together on a project and now we're going to present it to the class.*
Present perfect tenses vs past simple	• to show the difference between an unspecified time and a known time in the past	*My dad **has visited** lots of different countries. In October, he **went** to Japan.*

Notes

1 Time phrases

- Commonly used with the present perfect:
  already, yet, just, ever, never, for, since, How long?

- Commonly used with the present perfect continuous:
  How long?, for, since, all morning/afternoon/day/week

2 *been / gone*

Remember the difference in the present perfect simple between *been* and *gone*.

*I've **been** to London.* (= I've visited London in the past, but I'm not there now.)

*She's **gone** to London.* (= She is visiting London and is there now.)

3 The present perfect simple is **not** used

- to narrate past events. We use the past simple for this.
  *We **walked** along the river and **had** a picnic.*
- to describe completed events in the past. We use the past simple.
  *I **saw** Max last night.*

4 Remember! The present perfect simple focuses on the **completion** of the action while the **present perfect continuous** focuses on the **continuation** of the action.

*I'**ve spoken** to Patricia about the party.* (= completed action – the conversation is finished)
*I'**ve been writing** letters all afternoon.* (= continuous activity – we don't know if the action is finished)

5 We do not use the present perfect continuous when we talk about how many of something.

*I'**ve** written five letters this morning.*
*She'**s phoned** twice since 2 o'clock.*

Stative verbs

feelings	dislike, hate, like, love, trust
thinking / believing	agree, believe, doubt, expect, find (= think, feel), guess, imagine, know, realise, remember, suppose, think, understand
wants	hope, need, prefer, want, wish
senses (often used with can)	feel, hear, see, smell, sound, taste
being / having	appear, belong to, contain, depend, have, include, look (= seem), owe, own, possess, represent, seem, tend
measurements / cost	cost, fit, measure, weigh

Notes

1 Some stative verbs are also used in the present continuous to describe actions. There is a change of meaning.

*I **think** she's really nice.* (= have an opinion)
*I'**m thinking** about the test tomorrow.* (= considering)

***Do** you **see** that boat over there?* (= ability to see something)
*We'**re seeing** our friends next weekend.* (= meeting)

*I **have** some good DVDs.* (= own)
*I'**m having** pizza with my friends tonight.* (= eating)

2 Some stative verbs mean the same whether they are in the simple or the continuous tense.

*You'**re looking** tired. Have a rest.*
*You **look** tired. Have a rest.*

***Are** you **feeling** unwell?*
***Do** you **feel** unwell?*

3 Confusing verbs

- ***See** and **hear** are stative verbs and are often used with **can.***
  *I **can see** you.*
  *I **can't hear** the TV.*
- ***Listen** and **look** describe actions.*
  *Yes, I'**m listening** to you.*
  *You'**re looking** well.*

157

Unit 2
Past tenses

Form	Use	Example
Past simple I played He/She played Did you play? Did he/she play? He/She didn't play They didn't play **Passive:** It was played	• finished actions in the past • repeated actions in the past • past habits • past situations or states	*He **got** in the car and **drove** off.* *We **went** swimming every day.* *I always **got up** at seven o'clock.* ***Did** you **live** in France when you **were** younger?*
Past continuous I was singing He/She was singing We were singing Were you singing? Was he/she singing? I wasn't singing They weren't singing **Passive:** It was being sung	• an action in progress in the past • background description	*At ten o'clock they **were swimming** in the lake.* *It **was raining** and people **were hurrying** to work.*
Past continuous vs past simple	• an event in progress when another event interrupted it	*I **was sitting** in the caravan when suddenly it **started** to rain hard.*
Past perfect simple I had eaten He/She had eaten Had you eaten? Had he/she eaten? We hadn't eaten They hadn't eaten **Passive:** It had been eaten	• an action that happened before a certain time in the past • a past action that happened before a second past action	*It was nine o'clock. My parents **had finished** their meal and they were watching TV.* *By the time we arrived, most of the guests **had** already **left**.*
Past perfect continuous I had been playing He/She had been playing Had you been playing? Had he/she been playing? We hadn't been playing They hadn't been playing	• an action in progress over a period of time before a certain time in the past • an action in progress over a period of time before a second past action	*We **had been walking** for half an hour when we reached the village and we were very tired.* *We **had been going out** for three months when she told me she loved someone else.*

Notes

1 In sentences containing both the **past simple** and **past continuous**, we usually use either *while* before the past continuous or *when* before the past simple.

2 When the time phrase is used in the middle of the sentence, no comma is needed. When it is used at the start of the sentence, we combine the two clauses with a comma.

   While I was waiting for the bus, I saw Janet.
   *I was waiting for the bus **when I saw Janet.***

3 When the order of events is clear from the context of the sentence, the past perfect is not necessary.

   *I **locked** the door before I **left** the house.*

4 If two events happened before another past action, the auxiliary *had* is only used once.

   *By the time my mum got home, I **had done** the washing up and **cooked** dinner.*

5 In dependent clauses, the past simple can be used after a past perfect verb.

   *I arrived home and realised that someone had stolen the TV while I **was out** / **had been** out.*

6 The past perfect continuous is not generally used in the passive form.

Form	Use	Example
I used to walk He/She used to walk Did you use to walk? Did he/she use to walk? He/She didn't use to walk They didn't use to walk	• past habits that don't happen any more • regular past actions that don't happen any more • past states and situations that are no longer true	*Gran **used to walk** to school when she was a child.* *My friends and I **used to play** online computer games.* *There **didn't use to be** so many cars on the roads.*
I would wear He/she would wear	• past habits that don't happen any more • regular past actions that don't happen any more	*Every summer we **would stay** in a caravan by a lake.*

Notes

1   *Used to* acts like a normal, regular, past simple verb. It forms questions and negatives with the auxiliary *did* and drops the final -*d* in both forms.

2   *Would* with a past meaning is not commonly used in the question or negative form.

3   *Would* is not used to describe past states and situations.

Future in the past

Form	Use	Example
I was going to phone You were going to phone He/She was going to phone Were they going to phone? Was he/she going to phone? I wasn't going to phone We weren't going to phone	• a plan that you had (in the past) for the future which you did not carry out	*I **was going to send** you an email, but I forgot.* *We **were going to spend** the day at the beach, but it rained.*

It's time, I'd rather

Form	Use	Example
It's time + past simple	• for something that should happen now or should already have happened	***It's time you went** to bed.* *(= You should go to bed.)* ***It's time you were** in bed.* *(= You should be in bed already.)*
I'd rather + past simple	• for preferences about what somebody does generally or now	***I'd rather we didn't go** by bus.* *(= I don't want to go by bus.)*
I'd rather + past perfect	• for something you wish you had done differently in the past	***I'd rather we had seen** a different film.* *(I wish we had seen a different film.)*

Notes

1   We can also use *it's time* with the infinitive if we are talking about the actual time rather than what should happen. We use *for* to show the person.

*It's 10 p.m. **It's time to go** to bed.*
***It's time for you to leave** now.*

2   We can use *I'd rather* with the bare infinitive if there is only one subject for both verbs in the sentence.

***I'd rather (not) go** by bus.*

Form	Use	Example
Present simple	• timetables and programmes	What time **does** the concert **start**?
Present continuous	• future arrangements	We**'re meeting** at 9 pm.
Future simple I will visit He/She will visit Will you visit? Will he/she visit? He/She won't visit They won't visit **Passive:** He will be visited	• predictions • decisions made at the moment of speaking • offers, promises, requests, refusals	Most factories **will employ** fewer people in the future. 'I**'ll get** my camera.' I**'ll help** you with your case. I **won't tell** anyone your secret. **Will you phone** me when you arrive? 'No, I **won't** lend you my iPod!'
Future continuous I will be travelling He/She will be travelling Will you be travelling? Will they be travelling? I won't be travelling He/She won't be travelling	• an event in progress at a point of time in the future • predictions about something that is happening now • planned future events or actions	This time next month, we**'ll be skiing** in Switzerland! I can't call Jack now. He**'ll be having** his lunch. What **will** you **be doing** for your birthday this year?
going to I am going to travel We are going to travel Is he/she going to travel? Are they going to travel? I'm not going to travel He/She isn't going to travel **Passive:** She is going to be met	• future plans and intentions • predictions based on present circumstances	What **are you going to** get your sister for Christmas? Slow down. You**'re going to** cause an accident.
Future perfect I will have finished He/She will have finished Will you have finished? Will he/she have finished? I won't have finished He/She won't have finished **Passive:** It will have been done	• events finished or completed by a point of time in the future	I**'ll have finished** my homework by nine o'clock.

Notes

1 Time phrases

- Commonly used with the future simple
  probably, I'm sure, I think, I expect, I hope
- Commonly used with the future perfect
  by the time, by 2020, by next year, by the end of the week
- Commonly used with the future continuous
  in five years' time, this time next week

2 *Shall* is used for offers and suggestions, instead of *will*.

  ***Shall** I take the dog for a walk?*
  *Where **shall** we meet tomorrow?*

3 The present continuous and *going to* are used for future plans and arrangements. With the present continuous, the focus is on the 'arrangement' and with *going to*, the focus is on the decision or intention to do something.

*I**'m getting** a new bike. (It's been arranged)*
*I**'m going to** get a new bike. (I've decided or intend to)*

Future time clauses

After certain linking words (*after, until, when, while, as soon as, until, once*), present tenses are used to refer to future actions or completed actions in the future.

I'll come home **after** the basketball match **finishes**.
I won't start watching the DVD **until** you **get** here.
As soon as I **see** him, I'll give him the book.
While you **are eating** dinner, I'll tidy up.
By the time I get there, you will have left.

Comparative structures

Regular adjectives		
Adjective	Comparative	Superlative
quick	quicker than	the quickest
big	bigger than	the biggest
nice	nicer than	the nicest
happy	happier than	the happiest
impressive	more impressive than	the most impressive
Irregular adjectives		
good	better than	the best
bad	worse than	the worst
far	further/farther than	the furthest/farthest
little	less than	the least
much/many	more than	the most

Notes

1   We use the comparative form to compare one thing or group of things with another.

My brother's **taller than** me.
These books are **more difficult than** last year's books.

2   We use the superlative form to compare one thing or group of things with a number of others.

My friend Maria is **the best** in the class.
The most important thing is to be confident about what you can do.

3   We use *as … as* to compare two things which are the same.

We use *not as … as* to say what is different about two things.

He's **as intelligent as** his sister.
Their new flat **isn't as big as** their old one.

4   We can also use *less … than*, *the least* (+ adjective) to compare one or more things with other things.

These boots are **less heavy than** those boots.
The least difficult part of the test is the Speaking, I think.

5   We use *the -er/more … the -er/more …* to compare things that change at the same time or when one thing depends on another.

The slower you walk, **the later** we'll get there.
The harder he studies now, **the better** he'll do in the exam.

Quantifiers

Form	Example
some, lots of, a lot of, plenty of + plural countable and uncountable noun	**Some** of the students are doing a project about design. **Plenty of** information is available.
a few, few, (not) many + plural nouns	There are **a few** tickets left.
a little, little, (not) much + uncountable nouns	Here's **a little** advice for you.

	Form	Example
too	*too* + adjective/adverb (+ *for* + object / + *to* infinitive) *too* + *much/many* + noun (+ *to* infinitive) *too* + *few/little* + noun (+ *to* infinitive)	*These shoes are **too small** for me.* *You're **too young to fly** on your own.* *He was driving **too fast to stop** in time.* *There were **too many** people **to get** into the bus!* *You can never have **too much** money.* *We had **too little** time **to** really **relax**.* *There were **too few** guides **to show** us round.*
enough	*(not) enough* + noun (+ *to* infinitive) *(not +) adjective/adverb + enough* (+ *to* infinitive)	*There weren't **enough sun beds** around the pool.* *We hadn't read the brochure **carefully enough**.* *It wasn't **hot enough to go** in the sea.*
so	*so* + adjective/adverb (+ *that*) *so* + *many/much/few/little* + noun (+ *that*)	*The cruise was **so popular that** there were no places left.* *There were **so many people** in the restaurant **that** we had to go elsewhere.* *We had **so little** food for breakfast **that** we needed lunch before midday.*
such	*such* + adjective + noun (+ *that*)	*It was **such a great holiday that** we've booked again for next year.*

Notes

1 *Too* and *not enough* are used to talk about problems.

*The food was **too** spicy to eat.* (= The spicy food is a problem.)
*The food is **very** spicy.* (= This is a fact but not a problem.)

2 *So* or *such* are used to show cause and effect.

*The sea was **so** rough **that** we all got seasick.* (= The rough sea caused the seasickness.)
*It was **such** a warm day **that** we all went swimming.* (= The warm day made it possible for us to go swimming.)

Inversion

Usual word order	Inverted form
I was tired and hungry.	**Not only was I** tired, **but** I was also hungry.
We left late and we got held up by traffic.	**Not only did we leave late, but** we also got held up by traffic.

Notes

1   We use this form of inversion to emphasise two unusual or special actions that are normally linked by an addition clause. It is NOT used to link ordinary, everyday activities.

~~Not only did I fail my exams, but I also won the tennis tournament.~~
It is NOT used to link unexceptional, normal activities.
~~Not only did I get up, but I also got dressed.~~

2   When the first action is in the present or past simple, the auxiliary *do* or *did* is needed to form the inversion.

Not only does my father work ten hours a day, but he also goes to evening classes three days a week.
Not only did she come late but she also forgot her book.

3   If there are three or more actions, only one is inverted.

Not only are we lost, but we have no money, it's raining and it's getting dark.

4   Other common words and phrases which require inversion of the subject and verb when they are placed at the beginning of a sentence are: *never, no sooner, only if, only after, not until.*

Never had I seen such a strange person!
No sooner had we closed the door **than** I remembered my key was inside!
Only when I saw him **did I remember** his name.
Not until I saw him **did I remember** his name.

So do I / Neither do I

Initial statement	Response
I love skiing. I don't often eat out.	**So do I.** **Neither do I.**
I went to France last year. My sister didn't like the concert.	**So did we.** **Neither did mine.**
I'm going to study Spanish. I'm not going to worry about the exams.	**So am I.** **Neither am I.**

Notes

1   These responses are for agreement with a positive or negative statement. If the responder doesn't agree, they use either a positive or negative auxiliary verb.

'I love skiing.' '**I don't**.'
'My sister didn't like the concert.' '**Mine did**.'

Unit 5
Modal verbs

Modal	Use	Example
must *have to* *need to*	• obligation • necessity	You **must** eat well in order to stay healthy. I **have to** be home by 11 p.m. He **needs to** get his eyes examined.
mustn't	• prohibition	You **mustn't** eat chocolate before lunch.
don't have to *don't need to* *needn't*	• lack of obligation or necessity in the present or future	We **don't have to** arrive till midday. You **don't need to** pay me back yet. You **needn't come** if you don't want to.
had to	• obligation or necessity in the past	Paul missed his train and **had to** wait for the next one.
didn't have to *didn't need to*	• lack of obligation or necessity in the past	We **didn't have to** do the test in the end. She **didn't need to** show her passport.
needn't have + past participle	• past action that wasn't necessary	He **needn't have** worried about the exam. He got a good mark.
should *ought to*	• mild obligation • advice	He **should** be resting after his long run. You **ought to** tell her the truth.
should have *ought to have* + past participle	• criticism or regret about a past situation	You **should have come** camping with us. It was great! We **ought to** have helped Mum when she was ill.
may	• permission	**May** I go to Jane's party at the weekend?
can	• ability • permission	Jocelyn **can** cook really well. **Can** Joe and Dan stay here tonight?
could	• ability in the past	Ten years ago, Dad **could** touch his toes, but he can't now!
be able to	• ability • successful result in the past	Dan **is able to** teach us yoga. I **was able to** sell my old computer.
could have + past participle	• unfulfilled ability for a past situation	Peter **could have broken** the window when he was playing football in the garden.
may *might* *could*	• present or future possibility	It **may** snow tonight. It **might** rain later. Yes, that **could** be the new gym teacher.
may have *might have* *could have* + past participle	• possibility for a past situation	I didn't see Anna at the party. She **might have stayed** at home.
must	• deduction	You **must** be hungry after the long journey.
must have + past participle	• deduction in a past situation	He looks tanned. He **must have been** on holiday.
can't *couldn't*	• impossibility	That **can't** be your mum! She's so young! That **couldn't** be true! It's unbelievable!
can't have *couldn't have* + past participle	• impossibility for a past situation	He **can't have taken** your purse! He wasn't even sitting near you. They **couldn't have finished** it in 2 minutes! It was too difficult.
will	• predictions	There**'ll** be more strikes next month. This time tomorrow I**'ll** have my new car. We**'ll** never eat all this food.

Notes

1   Most modal verbs have one form and don't change.

   He **must** *take more care about what he eats.*

2   The semi-modals (*have to, need to* and *be able to*) change according to person and tense.

   He **doesn't have to** *go to work today.*

3   There is little difference between *must* and *have to.* We use *must* more often to talk about a decision we have made ourselves about what is necessary and *have to* for a decision someone else has told us is necessary.

   I **must** *eat less fast food.* (= I want to)
   The doctor says I **have to** *improve my diet.* (= My doctor thinks it is necessary)

4   *mustn't* does not mean the same as *don't have/need to* and *needn't.*

   You **mustn't** *go into that room.* (= It isn't allowed.)
   You **don't have to** / **needn't** *go into that room.* (= It isn't necessary.)

5   *Didn't have to* and *didn't need to* do not mean the same as *needn't have done.*

   I **didn't need to** *take the test.* (So I didn't take it.)
   I **needn't have taken** *the test.* (I took it but then discovered it wasn't necessary)

6   We use *wasn't/weren't allowed to* to talk about prohibition in the past.

   When I was ten I **wasn't allowed to** *stay up after ten o'clock.*

7   We use *was/were able to* to say that somebody did something on one occasion (usually something that was not easy). We do not use *could* in this case.

   He **was able to** *pass his exams the second time.*

8   We also use *able to* for future or past ability.

   I **haven't been able to** *go out much because of my exams.*
   We'**ll be able to** *practise our French this summer.*

9   *manage to* is not a modal verb but we often use it instead of *able to* to talk about ability where there is some difficulty.

   I don't know how you **manage to** read so many books.
   I **haven't managed to** fix my computer yet.

10   For possibility, *may* is a little more certain than *might.* We use both to talk about present and future possibility.

11   To form the passive we add *be* + past participle after the modal verb.

   It **must be done** by a student.
   They **can't have been told** to do that!

Unit 6
Conditionals

Form	Use	Example
Zero conditional *if* + present simple / present simple	• general truths	*Food **goes** off if you **don't keep** it in the fridge.*
First conditional *if* + present simple / *will* or modal + infinitive / imperative	• possible future situations • suggestions • advice • threats • promises	*If she **doesn't like** the present, I'**ll buy** her something else.* *If you **are** free tomorrow evening, we **could go** to the cinema!* *If you **like** the CD, **buy** it!* *If you **do** that again, I **won't let** you watch TV.* *If you **help** me with my homework, I'**ll lend** you my new CD.*
Second conditional *if* + past simple / *would* / *could* / *might* + bare infinitive	• unlikely / unreal situations in the present or future • advice	*If my dad **knew** how to fly a plane, he'**d have** his own helicopter!* *If I **were** you, I'**d buy** those trainers.*
Third conditional *if* + past perfect / *would* / *could* / *might have done*	• regret • unreal situations in the past	*If he **had played** in the match, we **might have won**.* *If I **hadn't been** ill yesterday, I **wouldn't have missed** the Maths test!*
Mixed conditionals *if* + past perfect / *would* / *could* / *might* *if* + past simple / *would* / *could* / *might have done*	• imaginary present situation caused by an unreal past situation • imaginary past event caused by an unreal present situation	*If I **had studied** harder, I **might be** at university now.* *If you **didn't live** so far away, you **could have cycled** to my party last week.*

unless, provided, on condition, as long as, suppose

unless *provided (that)* *on condition (that)* *as long as* *suppose*	• unless = if not • provided (that) = only if • on condition (that) = only if • as long as = only if • suppose = what if	*He won't pass his exams **unless** he works hard.* *I'll go **provided** you give me a lift.* *I'll lend you £10 **on condition that** you pay me back.* ***As long as** it doesn't rain, we'll go out for a walk.* ***Suppose** no-one turns up to the party? How will you feel?*

Notes

1   *Unless, provided* (**that**) and *on condition* (**that**) are generally used with the first conditional. *Suppose* can be used with the first, second and third conditionals.

   ***Suppose** you **won** the lottery, what **would** you do?*
   ***Suppose** you **had been caught** cheating in your exams, what **would** your parents **have said**?*

2   The *if* clause can come second in the sentence. If it comes second, you don't need to use a comma.

   If we had a dog, I'd be really happy.
   I'd be really happy if we had a dog.

Form	Use	Example
I wish / If only + past simple	• a wish about a present situation	*I wish I **had** an electric guitar!* *If only the holidays **were** longer!*
I wish / If only + could	• a wish about a present or future ability	*I wish I **could run** really fast.* *If only I **could speak** lots of languages!*
I wish / If only + would	• a complaint about a present habit or situation	*I wish they **would stop** shouting!* *If only the weather **would get** warmer!*
I wish / If only + past perfect	• regret about the past	*If only I **had studied** harder for my exams.* *I wish I **hadn't spent** all my money!*

Notes

1   Don't confuse *wish* and *hope*.

*I **wish** (hope) you happiness!*
*I **hope** (wish) you will be happy!*

2   We do not use *wish* + *would* to talk about our own habits. We use *could*.

*I wish I **could stop** biting my nails. NOT would stop*

	Direct speech	Reported speech
Present simple	*I am hungry.*	*She said (that) she **was** hungry.*
Present continuous	*We are waiting for a friend.*	*They claimed (that) they **were waiting** for a friend.*
Past simple	*I saw the accident.*	*He told us (that) he **had seen** the accident.*
Past continuous	*I was reading a comic.*	*She said (that) she **had been reading** a comic.*
Present perfect simple	*We have lost the money.*	*They explained (that) they **had lost** the money.*
Present perfect continuous	*I have been sunbathing all day.*	*She said (that) she **had been sunbathing** all day.*
Past perfect simple	*We had finished dinner.*	*They told us (that) they **had finished** dinner.*
Past perfect continuous	*They had been working on it for ages.*	*He said (that) they **had been working** on it for ages.*
am/are going to	*I am going to send an email.*	*He confirmed (that) he **was going to send** an email.*
will	*I will call later.*	*She said (that) she **would call** later.*
can/could	*We can do better.*	*They insisted (that) they **could do** better.*
may/might	*I may arrive late at the party.*	*She said (that) she **might arrive** late at the party.*
must/have to	*I must go to bed earlier.*	*He agreed (that) he **had to go** to bed earlier.*
should/could/might/ ought to/would	*She should relax more.*	*He told her (that) she **should relax** more.*

Notes

1 After present, future and present perfect reporting verbs, e.g. *says, has asked,* etc., the verb form is generally the same as in direct speech.

*'I**'ve found** the keys.'*
*Ben **says** he**'s found** the keys.*

2 We can use *say* and *tell* (and other verbs) to report statements. When we use *say* we don't use an object. When we use *tell* we use an object.

*Ben **said** he would bring a picnic.*
*Ben **told me** he would bring a picnic.*

3 If the sentence is still true, we don't have to change the tense.

*She said she **lives** in Paris.* (= She still lives in Paris.)

4 We often need to change the pronoun (*I, he, us,* etc.) and possessive adjectives (*my, his, her,* etc.).

'I wasn't enjoying the festival.'
*Ben said that **he** wasn't enjoying the festival.*

5 Place/time words may change.

Direct speech	Reported speech
yesterday	**the day before/the previous day**
tomorrow	**the following day/the next day**
now	**then/at that time**
today/tonight	**that day/that night**
next week/month/ year	**the following week/month/year**
last week/month/ year	**the previous week/month/year the week/month/year before**
two days ago	**two days previously/before**
this/these	**that/those**
here	**there**

Reported questions

	Direct speech	Reported speech
Wh- questions	*Where are you going?*	*I asked him **where he was going.***
Yes/No questions	*Can you help me?*	*I asked him **if/whether he could help me.***

Notes

1 For reported questions/offers with *shall*, *shall* changes to *should*.

*'**Shall** I open the window?'*
*She asked if/whether she **should** open the window.*

2 We don't use the auxiliary verb in reported questions.

Where do you live?
*She asked me **where I lived**.*
NOT *She asked me where ~~did I live~~.*

Reported commands and requests

	Direct speech	Reported speech
Commands	*Go away!*	*They told us **to go away**.*
Requests	*Can you help me?*	*She asked us **to help her**.* *She asked us **if we could** help her.*

1 To report an order or command, we use verb + object + *to* infinitive.

'Leave me alone.'
*She **told him to leave** her alone.*
'Be quiet!'
*He **ordered the class to be** quiet.*

2 To report a request, we use *ask* + *whether/if* or *ask* + *to* infinitive

'Can I see your photos?' Sandra asked me.
*Sandra **asked if she could** see my photos.* OR
*Sandra **asked to see** my photos.*

3 If the order or request is negative, we use *not* before *to* infinitive.

*He told me **not to** sit there.*
*She asked me **not to** tell anyone.*

Reporting verbs

1 The most common reporting verbs are *say* and *tell*:

	Direct speech	Reported speech
say + that	*I like rock music.*	*She **said that** she **liked** rock music.*
tell + object + that	*I am leaving.*	*She **told him that** she **was leaving**.*

2 verb + *that*

admit*, agree*, announce, believe, boast, claim, complain, decide*, deny*, explain, imagine, insist*, notice, promise, recommend*, reply, state, suggest*, think
*James **announced that** he was getting married.*
*They **boasted that** they were the best players in the team.*

3 verb + object + *that*

advise*, persuade*, promised*, remind*, warn*
*She **reminded her friends that** they had to leave at 8 a.m.*
*He **advised Sam that** he would be late.*

4 Different structures*

- **verb + *to* infinitive:** *agree, decide, promise, threaten*
  *He **promised to tidy** up the room.*
- **verb + *-ing*:** *admit, deny, imagine, recommend, suggest*
  *Jamie **denied stealing** the money.*
- **verb + preposition + *-ing*:** *apologise for, insist on*
  *He **apologised for being** late.*
- **verb + object + *to* infinitive:** *advise, ask, encourage, order, persuade, remind, warn*
  *Julia **ordered the children to leave** the room.*
- **verb + object + preposition + *-ing*:** *accuse of*

Unit 8
Passive voice

	Active	Passive
Present simple	Our teacher **gives** us homework twice a week.	We **are given** homework twice a week.
Present continuous	They **are testing** some new GM crops here.	Some new GM crops **are being tested** here.
Present perfect simple	They **have published** an article about pollution in the paper.	An article about pollution **has been published** in the paper.
Past simple	Someone **stole** our new electric car last night.	Our new electric car **was stolen** last night.
Past continuous	They **were making** a film.	A film **was being made**.
Past perfect simple	No one **had** ever **seen** the monster.	The monster **had** never **been seen**.
Future simple	Thousands of people **will visit** Stonehenge this summer.	Stonehenge **will be visited** by thousands of people this summer.
Future with *going to*	A meteorite **is going to hit** the Earth soon.	The Earth **is going to be hit** by a meteorite soon.
Modals	You **mustn't use** the shower after 10 p.m.	The shower **mustn't be used** after 10 p.m.
Gerunds	Celebrities **like people recognising them** in the street.	Celebrities **like being recognised** in the street.
Infinitives	We **have to return** these library books.	These library books **have to be returned**.

Notes

1. We use the passive when we want to focus on the action rather than the person who did it. It is often used in news reports and historical accounts.

2. To form the passive, we use *to be* + the past participle.

3. Intransitive verbs (e.g. *arrive*), which have no object, don't have a passive form.

4. When there are two direct objects in a sentence the passive can be expressed in two different ways:

   Dan's brother sent him a text.
   ***Dan** was sent **a text** by his brother.*
   ***A text** was sent **to Dan** by his brother.*

5. It is not always necessary or possible to say who did the action. If it is important to say who completed the action, then we use *by* added to the end of the sentence.

   *The pyramids were built **by the Egyptians**.*

Impersonal structures

It + passive	**It is believed that** the dinosaurs were killed by a meteorite. **It is known that** eating carrots is good for your eyesight. **It was thought that** the Earth was flat.
subject + passive + infinitive	Dinosaurs **are believed to have been killed** by a meteorite. Carrots **are known to be** good for your health. The Earth **was thought to be** flat.
subject + passive of verb *expected* + infinitive	Fossil fuels **are expected to run out** in the middle of this century.

Notes

1. Several different verbs can be used with this structure:

   consider, say, understand, claim, realise, etc.

2. This structure is used when it isn't important to state who the people making the claims are.

Causative *have*

Present simple	They **have** the house **painted** every three years.
Present continuous	We **are having** the television **mended** at the moment.
Past simple	She **had** extensions **put** in her hair last week.
Past continuous	They **were having** the windows **cleaned** when it started to rain!
Present perfect	We**'ve had** a special area **made** in our garden for all our recycling bins.
Past perfect	We **had had** our computer **looked at** three times before we realised there was a virus on it.
Future simple	Do you think they**'ll have** a swimming pool **built** in the garden?
Modals	You **should have** your satellite **moved**.
Gerunds	I **hate having** my teeth **cleaned**.
Infinitives	I**'d like to have** my photo **taken**.

Notes

1 We use the form *have something done* when something is done for us by someone else, usually because we ask them to. You can usually replace *have* with *get*.

He**'s getting** the car **washed** at the moment.

2 Causative *have* is also used to describe something that is done to us that we didn't want to happen. In these cases we can't use *get* in place of *have*.

He **had** his blog **closed** down because he offered illegal downloads on it.
He **got** his bike **stolen** when he left it unlocked outside the café.

3 Be careful of the word order in the sentence!

have my hair **cut**
have my bedroom **painted**

Unit 9
Gerunds and infinitives

Form	Use	Example
Gerund	• as the subject of a sentence • after certain verbs • after prepositions • after phrases that end with prepositions • after certain expressions • after determiners	**Watching** too much TV isn't good for you. Jamie **enjoys chatting** to friends online. **Without meeting** him, I can't tell if he's nice. Are you **good at making** things? **It's no use trying** to talk to him. **The opening** of the new shop is on Saturday.
Infinitive with *to*	• after certain verbs (+ object) • to express purpose	I **expect** you **to be** more responsible. We came **to see** if you're feeling better.
Bare infinitive	• after certain verbs • after most modal verbs • after certain phrases • after 'Why/Why not',	Let's **take** a break now. We **should go** home now. I'**d rather study** in the library. **Why not eat** at home tonight?

Notes

1 Some common verbs followed by a gerund are:

admit, avoid, begin, can't stand, consider, delay, deny, discuss, dislike, enjoy, feel like, finish, give up, hate, imagine, keep (on), mind, miss, practise, prefer, remember, report, risk, start, stop, suggest, understand
She **misses seeing** her old friends.

2 Some phrases that end with prepositions that are followed by a gerund are:

advise (sb) against, apologise for, fed up with, fond of, good/bad at, interested in, keen on, mad about, tired of
He **apologised for playing** his music so loud.

3 Some expressions that are followed by a gerund are:

can't stand, it's great, it's no use/good, it's worth/not worth, there's no point in, look forward to, don't mind, spend time, waste time
Don't **waste time watching** TV.

4 Some common verbs followed by *to* infinitive are:

afford, agree, appear, arrange, ask, begin, choose, continue, decide, expect, fail, forget, hate, hope, learn, like, manage, offer, plan, prefer, prepare, pretend, promise, refuse, seem, start, stop, threaten, try, want, wish, would like
Ben **offered to wash** up for me.

5 Some verbs followed by an object + *to* infinitive are:

advise, allow, ask, encourage, expect, forbid, force, help, order, permit, remind, teach, tell, tempt, want, warn
I **forbid you to go** out at this time of night.

6 Some verbs followed by the bare infinitive are:

hear, feel, let, make, notice, watch, see
I **heard** you **tell** him about the party.

7 Some verbs can be followed by either the gerund or the infinitive with little or no change in meaning:

begin, continue, hate, hear, intend, like, love, prefer, see, start, watch
I **like swimming** in the sea. (Generally I like it)
I **like to swim** in the sea. (Something that I do regularly)
I **heard him shout**. (He shouted once.)
I **heard him shouting**. (He shouted several times.)

8 Some verbs can be followed by either the gerund or the infinitive, but with a change in meaning: *forget, remember, try, stop*

He **remembered locking** the doors. *(He locked the doors and then he remembered that action.)*
He **remembered to lock** the doors. *(He remembered first and then he locked the doors.)*
She **stopped running** after three minutes. (She ran for three minutes, then stopped)
She **stopped to talk** to Dan. (She was doing something, then stopped it, in order to talk to Dan)
I **tried to open** the window, but it was stuck. (I couldn't open it.)
I **tried opening** the window, but hot air came in. (I opened it as an experiment)

be allowed to, let, make

be allowed to + infinitive I'm not **allowed to go** out during the week.
let + object + bare infinitive Jack's parents **won't let him try** parkour.
make + object + bare infinitive be made + to infinitive The teacher **made the students do** the exercise again.

Notes

1   We can use *allow* in the active or passive form, but *let* can only be used in the active form.

2   If we use *make* in the passive, we use the full infinitive of the verb:

*I'm **made to tidy** my room every weekend.*

would rather, prefer to, had better

Form	Use	Example
would rather + bare infinitive *prefer* + *to* infinitive	• personal preferences	*I'd **rather go** swimming when the weather's nice.* *I **prefer to do** my homework in my bedroom.*
had better + bare infinitive	• advice	*You'd **better get** ready. We're going out soon.*

Notes

1   We use *would rather* + person + past simple for something we would (not) like somebody else to do.

*I'd **rather you didn't borrow** my new jacket.*

Articles

Form	Use	Example
the	• something specific or when there's only one • before collective nouns, times of the day, musical instruments, some countries	*I can't go to **the** gym today.* ***the** staff, in **the** morning, She plays **the** piano, **the** UK*
a/an	• when something is mentioned the first time • before job titles, certain measurements	*I'm reading **a** good book.* *She's **a** psychiatrist. He's **an** architect.* ***A** thousand new houses* *4 euros **a** kilo, 60 km **an hour***
no article	• before plural countable nouns • before uncountable nouns • before subjects • with certain expressions	*Dogs make better pets than cats.* *Fame is difficult to deal with when you're very young.* *I love Maths, but I hate Science.* *at home, in bed, for breakfast, on foot*

Notes

1   We use *a* before *u* when it has a consonant sound: *a university*.
    We use *an* before *h* when it is not sounded: *an hour*.

Determiners

Form	Example
each, *every* + singular countable noun	*It gets hotter **every** day.*
(not) many, a few, few, most (of), each of, both of, neither of, either of, none of + countable nouns	***Either of** the films is worth seeing.* ***None of** the students like homework!*
(not) much, (a) little, a bit of, a large amount of, a great deal of + uncountable nouns	*I don't have a **great deal of** enthusiasm for football.*
some, any, lots of, a lot of, plenty of, all, no, none, hardly any + plural countable and uncountable nouns	***Lots of** teenagers go to festivals in summer.* ***Hardly any** people came to the meeting.*

Notes

1   *Few* and *little* have a negative meaning = *not many, not much*

***Few** people know how difficult a star's life can be.*

Unit 10
Relative clauses

Relative pronoun	Use	Example
who	• to refer to people	*I know some people **who** spend all their free time watching TV!* *Terry Jones, **who** lives in Brighton, is an excellent guitar player.*
that	• to refer to either people or things	*Have you got the book **that** I lent you last week?* *Have you met the woman **that** lives next door?*
which	• to refer to things	*Where's the CD **which** I was listening to?* *These football cards, **which** I collected when I was young, are worth a lot now.*
whose	• the possessive of **who** or *which*	*I met someone **whose** brother is a famous photographer.* *Henry, **whose** new book I am reading, won a prize in a writing competition.*
where	• after nouns to refer to places	*That's the house **where** we used to live.* *London, **where** my cousin lives, is a great city to visit.*
when	• after nouns to refer to time	*Do you remember the day **when** there was a fire at the school?* *Last July, **when** they were in Paris, John asked Polly to marry him!*

Notes

1 Defining relative clauses

- We use defining relative clauses to define or identify a noun. They tell us exactly which person, thing, time or place we are talking about. The information cannot be left out of the sentence or it won't give us all the information we require.
  *The boat **that Martin bought** is bigger than this one.*
  The boat is bigger than this one. (which boat?)
- No commas are used.
- In defining relative clauses, *that* can replace the relative pronouns *who* or *which*.
- We can omit the relative pronoun when it is the object of the relative clause.
  *Where's the book (**that**) I was reading?*

2 Non-defining relative clauses

- We use non-defining relative clauses to give extra information about a person, thing, time or place.
- Commas are used before and after the relative pronoun. This information can be left out of the sentence and it will still make sense.
  Our favourite beach, which has won several awards, is about 5 km from here.
  Our favourite beach is about 5 km from here.
- We don't usually use *that* in non-defining relative clauses.
  The man over there, who I was talking to, is from Hungary.
- Sometimes *which* refers to a whole idea not just a word.
  *My sister hates travelling, **which** is strange.* (which = the fact that she hates travelling)

3 In formal writing, we often write the preposition before the relative pronoun. In such cases, *whom* is used instead of *who*.

*The person **who** I complained **to** …*
*The person **to whom** I complained …*

Participle clauses

	Use	Example
Present participle verb + *-ing*	to describe two actions taking place at the same time or shortly after one another	***Walking** round town, Sarah met her friend, Luke.*
Past participle *having* + past participle	to describe one past action that happened before another	***Having finished** my exams, I was free to start planning my summer holidays.*

Notes

1 Participle clauses are often used at the start of sentences but can also be used as reduced relative clauses, i.e. a relative clause with no relative pronoun and only the participle of the verb.

*We saw our plane (which was) **taking off** as we arrived at the airport.*

2 Present participle clauses are often used after a preposition.

***By checking** the Internet, we were able to find the cheapest flights.*
***On finishing** my homework, I switched on my computer.*

3 The subject of the participle clause must be the same as the subject of the main verb.

Walking round the zoo, *we* saw the lions eating their dinner. (We were walking and we saw the lions.)
Walking round the zoo, *the* lions were eating their dinner. (The lions are the subject of the main clause, therefore the sentence says that it was the lions who were walking round the zoo.)

Question tags

> I *am* in the right place, *aren't* I?
> It*'s* a nice day, *isn't it*?
> Your mum *knows* how to send a text, *doesn't she*?
> You *don't live* near here, *do* you?
> He *forgot, didn't* he?
> You *didn't tell* her, *did* you?
> Your friends *have been* here before, *haven't they*?
> We*'ll* be on time, *won't we*?
> I*'m not* going to lose, *am* I?
> You *couldn't* help me, *could* you?
> *Give* me a hand, *will* you?
> *Don't* forget, *will* you?

Notes

1 Question tags have two main uses.

- to check information that the speaker is not sure about. In these cases the intonation rises at the end of the sentence.
- to confirm information that the speaker already knows or to ask the other person to agree. In these cases the intonation falls at the end of the sentence.

  You're Mr Davies, the new teacher, aren't you? (I'm not sure)

  Billy Davies. You're late again, aren't you? (I know)

2 Question tags usually take the form:

positive statement – negative tag
negative statement – positive tag
However, they can take the form:
positive statement – positive tag to express emotions such as anger, surprise or excitement.
You*'re wearing* my dress, *are* you?
You*'re going* out again, *are* you?

3 Words such as *no one* and *everyone* take a singular verb form but a plural tag. With *no one*, a positive tag is used with a positive verb form.

No one likes me, *do* they?
Everyone wants to come, *don't* they?

4 *Let's* forms an irregular tag with *shall we*?

Let's go out tonight, *shall* we?

5 Imperatives can form a tag with *would* or *will*. *Would* is more polite than *will*.

Help me with this email, *would* you?
Get some milk while you're at the shop, *will* you?

With negative imperatives, only *will* is possible.

Don't stay up too late, *will* you?

Echo questions

Statement	Echo question
I'm late for work.	**Are you?**
I don't often go swimming.	**Don't you?**
We'll be there soon.	**Will we?**
Paul didn't email.	**Didn't he?**

Notes

1 Echo questions use the same auxiliary as was used in the statement being responded to. For present and past simple affirmative statements, the auxiliary *do* is needed in the echo question.

2 Echo questions are used to show interest in or surprise about what the speaker has said.

Pearson Education Limited
Edinburgh Gate
Harlow
Essex CM20 2JE
England
and Associated Companies throughout the world.

www.pearsonelt.com

© Pearson Education Limited 2011

The right of Rod Fricker and Suzanne Gaynor to be identified as author(s) of this Work has been asserted by him/her in accordance with the Copyright, Designs and Patents Act 1988.

Thirteenth impression 2020

ISBN: 978-1-4082-7282-4

Printed in Slovakia by Neografia a.s.
Set in: Myriad Pro 10/14pt

Illustration Acknowledgements

Illustrated by **Beehive Illustration Limited** (**Richard Jones** pages 68, 92,100; **Chris Simpson** pages 46, 67, 99, 117; **Norbert Sipos** page 97); **The Bright Agency** (**Michael Garton** pages 12, 21, 26, 113); **Akis Melachris** pages 8, 65, 71, 74, 81, 99, 101; **David Semple** pages 20, 41, 44, 60, 68, 70, 72, 76, 89, 122.

Picture Credits

The publisher would like to thank the following for their kind permission to reproduce their photographs:

(Key: b-bottom; c-centre; l-left; r-right; t-top)

Alamy Images: Alibi Productions 53c, Alvey & Towers Picture Library 29/5, Angela Hampton Picture Library 5t, 6b, 12tl, Big Cheese Photo LLC 38br, Blend Images 109/4, Bubbles Photolibrary 79 (Theo), Chris Rout 14c, 78/4, 113, 114t, 120, D. Hurst 49 (ipod), David L. Moore 37br, 125b, Design Pics Inc 109/5, don jon red 53br, eddie linssen 24b, Fancy 108, Heather Delaney 49 (photography), i love images 25tl, James Boardman 96c, Jim West 38l, Jochen Tack 78/1, Juice Images 97b, Mark Bassett 29/1, MBI 95b, Moviestore collection Ltd 18t, Nicholas Pitt 114br, Pablo Paul 78/2, PCN Photography 5/3, PhotoAlto 87, Radius Images 65, 66, 72, Richard G. Bingham II 37tr, 125t, Rolf Richardson 25br, Roman Snytsar 85c, studiomode 49 (boots), 49 (map), Wendy Johnson 115b; **Art Directors and TRIP Photo Library:** Helene Rogers 48 (windsurfer), 49 (book), 102b , Joseph Okwesa 49 (martial arts); **Comstock Images:** 53bl; **Corbis:** Brian Summers / First Light 109/2, Edith Held 79 (Natalia), I Love Images 17t, 18b, 24t, Image Source 86r, JLP / Jose L. Pelaez 109/1, Josh McCulloch / All Canada Photos 48 (jogging), Najlah Feanny 77 (B), Tetra Images 11, Vstock LLC / Vladimir Godnik / Tetra Images 78/3; **Fotolia.com:** Eray 121l, Jonathan Larsen 119, Luminis 47b; **Getty Images:** AFP 96t, Bob Thomas 84 (B), George Frey / Bloomberg 77 (C), JUAN BARRETO / AFP 90 (Earthquake), Kimberly White / Bloomberg 77 (D), Langenberger / Barcroft Media 90 (volcano), Mark Wilson 84 (C), Matt Cardy 25bl, Photographer's Choice / Yellow Dog Productions 5/4, SAEED KHAN / AFP 110b, Stone / Betsie Van der Meer 103b, Stone / John Eder 25tr, Stone / Siri Stafford 105, The Image Bank / Richard Ross 101, 102, 108t, 110t, YURI GRIPAS / AFP 90 (White House); **Randy Glasbergen:** 10, 27, 32, 58, 59, 82t, 82b, 107; **Robert Harding World Imagery:** 114bl; **ICYS:** 95t; iStockphoto: Catherine Yeulet 84 (E), Chris Schmidt 86l, Christopher Futcher 14b, David Lentz 97t, Deborah Maxemow 118, digitalskillet 29t, 30, 36, Ekaterina Monakhova 38tr, Forest Woodward 48 (tennis), James Pauls 29/4, Jan Paul Schrage 49 (wall climbing), Juanmonino 5/1, 41, 42tl, 48b, 89, 90t, 96b, kristian sekulic 48 (gym), Larisa Lofitskaya 54b, Nicholas Monu 109/3, Nikolay Pozdeev 6t, Pattie Steib 67, Redgoldwing 7, robert van beets 121r, RTimages 29/2, S. Greg Panosian 34, Zuki 94-95; **Pearson Education Ltd:** Photodisc 98; **Photolibrary.com:** 17cr, Blend Images 111, Corbis 73, Edward Staines 51, fstop / Sven Hagolani 29/3, GoGo Images 5/5, Image Source 62-63, Pacific Stock 48 (surfer), Photoalto / Sigrid Olsson 37tl, Stockbroker 53t, 54t, 60; **Press Association Images:** Barry Batchelor / PA Archive 43b, Chris Radburn / PA Archive 5/2, Niall Carson / PA Archive 42b, Tone Georgsen / Scanpix 42tr; **Rex Features:** 23, Bill Stevenson / Stock Connection 47t, Brian J. Ritchie / Hotsauce 19t, Charles Sykes 35, Design Pics Inc 77 (A), Doug Blaine 43t, Image Source 49 (computer games), Jonathan Hordle 19b, Monkey Business Images 37bl, 78 (Aleksander), 109/6, NBCUPHOTOBANK 17br, Neale Haynes 48 (wakeboarding), Paul Cooper 103c, Picture Perfect 17cl, Quirky China News 103t, Richard Jones 61, Richard Young 18c, Sipa Press 17bl, 84 (A), Startraks Photo 19c, Voisin / Phanie 77t, 78t, 84b; **Shutterstock.com:** bajars 115t, Rui Saraiva 85t, s-eyerkaufer 6c; **Thinkstock:** Brand X Pictures 14t, Creatas 22, 84 (D), Digital Vision 29/6, 38c, Digital Vision 29/6, 38c, iStockphoto 15, 49 (film making), Photos.com 49 (rope), Pixland 79 (Monika); **TopFoto:** 91

Cover images: *Front:* **Comstock Images; Photolibrary.com:** Pacific Stock**; Rex Features:** Denkou Images; *Back:* **Alamy Images:** i love images; **Photolibrary.com:** Tim Parnell / Corbis

All other images © Pearson Education

Picture Research by: Louise Edgeworth

Every effort has been made to trace the copyright holders and we apologise in advance for any unintentional omissions. We would be pleased to insert the appropriate acknowledgement in any subsequent edition of this publication.